Spartan Seasons

SPARTAN SEASONS

HOW

Baseball Survived the Second World War

Richard Goldstein

Macmillan Publishing Co., Inc.

NEW YORK

Macmillan Publishing Co., Inc.
866 Third Avenue, New York, N.Y. 10022
Collier Macmillan Canada, Ltd.

Library of Congress Cataloging in Publication Data

Goldstein, Richard, 1942–
    Spartan seasons.

    Bibliography: p. 281
    Includes index.
    1. Baseball—United States—History.
2. World War, 1939–1945—United States.
3. World War, 1939–1945—Influence and results.
I. Title.
GV863.A1G64   796.357'0973   80-10597
ISBN 0-02-544600-2

First Printing 1980

The photographs in this book are from the files of
United Press International.

Printed in the United States of America

DESIGNED BY RON FARBER

To Mom, Dad, and Marcia

Contents

V

On Foreign Fields

VI

The Road to Peace

Acknowledgments

The events in this book go back almost four decades. But listening to the recollections of the men who were there, baseball's wartime era seems like only yesterday.

For sharing with me memories that remain remarkably vivid, a special word of thanks to Red Barber, Zeke Bonura, Lou Boudreau, George Case, Preston Gomez, Calvin Griffith, Babe Herman, Tommy Holmes, Tex Hughson, George Kell, Danny Litwhiler, Frank McCormick, Len Merullo, Hugh Poland, Virgil Trucks, Harry Walker, Lloyd Waner, and Phil Weintraub.

I'm grateful to Milton Richman, sports editor of United Press International, where I was formerly a reporter, for reviewing the manuscript.

Dan Gallagher and his staff at the UPI photo library were most helpful pointing me in the right directions among their extensive collection.

Richard Goldstein

Introduction

When the New York Yankees opened their 1979 season against the Milwaukee Brewers, the pregame ceremonies went a bit beyond the obligatory patriotic pomp of a small color guard and a live rendition of the national anthem.

Some very special guests of honor were brought out to home plate —ten middle-aged men receiving a belated tribute for heroic actions of thirty-five years past.

That cold, blustery Thursday had been declared "Incident at Lanzerath Recognition Day."

The ball club was honoring surviving members of a small band of GIs who, by halting a vast column of German tanks, paratroopers, and SS forces in an eighteen-hour battle at the Belgian village of Lanzerath, had blunted a surprise attack that might have altered the outcome of the Battle of the Bulge.

Somehow, only the commanding lieutenant of the tiny reconnaissance unit received a commendation—the exploits of the rank-and-file troops had been overlooked. The seeming injustice had been brought to light by Jack Anderson in a *Parade* magazine article and now George Steinbrenner decided he would show his appreciation by bringing the veterans before the Yankee Stadium throng.

For those in the crowd of 52,719 who could remember far enough back, the scene might have seemed a throwback to the baseball world of the early 1940s—when a day at the ballpark could hardly be considered complete without a glimpse of a war hero on hand.

On any afternoon a Medal of Honor winner might be introduced by the public address announcer and asked to take a bow from his box seat. One rainy June day in 1945, there was a beaming Dwight D. Eisenhower, finding time on his triumphal return home to visit the Polo Grounds and watch the lackluster Giants take on the equally uninspiring Braves.

And the military presence on occasion was a massive one—tanks rolling over the outfield terrain, perhaps white-clad sailors forming a giant "V for Victory" with its apex at home plate. Patriotic spectacles were favorite devices for boosting attendance on special days when gate receipts would go to aid a servicemen's relief agency or be funneled into war bonds.

The caliber of play may not have been much to behold, but the wartime ball clubs sure could put on a show, testifying to the role the "national pastime" was playing in America's battle for survival.

This is the story of those days—the era of World War II baseball, when the major leagues managed to carry on while beset by home front hardships, stripped of talent by the Army and Navy, and driven to patriotic hyperbole by intimations the sport was a frivolity that might well be dispensed with.

It was a time when travel restrictions drove spring training to the snowy North, when night games became a casualty of blackouts, when an ersatz baseball deprived of strategic natural rubber turned out to be "dead," when the St. Louis Browns had an outfielder named Pete Gray who took a bit more time than was desirable to peg the ball back —it wasn't easy to maneuver when you had only one arm. And these were days when a ballplayer might spend his free time visiting a war plant to spur production or volunteering to watch the night skies for enemy planes.

There isn't a great deal in this book about who won what, about the number of victories pitcher X achieved or how many home runs batter Y managed to slug. It was not, after all, a time for glorious exploits. The prewar heroes were gone—Bob Feller did his pitching against the Japanese, firing .40-millimeter shells from his antiaircraft station aboard the battleship *Alabama*; Joe DiMaggio traded pinstripes for sergeant's stripes; Ted Williams utilized his remarkable eyesight and reflexes to win the wings of a marine pilot. The game would limp along, at times bordering on comedy, with a collection of draft rejects, old-timers, and youngsters whose main asset seemed to be the fact they were civilians.

For the record, here's how it went.

Preeminent were the St. Louis Cardinals whose Branch Rickey-developed farm system, while decimated by war, was still able to produce some decent replacements for the players lost to military service. The Cards took the National League pennant in '42, '43, and '44, then finished a strong second to the Chicago Cubs in the last wartime season.

In the American League, the Yankees, the class of baseball since the Ruth era, retained their winning habit in '42 and '43, dropping the World Series to the Cardinals the first wartime year but taking the championship the following season. In 1944, there occurred an event only a world war could bring about. The St. Louis Browns, doormats for years, won what was to be the sole pennant in their history. The Brownie 4-Fs—men unfit for military service but not so lame they couldn't hit, run, and throw—were just a bit better or luckier than the draft-deferred ballplayers on the other clubs. The Browns ran out of miracles, however, in the "Streetcar Series," losing to the Cards in six games. They would finish third in 1945—the Detroit Tigers taking the AL pennant and defeating the Cubs in the World Series—then descend in the postwar years to their accustomed depths before being transplanted to Baltimore.

The wartime ballplayer did his best, but it seemed even the most extraordinary efforts might bring nothing more than ridicule from the press box.

As the 1944 pennant races entered their final weeks, a national magazine profiled "The Unbelievable Browns." Kyle Crichton wrote in *Collier's*: "They have a rickety-looking pitching staff and an outfield that has the appearance of something discarded from the Salvation Army, but these are war times and the rest of the league is no better."

Stanley Woodward, sports editor of the *New York Herald Tribune* and decidedly not a member of the "Gee whiz" school of sportswriting, commented one wartime spring on how the New York Giants were exuding optimism upon the conclusion of their exhibition season. The Giants, Woodward told his readers, "have been promising in press releases that they are less lousy than heretofore—or anyway that the rest of the major league clubs have so increased their lousiness that the native, intrinsic Giant brand no longer will be noticeable."

How bad was wartime baseball?

The 1946 big league rosters provide a clue. Of the 128 men considered starters during 1945, only 32 were still playing regularly for the same clubs in the first postwar season.

Asked to contrast the caliber of play with the immediate pre- and postwar years, Red Barber, a close observer of the wartime baseball scene from his "Catbird Seat" at Ebbets Field, says: "It's like apples and oranges, you can't compare it. It was just a matter of playing anyone who was breathing."

He adds, however, "Nobody asked too much. It was interesting and it gave people something to do."

Indeed, the last wartime season saw an all-time attendance mark set. Many of the ballplayers didn't really belong in big league uniforms, but there were two hot pennant races.

Lou Boudreau, who managed the Indians through the war years while playing shortstop on an ankle not quite up to the military's standards, agrees with Barber that baseball was still entertaining.

The level of play, Boudreau acknowledges, "was inferior because we lost a lot of fellows." But he notes, "The fan is still loyal. And he's out there for a little relaxation, a little enjoyment."

And that—lest it be forgotten in an era of free agents and multi-million dollar contracts—is what the game is supposed to be all about.

I

The Road to War

1

A Green Light from the White House

Interrupting a duck-hunting trip, he stopped off in Cleveland and joined 150 others queued up before nine o'clock in the morning. He lived on an Iowa farm for much of the year and was not quite twenty-two years old, but his plans were of interest to millions and so reporters were on hand.

"I'll be all right," he said. "I've got more control with that shotgun in my car than I have with a baseball."

In San Francisco, another celebrity, just a few years older than the first, was stumped for a moment by one of the eleven questions on the form before him. What was the legal name of his employer? "American League Baseball Club of New York" would do.

A motorist passing through the upstate New York community of Geneva decided to pull over outside City Hall. That would be as good a place as any to provide his particulars.

It is Wednesday, October 16, 1940. Bob Feller, Joe DiMaggio, and Hank Greenberg have joined fellow Americans between the ages twenty-one and thirty-five registering for the first peacetime draft in the nation's history.

Peacetime for the United States—Pearl Harbor is more than a year away. But it is now thirteen and one-half months since Hitler's blitzkrieg attack on Poland launched the war in Europe and four months past the fall of France.

Thirteen days after 16,316,908 men have answered the summons to register with their draft boards, Secretary of War Henry L. Stimson stands on the stage of the War Department auditorium along Constitution Avenue in downtown Washington, his eyes covered with a strip of yellow linen taken from a chair used by signers of the Declaration of Independence. Stimson reaches into a huge fishbowl that served a similar purpose twenty-three years earlier and takes out a one-inch-

3

long bright blue capsule. It is passed to President Franklin D. Roosevelt, who opens the capsule, removes a slip of paper, and calls out "One Five Eight" into a battery of radio network microphones. The first number has been selected in America's draft lottery. For many hours, cabinet members, Selective Service officials, congressmen, and just ordinary citizens will draw 9,000 capsules—each with a number corresponding to those assigned to registrants by the 6,175 draft boards—to determine the general order in which the nation's manpower will be called for military service.

Feller and DiMaggio would find their lottery numbers well down on the priority list; the Cleveland Indians' strikeout king and the Yankees' star outfielder would not be of interest to their draft boards for a while. Greenberg, however, had the 621st number to be drawn and he was a bachelor. No matter, they all would go in time. The Detroit Tiger slugger would be the first, entering the Army the following May. Feller would enlist in the Navy three days after Pearl Harbor and DiMaggio would join the Army Air Corps in February 1943.

As the nation began to mobilize for war in this autumn of 1940, baseball wanted to set the record straight—it would be in there pitching with the rest of America. Commissioner Kenesaw Mountain Landis, the stern, white-haired former federal judge who had ruled the game with an iron hand since 1921, was determined that no special treatment be sought.

National League President Ford Frick declared, "Baseball is ready, yes eager to do its duty in national defense. We are not going to Washington with any appeal or even a request for information as to what the authorities intend to do about the players."

Baseball didn't have to go to the capital; Clark Griffith was already there. The seventy-year-old owner of the Senators had built a friendly relationship with the president beginning in 1917 when, as the wartime assistant secretary of the Navy, Roosevelt marched to the flagpole on the opening day of the baseball season in step with the Griffith-managed Washington team. "The Old Fox" would do some quiet lobbying at the White House.

Just before the 1941 season got under way, Griffith had some public thoughts. He speculated in an interview with Dan Daniel of the *Sporting News* that the government "is willing to help us" although "baseball has not gone to the War Department for relief."

Griffith understood that Selective Service officials might limit their pickings to one or two players per club until the '41 pennant race concluded or perhaps wouldn't draft any big leaguers during the season if the teams agreed to drill under military personnel.

"Every club would be placed under a drill sergeant who would work with the men at least one hour every morning and put the squad through a public demonstration before every game," he envisioned. "When you consider that our players are in fine physical condition to begin with, I feel sure that by October we would show at least as well trained a body of men as you could find in any Army camp across the country."

Griffith didn't say where he got the idea players might be permitted to trade public drills for draft deferments, and if anyone in the War Department had such a plan in mind, it was never implemented.

There had, however, been some fancy stepping during World War I. The Senator players who paraded with Roosevelt that April day twenty-four years before had carried bats on their shoulders simulating rifles. Army sergeants had supervised drilling at the ballparks, with the St. Louis Browns winning a $500 prize put up by American League President Ban Johnson in August 1917 for the club with the snappiest formations. (The Brownies seemed to thrive in wartime—they would win their only pennant in 1944.)

Griffith then turned from the fate of individual ballplayers to the larger question of whether baseball itself could justify continuing amid the austerities a war would bring. He concluded, "We deserve some consideration" on two counts: "There is the question of national morale and baseball. In times of trouble, people want to be entertained. There is the status of baseball as a vast business with big investments and appreciable revenues for the government through the various forms of taxes."

There were other rumblings from baseball men as the game moved into what would be the final prewar season. Brooklyn Dodger President Larry MacPhail, never one to shy from controversy, complained that the draft might work a particular hardship on ballplayers. While men were being called for just twelve months' service, a player who entered the military in the summer of 1941 would not only miss part of that baseball year but would be returning, presumably without having had a chance to resharpen his skills, in the midst of the next season. It would be more equitable, MacPhail suggested, to hold off on calling up ballplayers until perhaps October 1. Then they would miss just one full season.

"The draft, as it is going to affect our young baseball players, is unfair," he contended. "By drafting them into service in June they are knocking our boys out of two years' play. It cuts deeply into a young boy's baseball career."

The *Sporting News,* weekly bible of baseball, urged that ballplayers taken into the armed forces be given a chance to practice their trade.

"Men qualified as specialists ought not to be held to the routine of barracks or field duties," suggested a May 1941 editorial. An outfielder-turned-soldier assigned to "slugging the ball for some camp team" would be "giving more material aid to the upbuilding of esprit de corps than merely shouldering a rifle or squinting behind a machine gun."

The first man from the ranks of organized baseball to be drafted was Bill Embick, an outfielder for the Harrisburg Senators of the Interstate League who went into the Army on November 25, 1940. Billy Southworth, Jr., another minor league outfielder and son of the St. Louis Cardinals' manager, took honors as the first ballplayer to enlist, joining the Army Air Corps in December 1940. He would become a highly decorated pilot and complete numerous bombing missions over Europe unscathed, only to be killed in a crash at New York's LaGuardia Field a few months before the end of the war.

Another milestone was recorded on January 10, 1941, when Gene Stack, a promising twenty-two-year-old pitcher in the Chicago White Sox organization, entered Camp Custer, Michigan. Stack, who otherwise would have gone to spring training with the Sox, was the first man on a major league roster to be called into the service. He, too, was ill-fated. After pitching for the Army post in a June 1942 game against a semipro team at Michigan City, Indiana, Stack stopped with his teammates at a roadside diner. He put a few nickles into a jukebox. Then, suddenly, the young man slumped to the floor and died of a heart seizure.

As for genuine major leaguers, there were rumors in the weeks following the draft lottery that Tiger pitcher Johnny Gorsica—born John Gorczyca—had joined a Polish air squadron training in Canada for duty with the British Royal Air Force. But Gorsica turned up in Beckley, West Virginia, where he was spending the winter with his wife and son, working in a drugstore.

"The only bombarding he contemplates is on the pins at the bowling alley in Beckley," said a news dispatch from the scene.

In 1941 the nation was just beginning to marshal its manpower; draft calls were relatively light and dependency deferments common. Since many ballplayers were married men with children, the major league rosters would be virtually intact during the last peacetime season.

Hugh "Losing Pitcher" Mulcahy—he'd earned the nickname for his seventy-six defeats with the lowly Phillies from 1937 through 1940 —was the big leagues' initial contribution to the military, going to Camp Edwards, Massachusetts, on March 8, 1941, with 270 others from the Boston area. Four more major leaguers were to join the

Billy Southworth, Jr., at Randolph Field, Texas, preparing to take a few swings against the Nazis.

service before the '41 season concluded, three of them rather obscure. Pitchers Oad Swigart of the Pirates and Lou Thuman of the Senators and outfielder Joe "Muscles" Gallagher of the Dodgers wouldn't be especially missed.

The war really hit home for baseball on May 7 with the drafting of Hank Greenberg, the game's premier long ball hitter and the American League's Most Valuable Player in 1940, when he led the Tigers to a pennant with 41 homers, 150 RBIs—both league highs—and a .340 average. At his first draft physical in Lakeland, Florida, during the Tigers' '41 spring training camp, Greenberg was found to have flat feet. The doctors recommended he be considered for limited duty only, but a second examination on April 18 in Detroit, ordered by the thirty-year-old slugger's Michigan draft board, found him fit for full military service.

Great hoopla surrounded Greenberg's trading of a $55,000-a-year job in the Detroit outfield for the $21-a-month pay of an Army private. Two days before he was to report for duty, his teammates threw a farewell party at the Franklin Hills Country Club, inviting the Yankees, who were in town, to come along, and presented the star with an inscribed gold watch.*

Greenberg went out in grand style on May 6 with two homers, powering the Tigers to a 7–4 victory over the Yanks. He entered the Army the next morning, turning down a last moment offer to delay things a day so that he could attend ceremonies at which the Tigers raised their 1940 pennant flag.

"I have been ordered to report May 7 and will do so," said Greenberg. "I want no favors."

There was bedlam at the Detroit induction center. The new GI posed for newsreels and signed one thousand autographs for fellow recruits, sergeants involved in processing duties, and women workers from a nearby corset factory.

When Greenberg arrived later that day at Camp Custer in Battle

---

*The Tigers were not the first club to think up the idea of giving a watch to a departing serviceman. During World War I, the Dodgers established a fund to aid the dependents of ballplayers called into the military, with donations coming from owner Charles Ebbets and the men remaining behind. In the winter of 1918, when he heard that pitcher Jeff Pfeffer had enlisted in the Navy, Ebbets took some of the cash, bought a wristwatch, had it suitably engraved, and sent it to the hurler. The story did not end there. No sooner had the Dodgers opened their 1918 spring training camp at Hot Springs, Arkansas, than in walked Pfeffer, proudly wearing the watch. The pitcher explained he had not joined the regular Navy but an outfit called the Naval Auxiliary Reserve Force. The gesture, however, wasn't for naught—Pfeffer was soon called by the real Navy and sent to the Great Lakes training base.

Pvt. Henry Greenberg on his first day in the Army.

Creek, one-third of the 15,000-man Fifth Division was at the train station to say hello. After checking in at the reception company, Greenberg led the other inductees in a march to the mess hall where he had pork chops, mashed potatoes, green peas, fruit salad, and milk, and declared: "I'm glad to be here, they're treating me fine."

Assigned as an antitank gunner, Greenberg went on maneuvers for a time in Tennessee, but there was an opportunity for some baseball. Greenberg didn't play for Camp Custer, but got into a game in August when the post team visited the Michigan state penitentiary at Jackson. Loaned out as a first baseman for the prisoners, he had a perfect day with a 390-foot homer, two doubles, and a single, leading the inmates to a 10–2 victory. By November '41, having risen to the rank of sergeant and making all of sixty dollars a month, Greenberg was again hearing cheers from thousands—onlookers at a Detroit Armistice Day parade in which he rode on a gun carrier.

Under draft law provisions making men over the age of twenty-eight eligible for release after serving a minimum of 180 days, Greenberg was discharged from active duty on December 5. Two days later, the Japanese attacked Pearl Harbor. Without waiting for a formal summons, he went right back into the Army. Greenberg transferred eventually to the Army Air Corps, obtained a commission, and served in the China–Burma–India theater in an administrative capacity. He would not return to baseball until July 1945.

No one repeated the kind of gaffe said to have been made by Harry Weaver, a pitcher for the Chicago Cubs during World War I, who, according to the *Sporting News,* filed a request for a deferment with his Warren, Pennsylvania, draft board on grounds "we have a good chance to win the pennant."

But a situation potentially embarrassing to the baseball world was arising: a man might be sound enough to play major league ball yet physically unfit for military service.

Outfielder Morrie Arnovich, turned down for poor teeth, was among the first to be put on the defensive. Arnovich denied indignantly that he had sought a deferment. He displayed papers documenting his molar problems and one day offered incontrovertible evidence: he pulled out his upper and lower bridges to show the world he wasn't a malingerer. Although allowed to play for the Giants in 1941, Arnovich later went into the service, bad teeth and all.

An entire North Carolina local draft board and its medical examiner resigned in the summer of 1941 to protest the rejection by doctors at Fort Bragg of Irv Dickens, a minor league second baseman. Though certified by the board as physically fit, Dickens had been sent home by Army doctors because of varicose veins. He, too, would eventually find his way into the military, later joining the Army Air Corps.

Hank Gowdy, a Cincinnati Reds coach with impeccable patriotic credentials, decided to speak up for the athlete labeled a physical reject. The first ballplayer to enlist during World War I—he left his catching job with the Boston Braves to serve in the trenches in France—Gowdy presumably knew whereof he spoke when he explained: "A man should be physically perfect for military service because it calls for sustained action over a long period over exceedingly trying conditions. In baseball a man with a handicap often can meet the game's demands. Of course, he is not continually in action as frequently is the case in the Army."

Gowdy himself re-upped at age fifty-three, obtaining a commission as an Army captain after the 1942 season. He was assigned to

handle recreational activities at Fort Benning, Georgia, whose baseball field had been named in his honor years before.

Baseball, meanwhile, had a conscientious objector in its ranks as
war approached—pitcher Tom Ananicz of the American Association's Kansas City Blues. Then there was the Dodger fan who very
briefly claimed that status. Robert Anderson, a twenty-six-year-old
Brooklynite who hadn't missed an opener at Ebbets Field in ten years,
was scheduled to enter the Army on April 7, 1941, eight days before
the start of the season. To keep his attendance record intact, Anderson filed a claim as a conscientious objector, knowing his induction
would be delayed while an investigation was undertaken. He got to
see his beloved Dodgers open up—alas, they lost to the Giants, 6–4—
and the next day withdrew his plea for exemption from military
service.

Soon shipped to Camp Upton, Long Island, Anderson would miss
a season that proved eventful for the Dodgers and one of the most
memorable in baseball history.

Brooklyn won its first pennant in twenty-one years, thanks to a
series of sharp deals engineered by Larry MacPhail. The heavy-hitting Dolph Camilli, an ex-Phil, held down first base. Billy Herman,
obtained from the Cubs in exchange for two mediocre players plus
sixty thousand dollars, and young Pee Wee Reese, purchased from
the Red Sox farm system, formed a brilliant double-play combination.
Cookie Lavagetto, once a Pirate, capably handled third base. In center
field, marked for greatness (his famous encounter with an outfield
wall still a year off), was "Pistol" Pete Reiser, set loose by Landis from
the Cardinals' farm system as a penalty for infringement of minor
league operating procedures. Right field belonged to "The People's
Cherce," American League castoff Dixie Walker, perhaps the most
popular player ever to wear a Dodger uniform. In left field was Joe
Medwick of the old Cardinal Gashouse Gang, some good baseball still
left in him. Mickey Owen, another former Cardinal, was behind the
plate.

Camilli won the National League's Most Valuable Player award
with 34 homers and 120 runs batted in, both league highs. Reiser took
the batting championship with a .343 mark while Medwick hit .318
and Walker .311.

Kirby Higbe and Whitlow Wyatt won twenty-two games each; the
rest of the mound strength was provided by Freddie Fitzsimmons,
Johnny Allen, Curt Davis, Larry French, and Hugh Casey. Like the
everyday lineup, all the pitchers had previous baseball addresses.

Masterminding the Dodgers to the pennant by two and one-half games over the Cardinals was fiery Leo Durocher, in his third season as manager.

Joe McCarthy's Yankees, leaving the second-place Red Sox 17 games behind, swept to their fifth pennant and World Series championship in six years. DiMaggio took the American League's Most Valuable Player title with 30 home runs, 125 RBIs, and a .357 average. The rest of the outfield wasn't bad either. Charlie Keller in left produced 33 homers and 122 RBIs and right-fielder Tommy Henrich accounted for 31 home runs and 85 runs batted in. Anchoring the infield were Joe Gordon at second base and rookie Phil Rizzuto at shortstop. Veteran Red Rolfe was at third base, Johnny Sturm the first baseman. Bill Dickey, slowing down a bit at age thirty-four, did the catching.

The pitching staff was led by Red Ruffing and Lefty Gomez who had fifteen victories apiece, followed by Marius Russo with fourteen wins. Johnny Murphy handled the relief chores.

The Yankees dispatched the Dodgers in a five-game World Series best remembered for Mickey Owen's two-out, dropped third strike in the ninth inning, costing Brooklyn the next-to-last game.

Most of all, 1941 was the year of Joe DiMaggio and Ted Williams.

For the Yankee center fielder, in the prime of his career, it began on May 15 with a single off Edgar Smith of the White Sox. He would not go another game without a hit until the night of July 17 when two great stops by Indian third baseman Ken Keltner before a crowd of 67,468 at Cleveland's Municipal Stadium ended baseball's longest consecutive game hitting streak at 56. Left far behind was Wee Willie Keeler's 44-game mark set in 1897 with the old Baltimore Orioles.

Williams, in his third season with the Red Sox, went into the final day with an average of .39955, technically making him the first .400 hitter since Bill Terry batted .401 for the Giants in 1930. Manager Joe Cronin offered to let his young star sit out the season-ending doubleheader with the Athletics at Shibe Park, but Williams insisted on playing, went six for eight, and wound up at .406.

Bob Feller reigned as baseball's top pitcher, striking out 260 batters en route to a 25–13 record. His Indians finished in a tie for fourth place with the Tigers who, minus Greenberg, wound up 15 games behind their pennant-winning record of 1940, and down 400,000 in attendance.

Detroit would not, of course, suffer alone. By the midpoint of the war, Herman, Reese, and Reiser; DiMaggio, Rizzuto, and Dickey;

Getting ready for Finnish Relief Fund benefit game are (left to right) Mel Ott, Ernie Lombardi, Joe DiMaggio, and Jimmie Foxx.

Williams and Feller, and scores of their fellow ballplayers would be in Army khaki or Navy blue.

The baseball owners were well aware, meanwhile, that beyond the loss of their top talent, the very survival of the game, among other things, would be at stake if America went into battle. The so-called national pastime might be viewed as a wasteful frivolity, using manpower, materials, and transportation facilities needed for the war effort. A few moves to store up goodwill therefore were in order.

The first gesture was made in March 1940 when an all-star game was played in Tampa for benefit of the Finnish Relief Fund which, under the direction of Herbert Hoover, was aiding thousands of Finns left homeless by the three and one-half month Winter War with

Russia. A crowd of 13,180—the largest ever for a Florida baseball game—turned out to see the National League beat the American League, 2–1. The spring training spectacle raised $22,000.

More than $53,000 in receipts from the 1941 summer all-star game in Detroit went to the United Service Organizations (USO)—the agency providing recreational activities for servicemen. It was the first time since the midseason contest was inaugurated in 1933 that the gate did not go to aid needy retired ballplayers.

The clubs began to admit servicemen free of charge during the 1941 season with each team setting its own guidelines. The Yankees, Dodgers, and Giants hosted soldiers and sailors if they wore their uniforms and arrived in groups accompanied by officers.

Larry MacPhail, while pressing for ballplayer deferments until the '41 season was over, had no use for isolationism. He served as head of the Brooklyn division of the Committee to Defend America by Aiding the Allies. A request by the America First Committee to use Ebbets Field for a June 1941 rally to be addressed by arch-isolationist Charles Lindbergh was nixed by MacPhail on grounds that the park could not be a forum for "propaganda."

The Dodgers, with some help from a newspaper that was looking for a good human interest story, would be pleased, however, to identify themselves with the American fighting man, even if he wasn't fighting quite yet.

When Private Murray Waldenburg arrived at Camp Wheeler, Georgia, in late summer 1941, with a barracks bag labeled "Brooklyn," an officer inquired, "What do you have in there, son, the remains of the Dodgers' pennant chances?"

The story went that Waldenburg told the officer he could do with him as he wished, but "please don't make humorous remarks about the Dodgers."

The exchange made the rounds of the troops and got back to the *New York Journal–American* which, when the Dodgers clinched the pennant, prevailed upon the Camp Wheeler commander, Brigadier General John H. Hester, to grant Waldenburg a pass so that he could see a World Series game.

The Hearst paper sent a reporter down to the Georgia post during the final weekend of the season to accompany the loyal Brooklyn boy back home. Waldenburg was greeted at LaGuardia Field by the borough presidents of Brooklyn and Queens, then whisked via police escort to Ebbets Field, where he posed with the Dodger players and collected their autographs.

In a page one interview, Waldenburg had a prediction for *Journal–American* readers: "What is going to happen to the Yankees shouldn't happen to Hitler."

The young man sat with William Randolph Hearst Jr. in the publisher's Yankee Stadium box at the Series opener, and "to Mr. Hearst, Waldenburg murmured gratefully, 'this is the happiest moment of my life,' " the paper reported.

The Brooklynite returned to Camp Wheeler after the game, sparing himself the misery of watching the Dodgers go down to defeat.

As the nation moved into its final weeks at peace, Clark Griffith did a good turn on a grander scale. He converted the ballpark of the Senators' Charlotte, North Carolina, Piedmont League club into a camping ground for some 4,000 soldiers from nearby bases who were invading the town on weekend leaves but couldn't find accommodations.

Much of the baseball establishment got the news of Pearl Harbor in Chicago where the owners convened for their winter meetings. The session at the Palmer House opened on schedule the morning of Tuesday, December 9, when Ford Frick wired Roosevelt assurances that the National League "as its first order of business" had pledged "complete cooperation and assistance in this time of national crisis." Frick concluded, "We are yours to command."

A recess was called Tuesday night to hear a national radio address by the president piped into two large, adjoining dining rooms at the hotel. With Washington saying nothing to the contrary, the owners then went ahead with plans for the 1942 season, making no changes in the schedule or training sites.

A look back at World War I, however, would have given cause for concern.

Few ballplayers were called into the service during the 1917 season, the United States having stayed out of the war until April of that year. The majors retrenched, however, in 1918 as manpower losses began to mount, scheduling only 140 games instead of the traditional 154 and selecting spring training sites closer to home as a travel conservation measure. The worst was yet to come. The federal government declared baseball, along with other sports, to be nonessential activities, and on May 23, 1918, General Enoch Crowder, the provost marshal of the armed forces, issued a "work or fight" order setting July 1 as the deadline for men in such occupations to get war-related jobs or be drafted.

The baseball owners asked that the players be exempted from the

order until October 15 so that the season could be completed and the
World Series played. Secretary of War Newton D. Baker agreed to
extend the deadline, but only until September 1. The clubs could
have tried to play into October with men too young or too old for the
draft, but decided to call it quits on Labor Day, going twenty-four
hours past the new September 1 deadline to reap holiday gate receipts. (The Cleveland players, however, were taking no chances.
They refused to travel to St. Louis for their holiday weekend games,
which had no bearing on the American League pennant race.)

Baseball officials got the War Department to hold off on drafting
any players from the pennant-winning Cubs and Red Sox so that the
World Series could be held in early September. But as matters developed, the game would have been better off forgetting about the Series. While doughboys were dying in the trenches of Europe, the Chicago and Boston ballplayers, already privileged with a brief respite
from the "work or fight" order, decided to threaten a strike.

The three-man National Commission, which ran baseball then,
had indicated the winning World Series share would be at least $2,000
with the losers guaranteed $1,400 each, but as the Series progressed,
it became clear the players would wind up with a lot less. In 1918, for
the first time, members of the second, third, and fourth place teams in
each league were to receive a cut of the money previously earmarked
exclusively for the Series participants. In addition, attendance, down
by 40 percent during the season, was relatively poor at the first few
Series games—fan interest had been eroded by the war—and the
players had already pledged 10 percent of their shares to the Red
Cross.

The 24,694 spectators arriving at Fenway Park for the fifth game
of the Series were puzzled when the teams did not come out on time
for batting practice. And they wondered what mounted police were
doing prancing around the outfield. The players had balked at taking
the field, demanding a guarantee of $1,500 for the winners' share and
$1,000 to the losers, or a postponement of the revenue-sharing ar-
rangement with the also-rans until the following season. The police
were on hand to deal with a feared riot if the game were canceled.

Ban Johnson, said to have arrived at the ballpark a bit the worse
for wear after lingering in the Copley Plaza Hotel bar, pleaded with
player representatives Harry Hooper of the Red Sox and Les Mann
of the Cubs to call off the strike. A wartime walkout would give baseball a black eye, insisted Johnson, with great emotion.

Hooper countered at one point with a suggestion that the players give their entire share to the Red Cross and the owners similarly turn over their own profits. This was going a bit too far for management. Finally, seeing that Johnson was not in a state to be reasoned with, the players gave in. They took the field an hour past the scheduled starting time, issuing a statement that they would carry on "for the sake of the game, for the sake of the public, and for the sake of the wounded soldiers and sailors in the grandstand."

The Red Sox lost to the Cubs, 3–0, but clinched the Series the next day. Only 15,238 fans showed up for the finale, the strike threat apparently having disgusted a good many would-be customers.

When it was all over, each Boston player received $1,108 for his efforts, the smallest winning Series share ever, while Chicago got $671 per man, second tiniest loser's pot.

So the owners meeting at the Palmer House following Pearl Harbor could not have been comforted by baseball's wartime past.

They did, however, resurrect in altered form a program that had brought the game some goodwill amid its otherwise unhappy experiences.

Two weeks after the United States entered World War I, Senator manager Clark Griffith announced a public fund-raising drive to buy athletic equipment for servicemen. The nation's fifty-two thousand post offices were designated to receive donations, and contributors were to be rewarded by having their names listed in the *Sporting News.* The ball clubs also kicked in with some gate receipts. The first shipment to the American Expeditionary Force in France—fifty-one equipment kits—went down in the torpedoing of the freighter *Kansan,* but the fund eventually sent $95,000 worth of baseball sporting goods to military camps.

Another athletic equipment fund would be organized in World War II. Landis' office and the two leagues kicked things off at the December '41 meeting with a $24,000 contribution while earmarking proceeds from the following summer's all-star game for the drive.

Griffith and Frick, named to chair the fund, met in Washington on December 30 with representatives of major sporting goods firms and a joint Army and Navy recreation committee to place initial orders for 1,500 kits containing three bats and a dozen balls each. For catchers on service ball clubs, there would be mitts, chest protectors, and shin guards as well.

While announcing the manufacturers had agreed to cut their

Bob Feller takes Navy oath from Lt. Comdr. Gene Tunney.

prices, Griffith was quick to provide assurances that the equipment "is the best we can get—none of that cheap stuff for the soldiers and sailors, only the best for them."

A minor consequence of Pearl Harbor, meanwhile, was that southern California would be spared the St. Louis Browns. Don Barnes, president of the lackluster Brownies, had received informal approval from the other owners to shift his franchise to Los Angeles; final ratification was scheduled to come at the December meetings. But with the war leaving the game's future uncertain, the move was abandoned. Perhaps it was for the best. As one observer who preferred anonymity put it, "Here is Los Angeles threatened with bombing, with blackouts, and along comes Don Barnes. It's downright unpatriotic. He's destroying the morale of Los Angeles utterly."

By the time the December sessions concluded, Hank Greenberg was no longer the sole baseball star in military service. Bob Feller had been in his auto en route to the meetings when he heard the radio flash reporting the attack on Pearl Harbor. Classified 1-A—available for immediate service—Feller quickly contacted former heavyweight champion Gene Tunney who was recruiting athletes to serve in a Navy physical training program he headed. After bidding good-bye to reporters in the Palmer House pressroom, where it was said "he received his first wound of the war—he sat on a tack," Feller was sworn into the Navy by Lieutenant Commander Tunney on Wednesday, December 10. The noon ceremony at the Chicago courthouse was carried on radio and filmed for newsreels.

Feller reported to the Norfolk Naval Training Station in January '42, expressing hopes that he could "throw a few strikes for Uncle Sam."

On April 3, Feller began doing just that—blowing the ball past Richmond University batters in a three-inning debut for the naval station's baseball team. He spent 1942 pitching for the Norfolk club and military all-star units, then requested sea duty and saw extensive combat in the Pacific as an antiaircraft gunner aboard a battleship.

Soon after the nation went to war, baseball sought official word on whether it would be allowed to continue. Although Landis refused to visit Washington and argue the game's cause, he did sit down on January 14, 1942, to pencil a note to Roosevelt.

"Baseball is about to adopt schedules, sign players, make vast commitments, go to training camps," wrote the commissioner. "What do you want it to do? If you believe we ought to close down for the duration of the war, we are ready to do so immediately. If you feel we ought to continue, we would be delighted to do so. We await your order."

Roosevelt replied two days later in what became known as the "Green Light" letter. Expressing what he said was only a "personal" view and suggesting the final decision must rest with the club owners, the president felt baseball was worthy of continuing, citing its role as a morale booster. At the same time, Roosevelt stressed that individual players would have to take their chances with the draft like everyone else.

"I honestly feel that it would be best for the country to keep baseball going," FDR responded. "There will be fewer people unemployed and everybody will work longer hours and harder than ever before. And that means that they ought to have a chance for recreation and for taking their minds off their work even more than before. Baseball provides a recreation which does not last over two hours or two hours and a half, and which can be got for very little cost. . . . Here is another way of looking at it—if 300 teams use 5,000 or 6,000 players [here he was referring to the minor leagues as well as the majors] these players are a definite recreational asset to at least 20,-000,000 of their fellow citizens—and that in my judgment is thoroughly worthwhile."

Roosevelt continued: "As to the players themselves, I know you agree with me that individual players who are of active military or naval age should go, without question, into the services. Even if the actual quality of the teams is lowered by the greater use of older players, this will not dampen the popularity of the sport. Of course, if the individual has some particular aptitude in a trade or profession, he ought to serve the government. That, however, is a matter which I know you can handle with complete justice."

Although Landis hadn't asked his views on the matter, the president also put in a word for night baseball.

Play under the lights was still a matter of controversy seven years after its introduction in the majors at Crosley Field by Larry Mac-Phail, who was running the Reds then. Traditionalists like Yankee President Ed Barrow viewed night ball with distaste while have-nots such as the Senators and Browns plugged it as a spur to attendance.

At the time Landis wrote to Roosevelt, the tentative 1942 schedule limited each club to seven home night games. And the Yanks, Red Sox, Braves, Tigers, and Cubs (Wrigley Field a holdout to this day) still hadn't got around to installing lighting systems at their parks.

Though he may have been simply doing a favor for Clark Griffith, a convert to night ball, the president suggested in his letter that a continued heavy diet of day games would induce absenteeism at war plants, writing that he hoped "night baseball can be extended because it gives an opportunity to the day shift to see a game occasionally."

Properly grateful for Roosevelt's go-ahead, Landis responded, "I hope our performance would be such as to justify the president's faith."

American League President Will Harridge felt the White House confirmed "the conviction held by all baseball men that the 'national pastime' has a definite place in the welfare of our country, particularly in times of stress."

And three weeks after receipt of the Green Light letter, baseball granted Roosevelt's plea for additional night games, allowing the Senators to schedule twenty-one contests under the lights while raising the limit in other ballparks from seven to fourteen.

The outlines of Roosevelt's note to Landis would constitute the federal government's stance on baseball throughout the war years—sanction for the game itself but no favoritism toward individual players.

Landis, described by his biographer, J.G. Taylor Spink, the late publisher of the *Sporting News,* as "one of the nation's most bitter anti–New Dealers," was not about to keep after FDR personally to ensure that baseball remained in Washington's good graces as war pressures mounted. But Clark Griffith might, having developed an acquaintanceship with Roosevelt from annual White House visits to drop off a season's pass and from hosting season-opening first-ball ceremonies traditionally attended by the president.

George Case, who joined the Washington Senators in 1937 and played with the club for ten years, credits Griffith with a major role in keeping baseball alive during the war. Six times the American League's stolen base leader—a lifetime 349 steals to his credit—Case was serving as baserunning and batting instructor for the Seattle Mariners' minor league teams during the 1979 season. One spring day, at

FDR performs 1941 season-opening ritual at Griffith Stadium. Alongside the president is his military aide, Gen. Edwin M. "Pa" Watson.

*Clark Griffith presents Roosevelt with 1943 season's passes for himself and
First Lady.*

his home in Morrisville, Pennsylvania, a pleasant suburb of Philadelphia, the ex-outfielder reflected on his old boss.

"Clark Griffith was really instrumental in baseball surviving, he
was the guy responsible," says Case. "He spent considerable time im-
ploring Roosevelt to continue baseball. He kept getting assurances
from the White House baseball would continue—but there wouldn't
be any favors shown to baseball players."

Case continues: "During the winters, Mr. Griffith kept in contact
with the players. He implored everybody to stay with baseball until
they were called up. He kept reminding us they were in close contact
with the government."

Clark Griffith's son, Calvin Griffith, president of the Minnesota
Twins—as the Senators have been known for quite some time—
agrees his father had Roosevelt's ear.

Looking back to the eve of the 1942 season, he says, "Clark Griffith was at the White House and President Roosevelt questioned him as to what government could do for baseball. Mr. Griffith told him that the best thing would be to just give baseball permission to carry on the game for the recreation of the people in the United States. The president agreed that this was needed at that time."

And so baseball headed warily toward its first wartime season. Only a few big league ballplayers had joined the military by spring training, but complications and controversy were brewing.

There was the question of who was stuck with Don Padgett, a catcher-outfielder bought by the Dodgers from the Cardinals in December '41 for $25,000. Padgett played for Brooklyn during the early part of the '42 spring camp and then reported for his draft physical. Two weeks before the start of the season, he joined the Navy. The Dodgers tried to get their money back and have Padgett returned to the Cardinals, but Landis ruled a deal was a deal.

The Reds wanted to be sure their fans knew who might soon be exchanging a baseball uniform for a set of fatigues. So they listed each player's selective service classification in their 1942 brochure.

Ted Williams found himself under fire for being deferred as the sole support of his mother, who was divorced and spent much of her time as a Salvation Army worker. Soon after the close of his sensational 1941 season, the twenty-three-year-old Williams was given a 3A dependency deferment. But in January '42, while spending the winter hunting and fishing in Minnesota, he received notice of reclassification into 1A. With Williams' consent, a lawyer designated to handle appeals from the decisions of local draft boards in the state took the matter to a presidential appeals panel. Soon the young phenom was back in 3A classification.

Far from a popular figure in the press even in his early days, Williams was rapped by a couple of sports columnists for accepting reinstatement of the deferment. In his autobiography, *My Turn at Bat,* Williams contends that a Boston newspaper sent a private detective to his hometown of San Diego to find out if he really supported his mother, and that Red Sox owner Tom Yawkey felt it might be best it he didn't report to spring training. He also notes he had a four-thousand-dollar contract to endorse Quaker Oats and "I used to eat them all the time, but they canceled out on me because of all this unfair stuff and I haven't eaten a Quaker Oat since."

Under pressure, Williams considered giving up his deferment. He discussed enlisting in the Navy with Mickey Cochrane, the former star catcher and Tiger manager, who had been given a commission to run the baseball program at the Great Lakes Naval Training Station. But Williams says that when Cochrane warned he'd be booed out of every ballpark if he tried to play, his anger over being singled out for criticism grew and he decided to return to the Red Sox.

Upon checking in at the Boston training camp in Sarasota, Florida, Williams told reporters, "Anyone who knows the facts in my case will not condemn me. This is the toughest decision I've ever had to make. I realize I'm going to take a great deal of abuse from the crowds this year. I don't know why I should."

In fact, Williams' fears weren't realized. An envelope did arrive one day with a blank piece of yellow paper inside and there were scattered catcalls, but he generally got a good reception from the fans.

Williams soon decided that after playing out the 1942 season, he would become a Navy flyer.

"I'm glad it's all straightened out now," he said upon arriving at a Boston induction center May 22, tieless as usual, to be sworn in as a seaman second class. "It's a load off my mind even though I felt I was doing the right thing all the time. I'm tickled to death and I'm hoping I'll get into the air quick to start some slugging against the Axis."

While awaiting a call to active duty, Williams confined his slugging to the offerings of American League pitchers, taking the batting Triple Crown with 36 homers, 137 RBIs, and a .356 average. With the Red Sox finishing a distant second to the Yankees, the MVP award went, however, to New York's Joe Gordon.

Williams was otherwise kept busy taking evening math and science courses at Boston's Mechanics Art High School in the Navy's V-5 preflight training program. Among his 200 classmates was Johnny Pesky, the Red Sox's outstanding rookie shortstop.

After the '42 season, Williams left for the Navy, won his wings, and then spent most of the war as a flight instructor at the Pensacola, Florida, Naval Air Station. He was in San Francisco, awaiting shipment to the Pacific for combat duty, when Japan surrendered. Sent on to Hawaii, he finished out his hitch playing baseball at Pearl Harbor for a marine flight-wing team. Williams would get his share of action when he was recalled by the Marines for the Korean War. Almost shot down on one mission, he barely managed to return to base in a fighter crippled by antiaircraft fire.

Spring training during the first war year went pretty much as usual—the move from Florida and California to northern camps, necessitated by travel curbs, would not come until 1943—but there were signs of the times.

Ted Williams joins the Navy team, Lt. F. T. Donahue doing the honors.

The Phillie ballplayers were briefly put through drills by Army officers at the club's Miami Beach training site, visited a nearby base to inspect fighters and bombers, and were entertained by air corps stunts above their Flamingo Park diamond. In a throwback to World War I, the players marched with bats on their shoulders before an exhibition game with the Braves, then lined up in front of the Boston dugout to salute opposing manager Casey Stengel and his men. The visitors didn't return the compliment, beating the Phils, 6–2. The drills were the inspiration of manager Hans Lobert, no stranger to such maneuvers, having run the U.S. Military Academy baseball team from 1918 to 1925.

Danny Litwhiler, the left fielder on that Phillie team and himself a veteran of twenty-five years coaching college baseball—his protégés at Florida State and Michigan State universities include Yankee manager Dick Howser, the Dodgers' Steve Garvey, and the Angels' Rick Miller—remembers the drilling.

"Lobert had been the baseball coach at West Point and he had loyalty to the service, and the guys were starting to go in. It was to show that the ballplayers are thinking about the guys in the service," Litwhiler recalls, reminiscing about the war era from his home in East Lansing, Michigan. "But I think it was mostly a stunt for the papers, a publicity gimmick. They tried to give us some close order drill for a day or so, then it was forgotten."

As a public relations gesture, the drills were a flop. *Philadelphia Inquirer* sports columnist Perry Lewis wrote, "Any public drilling of players under the direction of Army officers whose services are required elsewhere would be getting out of step. May we be spared that ridiculous spectacle. A bat is no substitute for a gun and the place to drill is an Army camp."

Out at Anaheim, California, the Athletics were awakened in the pre-dawn hours of February 25 by an air raid siren. A few ballplayers ventured to the roof of the club's hotel and watched a spectacular display of antiaircraft fire light up the sky. The Western Defense Command, jittery after a Japanese submarine ineffectually lobbed a few shells at an oil refinery near Santa Barbara the previous night, had spotted a suspicious object aloft and figured southern California was about to be bombed. Before the counterattack was over, two people had died from heart attacks possibly induced by the excitement, three others were killed in a stampede of the panic-stricken, and dozens were hurt by shell fragment fallout. The mysterious craft setting off the commotion turned out to be a stray weather balloon.

Before the Chicago Cubs were permitted to depart via boat from Los Angeles to owner Phil Wrigley's Catalina Island training site, each of the players had to satisfy authorities that he was not an enemy alien.

The Pacific Coast League's Seattle Rainiers were required to show military passes to armed sentries before being admitted to their spring training diamond in San Fernando, California. The field happened to be located in a municipal park that had an encampment of the Fortieth Field Artillery. To display their gratitude for being allowed through the lines, the Seattle players helped coach the Army unit's baseball team after their own workouts.

There was also the case of the road secretary suspected briefly of being a spy.

The Dodgers held their early spring training workouts in Havana before finishing up at Daytona Beach, Florida. Well aware of the numerous opportunities for late night diversion in the Cuban capital, Larry MacPhail hired detectives to trail the more fun-loving ballplayers and file reports with road secretary John McDonald. As described by Frank Graham in *The Brooklyn Dodgers: An Informal History,* a U.S. intelligence officer, checking out McDonald's briefcase as the team was returning to Miami, found a curious document, reading in part:

"Trailed No. 15 to the Florida, where he was joined by two others. He had two Daiquiris. From there, he went to Sloppy Joe's, where he

Before long, some of the Dodger ballplayers on a spring '42 pigeon shoot at private club in Havana will be handling a different type of weapon. Ready to blaze away at the last warm weather training camp until 1946 are (left to right) Johnny Allen (the notorious number 15), Hugh Casey, Billy Herman, Augie Galan, Johnny Rizzo, Lew Riggs, Curt Davis, Freddie Fitzsimmons, and Larry French.

spent some time and had more drinks. No. 1 appeared and they walked together. No. 1 had a glass of beer. They left and walked toward Prado 86, but met No. 7 and No. 12 on the way. All of them got into a cab and were driven to the Nacional."

Suspecting he might have come upon a coded espionage report, the intelligence officer took McDonald out of line and questioned him. What was the meaning of the numbers? Who was being trailed?

McDonald explained the numerals corresponded to those on the uniforms of certain Dodger players—number 15 was pitcher Johnny Allen, for example—and convinced the official he was not on a spy mission.

Perhaps the atmosphere as baseball went into its first wartime season was best captured by John Kieran of the *New York Times*. Kieran wrote in an April '42 sports column:

"There's a different spirit in the dugout and on the diamond. . . . There is the matter of the selective service rating of many of the players who are currently scampering around in their baseball flannels, playing now, but wondering how long it's going to last. A man can't give all his thoughts to getting into shape to run, hit, and throw furiously to aid his team in a coming pennant race under such conditions. He must have somewhere in his mind the thought that maybe he will be in that pennant fight for only a short time, if at all."

Kieran observed, "It used to be that at this time of year, the important sundown reports were the late scores of the ball games. But players and fans, like every other citizen, are now asking at sundown and all other times: 'What's the latest from Bataan and Burma?' "

II

Baseball Pitches In

2

The Patriotic Pastime

The White Sox pitchers going through their drills on the Pasadena, California, ballfield had a very special incentive to hit their target. It being spring training, there was a manager to impress, but at this particular moment the stakes were higher. The deliveries would not be slamming into a catcher's mitt. They were aimed, rather, at a cartoon figure—the four-by-six-foot caricature of a bespectacled Japanese soldier.

Hurling their insults at the helpless backstop for the benefit of photographers one day in early March '42, the moundsmen were making a small contribution to what would become an unceasing propaganda offensive by baseball and its many friends.

Through torrents of rhetoric, baseball would tell America why the "national pastime" was needed more than ever by a nation in battle. And there would be numerous patriotic gestures by the game as it joined with the rest of the home front to help win the war.

First, there was the matter of keeping up the country's spirits.

"The game stands at attention, ready for whatever role it may be called upon to play in the emergency," editorialized the *Sporting News* in the wake of Pearl Harbor. Then, suggesting the role it envisioned, the paper declared, "War in the distant Pacific does not necessarily mean the suspension of all normal human activity. . . . Both citizen and military morale must be maintained by all possible means and sports represents one of the most effective of all morale-building agencies."

Previewing the 1942 season, American League President Harridge was a man with a mission. The way he explained it: "Baseball may be approaching the finest opportunity for service to our country that the game has ever had, providing a recreational outlet for millions of fans who will be working harder than ever to help achieve our common cause of victory."

31

White Sox pitchers find Japanese soldier an inviting target.

Perhaps the game's most eloquent spokesman could be found in Brooklyn. Branch Rickey would be struggling with baseball's wartime woes as president of the Dodgers, moving on after a long and successful tenure with the Cardinals to replace Larry MacPhail, who obtained an Army commission after the 1942 season.

As baseball prepared for its second wartime pennant race, Rickey was aroused by speculation that the government would step up the drafting of ballplayers on grounds their jobs were essentially of no benefit to the nation. (The game would, in fact, remain in a sort of limbo throughout the war—considered neither an essential industry nor an occupation so useless its employees should be drafted with no regard to dependency status.)

Issuing a six-hundred-word statement in February '43 aimed at those who would look on baseball with disdain, Rickey declared, "We need to hold on to all such diversions as tend to relieve us from the ever increasing sorrows of war. The good health of our people is not conserved by continuous and almost compulsory reflection upon their personal heartbreaking losses, which are bound to come and are coming even now. . . . We need to be cheerful fighters or as cheerful as we possibly can be. To die is to be glorified for the Japanese. To live hopefully and joyfully is the American objective and our fighting to live must match the religious frenzy of the Japs who fight to die."

Manufacturers of baseball equipment took a look at the situation and concluded happily that by selling more merchandise they would be supporting the war effort. An advertisement by the Wilson Sporting Goods Company placed in the *1943 Baseball Register*—a compilation of major league statistics—proclaimed "Baseball is America" in large letters superimposed over a diamond. The ad explained:

"In times of peace, baseball plays a vital role in the American way of life—on our sandlots, our playfields, our school diamonds; in our professional parks, our grandstands, and our bleachers. In times of *WAR*, baseball is even more important to the health and morale of our youth, our workers, and those on the home front."

Wilson promised, "As far as our war orders and available material permit, we will continue to supply finest quality baseball equipment for America's youth."

Vying with Wilson in patriotic fervor was the cover of the *Baseball Register*, depicting Uncle Sam holding a ball in one hand and a bat in the other with a huge baseball behind him which bore the signatures of Greenberg, Feller, Williams, Mulcahy, and former Cardinal pitcher Johnny Beazley—at that point the game's most prominent contributions to the armed forces.

In the political arena, Roosevelt was hardly alone in citing sports as a morale builder. FDR's old postmaster general, James A. Farley, a baseball fan who would be mentioned as a possible successor to Landis after the commissioner's death in November 1944, felt Americans should take their cue from the beleaguered Englishman. Noting in early 1942 how a British soccer game had drawn fifty thousand fans undeterred by the threat of a bombing attack, Farley counseled, "Interference with our sports might really retard our winning the war. Keep 'em playing, keep 'em active, keep the American people entertained and relaxed during whatever periods of play and rest they may find in these times. This is no time for hysteria, for panicky people to rule out our sports and our pastimes, which the great majority of Americans really and truly want continued."

Not long after Pearl Harbor, the Associated Press surveyed congressional attitudes toward the continuation of athletics. Baseball could take heart from the response.

"Morale must be maintained," said House Minority Leader Joseph Martin of Massachusetts, registering his stamp of approval on baseball so long as individual players were shown no favoritism in the draft.

"I don't believe in draping the whole country in black. Certainly professional baseball should be continued during the war. It helps preserve morale and provides outdoor recreation for thousands," declared Congressman James W. Wadsworth of New York, who happened to be co-author of the 1940 Burke–Wadsworth bill, which set up the selective service machinery. He may not have been entirely unbiased in the matter, however, having once made All-American playing first base for Yale.

When the Washington Board of Trade sponsored a luncheon at the Mayflower Hotel to help the local baseball heroes kick off their 1943 season, a couple of Senators of the Capitol Hill variety were on hand. Kentucky's Albert ("Happy") Chandler, a frequent visitor to Griffith Stadium and a cheerleader for baseball throughout the war— he'd be rewarded with the commissioner's job in April '45—told the gathering, "It would be a tragedy for baseball to stop. It's ridiculous to say we can't spare two hundred men in the American League and two hundred more in the National League."

Millard Tydings of Maryland saw baseball as an antidote for people's tendency to do a little too much thinking for their own good. He explained to the luncheon crowd: "We are all under tension we cannot appreciate and we must give our minds an occasional rest. Baseball's contribution to the war effort in that respect is enormous."

Tydings may have got carried away a bit in his enthusiasm. Burton Hawkins of the *Washington Evening Star* reported that the senator expressed joy over hearing baseball had been declared an essential industry, "a statement that remains his exclusive idea."

Late in the war, Congressman Melvin Price of Illinois was so impressed with a report by Cardinal owner Sam Breadon detailing how his club had contributed to the war effort (exhibition games were played at military installations, soldiers and sailors were admitted free to Sportsman's Park, funds were raised for servicemen's relief agencies, and players even left the team to join the service) that he inserted the document in the *Congressional Record*.

Baseball as a morale booster was not the only rhetorical theme. Although Jackie Robinson's day had yet to come, the game portrayed itself as the essence of democracy—doing it in would be tantamount to subverting the ideals that made the nation great, the principles for which our boys were fighting.

Boston Braves' President Bob Quinn, asked in December '42 for his assessment of the future, expressed confidence that baseball would survive during the war years and emerge afterward stronger than ever.

"It is the most democratic of games, for the governor's son may play alongside the son of humble parents and the only favoritism that either gets is what he earns by merit and playing," he declared.

Ford Frick, giving a talk in April '44 before the Advertising Club of New York, showed the image makers he was pretty good at the art himself. The nation would be well served by allowing baseball to carry on, contended Frick, since "the real example of genuine democracy is on the playing fields of America. It is the one place American youth meets on common ground and the real lesson of democracy can best be preached."

When the war was over, General Jacob L. Devers, an ex–West Point baseball and football star who had commanded the Sixth Army Group in Europe, reflected on how sports taught "team play" so essential for victory in battle:

"This war was not won by the few men we sent overseas but by a team—a team of men overseas and at home and baseball played its role for both. Why were we a great team, a great Army? Because we knew something of team play and we have the best competitive spirit of any nation in the world and baseball, football, and other sports teach that competitive spirit."

But there was a problem here—baseball happened to be a passion, too, for a certain enemy nation.

The game was introduced to Japan in 1873 by Horace Wilson, an American who taught at a Tokyo university, and flourished initially on a high school and collegiate level. Enthusiasm soared following a 1934 visit by a group of major league stars including Babe Ruth, Lou Gehrig, Jimmie Foxx, and Charlie Gehringer,* and by the time World

---

*While the troupe got a tremendous reception (its motorcade was mobbed in Tokyo's Ginza district), the specter of rising Japanese militarism was overshadowing mutual expressions of goodwill. And so Moe Berg, a journeyman ballplayer but a man with a brilliant mind, was sent along to carry out an assignment for U.S. intelligence authorities. As recounted in the biography *Moe Berg: Athlete, Scholar . . . Spy*, the Indians' catcher slipped away from his teammates one day, entered Tokyo's St. Luke's International Hospital on the pretext of visiting a patient, then went to the roof and photographed military, industrial, and transportation facilities. The pictures reportedly were utilized in Jimmy Doolittle's 1942 Tokyo bombing raid.

Babe Ruth and batboy friends in happier days, watching game at Osaka.

War II arrived, the eight-team Japanese Professional Baseball League was firmly established.

Could baseball really be emblematic of the ideals America cherished if the sneaky Japs loved it too?

The *Sporting News* solved the puzzle by concluding that despite surface appearances, the game had never truly taken root in Japan, explaining in an editorial shortly after Pearl Harbor:

"After looking at the seventy years of Japanese baseball in retrospect, this treacherous Asiatic land was never really converted to baseball. . . . Through our great game runs an inherent decency, fair dealing, love of the game, and respect for one's opponents. . . . It is the very soul of baseball. We may cut a few corners on the playing area, but we do not stab an 'honorable opponent' in the back. Nor do we crush out his brains with a bat while he is asleep. . . . No nation which has had as intimate contact with baseball as the Japanese could have committed the vicious, infamous deed of the early morning of December 7, 1941, if the spirit of the game had ever penetrated their yellow hides."

If the Japanese weren't sincere about loving baseball, they certainly fooled Hap O'Connor, a college and semipro umpire who had once made a barnstorming trip to the Orient. O'Connor viewed the Japanese connection as one more reason to keep the game alive in America.

"The Japs so envy us for our baseball prowess and our intense love for the game that to call it off during wartime would be like a tonic to them," he warned. "I think they would construe it to mean we were becoming panicky or something in this country."

Not only would American baseball go on, its boosters would strike back at the Japanese, perhaps to atone for our giving them the game. Besides the barrage fired by White Sox pitchers at the phantom soldier, there was the matter of a particular flag. The First National Bank in downtown Pittsburgh had for years employed a banner to advise fans whether there would be a game at Forbes Field on a given day. If the flag was flying atop the bank building, the game was on. If it came down, that meant a postponement due to bad weather. Trouble was, the thing had a red circle on a white background—the same design used by the Land of the Rising Sun. The flag quickly became a casualty of the war.

There would be many other gestures identifying baseball with the war effort.

In the minor leagues, the New Orleans Pelicans painted their grandstand seats red, white, and blue; the Indianapolis Indians rechristened Perry Stadium as Victory Field; and the Syracuse Chiefs decided Municipal Stadium would become MacArthur Stadium.

During World War I, the Minneapolis Millers of the American Association sported khaki uniforms with the Stars and Stripes embroidered across the shirt. Baseball fashion would reflect a patriotic spirit in the Second World War as well, though the impact was more subdued. Affixed to the left shoulder of every ballplayer's uniform was the insignia of the "Hale America" campaign. The patch, created by the U.S. Division of Physical Fitness, bore a one-word message: "Health." The Philadelphia Phillies and Boston Braves were a particularly colorful lot during a Shibe Park doubleheader in May '42. Their uniforms were decorated with poppies presented by an American Legion post.

The Phils put a photo of Hugh Mulcahy above a crossed bats "V for Victory" arrangement on the cover of their '42 brochure while the Cardinals chose the Statue of Liberty and the Reds selected the American Eagle to adorn their booklets.

Although fireworks shows like those traditionally put on by the Reds prior to night games seemed ideal for creating a martial air, the explosives might better be used in the war effort. So Cincinnati general manager Warren Giles sent postcards to regular patrons asking if they would feel particularly aggrieved by a halt to the pyrotechnics. Assured by a 50–1 margin the fans would come to the park anyway, if there was something to see on the field, Giles announced that his ballplayers would have to draw pregame inspiration from some other source.

In the interests of beautification, the Pirates liked to keep their outfield walls free of signs, but the policy would be suspended for the war. A Marine recruiting poster and a message urging the purchase of defense bonds were plastered on the Forbes Field fences.

Before World War II, "The Star Spangled Banner" had been played at ballparks only on special occasions such as opening day and the World Series. Now it would be heard prior to every game.

Jimmy Bloodworth of the Tigers had the ritual to thank for his getting on base in an April '42 exhibition contest against the Reds. Bloodworth banged the first pitch of the game back to the mound, the ball careening off Cincinnati's Elmer Riddle. As the pitcher and second baseman Lonny Frey scampered after the ball, the recorded strains of the national anthem boomed belatedly from the loudspeaker. Riddle and Frey stopped in their tracks, snapping to attention, but Bloodworth kept running and made first base. Patriotic niceties aside, umpire Al Barlick ruled Bloodworth was entitled to the bag.

The ball clubs used their public address systems to bring the fans important war news. The second game of a Yankee–White Sox Sunday doubleheader on July 25, 1943, was interrupted with an announcement to the Yankee Stadium crowd: "A flash has just come over the wires that Mussolini has resigned." The word brought cheers and dancing in the aisles. Later in the week, a night game at Forbes Field was halted in the third inning so that a half-hour speech by Roosevelt reporting on the fall of Mussolini could be piped into the park.

On Saturday, June 3, 1944, as a Giants–Pirates game at the Polo Grounds was about to enter extra innings, the 9,171 fans heard a momentous announcement over the loudspeaker—the invasion of northern Europe had begun. There was a brief roar and then the crowd and players stood for a moment of silent prayer. But it was not the real thing. Joan Ellis, a young teletype operator in the London bureau of the Associated Press, deciding to get in a little practice at her machine, had punched out "Flash—Eisenhower's Headquarters Announce Allied Landings France" just to see what it would look like. The dispatch had been transmitted inadvertently to the AP's New York office, which had sent it out to the nation. Moments afterward, realizing the flash was not authentic, the wire service frantically killed it, but not before the long-awaited news had been broadcast over many radio stations as well as to the crowd at the Polo Grounds.

The genuine D-Day flash reached the United States at 12:30 A.M. Eastern War Time on Tuesday, June 6, 1944. Two National League games, the only action scheduled for the majors that day, were postponed. At times, the man behind the play-by-play microphone was asked to do his bit to rally the home front. The Office of War Information, the federal agency charged with explaining why we fought— its labors ranging from straight news to thinly disguised propaganda —suggested in one memo that a baseball announcer might promote the USO by interviewing a ballplayer about an ex-teammate who had gone into the armed forces.

"Have him point out that his former teammate, the fans' former star, is now giving his all to the service. Make the fans want to contribute to his comforts and off-duty pleasures by contributing to the USO," urged the OWI.

Red Barber says he was never asked by the OWI to disseminate "propaganda," but he does recall with some amusement how sports announcers were required to help safeguard the home front in a negative fashion—they were banned by the government from mentioning weather conditions over the air for fear potential enemy bombing plans would be aided.

Reminiscing about the war era one day, after participating in a symposium on sports journalism before a group of New York college students, Barber explained, "You simply did not refer to the weather. It was just as though we were performing without weather. When there was a rain delay you would just say 'the game is stopped and when it resumes we'll let you know.' We'd play some phonograph records. The audience, of course, knew what was going on."

Barber remembers how the point was driven home to him early in the war:

"It was in '41; the Giants and Bears were playing for the football championship at Chicago. It was the first network sports broadcast after Pearl Harbor and I was the announcer. We were told before the game by a man from the armed forces, 'Look, you're not to mention anything pertaining to the weather.' During the game I said Mel Hein, the Giants' center, was using a towel. You see, they were playing in mud. Well, the broadcast was cut off. The man called and reminded me I was not to reveal anything about the weather. Later we were cut off again. I'd noted the team moving toward one of the goal posts had an advantage. The man said I was mentioning the wind."

On one occasion, Dizzy Dean, who broadcast the Cardinals' and Browns' games during the war, found the edict too preposterous to put up with. His radio partner, Johnny O'Hara, later told what happened:

"A game had been held up for about an hour by rain and we did our best to fill in the time with extemporaneous stuff, keeping away from the real reason for the game being held up. But finally Dizzy ran out of words and blurted out, 'If you folks don't know what's holdin' up this game just stick your heads out the window.'"

New York Herald Tribune sportswriter Rud Rennie poked a little fun at the bureaucracy in his story on the 1942 all-star game at the Polo Grounds, a twilight contest that was late getting under way because of a shower.

"Black clouds darkened the sky. The batteries of lights atop the stands had to be turned on shortly after six o'clock and a military secret crashed the party and caused a fifty-minute delay in the start of the game," he wrote. "Al Schacht, the baseball comedian, amused the crowd in the interim. Groundskeepers with brooms swept the spots left by the military secret."

Besides hailing the game as a booster of home front morale and embodiment of the American way, baseball's supporters had a third theme in urging continuation of play during the war: the boys overseas wanted athletics to carry on and anxiously awaited news of the sports scene as a link with the land they left behind.

Speaking at the annual dinner of the New York baseball writers in February '44, Landis made a point with a little story about a request for ticket reservations arriving at his office:

"Before I left Chicago, I received a letter signed by five men in the Army. They wanted to be sure that they would be at the next World Series. I am not given to prophesying, but this is my conviction. These boys away from home, they want this thing called baseball to continue as best it can."

A little later that month, Landis' sentiments were echoed by Braves' President Quinn in response to some gloomy words coming from a colleague.

Watching his roster being depleted by calls to military service, Alva Bradley, owner of the Indians, had suggested he might unilaterally shut down if the game became a "low form of comedy" played by a collection of 4Fs, oldtimers, and kids.

"Once the manpower situation becomes so acute that it's impossible to put a well-balanced team on the field, the game will develop into a farce and I, for one, won't tolerate that kind of baseball," warned Bradley.

Retorted Quinn, "We will go on no matter what our losses to do our bit for the lads in uniform."

That rationale was also presented by baseball's allies in the world of politics. Congressman Samuel Weiss of Pennsylvania, who had been a National Football League referee, urged in a March '43 speech on the floor of the House of Representatives that the government do nothing to curb professional athletics, buttressing his views by reading a letter from a soldier that stated, "I am willing to die for my country, but for God's sake, don't stop the sports that make America great."

Happy Chandler, upon being elected baseball commissioner in spring 1945, told soldiers and sailors via a Senate speech, "Because of the great victory you are winning over our enemies, we shall give you when you return home the greatest era of sport in the history of the world."

A host of stories came from the war theaters suggesting that next to his own survival, the fate of baseball was uppermost in the mind of the American fighting man.

Red Sox manager Joe Cronin, returning from a Red Cross–sponsored trip to Hawaii to visit hospitalized servicemen, remembered how "one poor kid who couldn't even sit up or move much, except his head, yelled 'keep 'em playing' when I went by."

Sergeant Charley McKenna, a Marine Corps combat correspondent visiting Bougainville field hospitals in January '44 to provide some news of the outside world, stopped to chat with a patient who had lost his left arm to a piece of shrapnel.

McKenna reported, "His first question was, 'Who won the Most Valuable Player award in the National League?'"

"The soldiers, sailors, and marines out here don't worry too much about changes in our national scene nearly as much as they do about the future of sports," McKenna told the United Press. "Sports is the lifeblood of these men, the connecting link between them and the United States left behind."

A similar scenario was recounted by Andrew Hodges, a Red Cross representative who helped arrange a November '44 exchange of American and German prisoners in the French fishing village of Le Mayour. Hodges said that as he came into sight of the GIs about to be repatriated, he heard a shout, "Who won the World Series?"

When they weren't busy with the Japanese, a pair of marines on Guadalcanal got into a dispute concerning Reds' pitcher Bucky Walters. At issue was whether Walters had played before the war with both the Braves and Red Sox, a contention advanced by one leatherneck but disputed by his buddy. Not having a record book handy in their foxhole, the marines bet sixty dollars—a month's pay—on the matter and sent a letter home seeking the answer. The note was passed on to Charles Doyle, a Pittsburgh sportswriter, who wrote back that Walters had, in fact, been a third baseman with both Boston clubs.

From somewhere in North Africa, Warrant Officer Bill Gold mailed the Phillies a one-hundred-franc note to buy his twelve-year-old son tickets for a game with the Dodgers.

A seaman used the following lingo to get around the censors and send home a report on the sinking of a sub: "We played one game on a wet field. Hit home run on second pitch."

Baseball terminology found favor even among the highest military circles. Army Chief of Staff General George C. Marshall designated "play ball" as the code words to signal the opening of fire in the North African invasion.

Knowledge of baseball could mean the difference between life and death.

The *Chicago Herald–American* noted how some American soldiers fighting in North Africa were a bit too clever for the enemy: "Two men were spotted and although they wore U.S. Army uniforms, their English was not too good. 'What's your favorite sport?' they were asked. They both replied, 'Baseball, of course.' A GI then said, 'Didya hear, Connie Mack pitched a shutout against Brooklyn and Tommy Harmon got two homers for the Bums?' "

Not having learned in their indoctrination courses that Mack was the octogenarian manager of the Athletics and Harmon a football hero, the infiltrators replied, "Yeah, we heard that on the shortwave broadcasts."

The newspaper reported, "Result: Two defunct Nazi parachutists."

During some of the heaviest fighting in the Battle of the Bulge, a woman wearing a GI helmet and overcoat but lacking proper identification drove her jeep into the American lines. Sentries, who had been warned against Nazi infiltrators, were skeptical over the girl's story that she was a Red Cross worker and had become lost, so they took her to their commander. Virginia Von Lampe of Yonkers, New York, later recounted: "I finally convinced the major I was an American when I rattled off the Brooklyn Dodgers' lineup for the 1941 World Series."

There was at least one enemy soldier who could have carried out an infiltration mission perfectly. Joseph Weinstein of the Bronx received a letter from his brother telling how he helped capture three Nazis on a reconnaissance patrol in the Italian theater. While marching the prisoners back to headquarters, the GI noticed one of them had a newspaper sticking out of his pocket. It turned out to be the overseas edition of the *Sporting News*. The German explained that he got the paper from an American POW, had spent some time in New York before the war, was an avid Dodger fan, and hoped one day to be back at Ebbets Field.

On New Britain island, Japanese troops were reported charging American lines with the battle cry, "To Hell with Babe Ruth." When contacted in New York, the Babe responded, "I hope that every Jap that mentions my name gets shot and to hell with all Japs anyway."

Ruth would have approved of one unorthodox method employed by some marines for dispatching the enemy. Sergeant William Blank, a marine combat correspondent on New Georgia island, reported "the usual weapon for standing silent and effective night guard here is a machete or a knife," but that in one unit, if the Japanese try to slip through the lines, "the men are prepared to conk them with a baseball bat."

The other side may have had a similar reception in mind for infiltrators of its ranks. Marine Corporal Charles Truitt discovered a baseball bat stamped "Made in Japan" and bearing the apparently forged signature of Paul Waner lying beside the body of a Japanese soldier on Namur. Truitt mailed the bat to his hometown newspaper, the *Wilmington Journal*, in Delaware, for shipment to Waner as a souvenir.

Back on the American side, the name of a baseball figure might be scrawled on a warplane to bring good luck. Giant manager Mel Ott got word in October '43 that a bomber christened "Ott's Big Bat" had returned from five successful raids. Billy Southworth, Jr., while declining to focus on any one baseball hero, dubbed his B-17 Flying Fortress "Winning Run," the idea being it was supposed to reach home safely from bombing missions over France and Germany.

A Liberty ship launched in June '43 from the Fairfield–Bethlehem

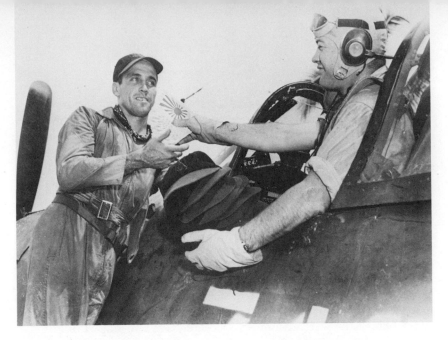

Maj. Gregory Boyington (right) with his St. Louis Cardinal caps.

yards in Baltimore was named the "Edward L. Grant" in honor of the only major leaguer to be killed in action during World War I. A Harvard graduate who went on to play third base for the Phils, Reds, and Giants, Grant died in the Argonne Forest a month before the armistice. Other Liberty ships were named for Lou Gehrig, Christy Mathewson, and John J. McGraw, and there was even one called the "Abner Doubleday," saluting the man credited by baseball folklore with inventing the game.

As baseball sought to back its patriotic rhetoric with home front gestures such as obligatory renditions of "The Star Spangled Banner," so, too, did it reach out to the men in combat.

The ball clubs shipped scores of baseball caps to pilots; the bills were said to be ideal for keeping the sun's glare out of their eyes. Major Gregory "Pappy" Boyington, the colorful marine air ace who commanded the famed "Black Sheep" fighter squadron, vowed his men would shoot down a Japanese Zero plane for every cap received from the winner of the 1943 World Series. Despite their defeat by the Yankees in the Series, the Cardinals sent twenty hats to the unit. More than making good on the promise, Boyington's squadron had bagged an additional forty-eight enemy craft by February '44. (Their commander was out of action by then. Shot down over Rabaul, Boyington spent the last twenty months of the war in a Japanese prison camp.)

The headgear wasn't, however, exclusively for pilots. A paratrooper about to go overseas wrote to Cubs' outfielder Bill Nicholson, "I've always admired your playing and I wonder if you'd be so kind as to send me a Cub cap. I'd like to wear it going into battle." He got the hat.

The Red Sox went capless at the opening drill of spring training one year because their hats had been given away to servicemen and replacements had not yet arrived.

The official World Series films were shipped abroad and the Armed Forces Radio Service carried the Series and selected regular season games to troops overseas. At its peak the service encompassed twenty shortwave stations along the East and West Coasts and beamed the play-by-play to 166 outlets around the world. Anything less than a full diet of World Series action might provoke a storm of protest. When the North African sector was provided with only fifteen-minute

Cardinal manager Billy Southworth and Yankee counterpart Joe McCarthy tell U.S. troops in England and Ireland what it's like at 1942 World Series, courtesy of British Broadcasting Corporation.

The '42 Series also comes to the jungles of Panama.

broadcast summaries of the first two 1943 World Series games, the howls of outrage were so great they reached Eisenhower's ears. He ordered that the remaining contests be carried in full. The '45 Series broadcasts received credit for speeding up deactivation of antisubmarine mines from waters around the Panama Canal. Soldiers who were promised afternoons off to listen to the action if they removed their day's quota of mines by noon were said to have made excellent progress.

The Phillies put out a weekly all-sports newsletter called *The Scoreboard* for shipment overseas, though the word from Philadelphia was always dismal, the town's two big league entries being perennial tailenders. (*Stars and Stripes* felt so sorry for servicemen from Philly that it printed the National and American League standings upside down one day during the 1945 season.)

When the war heroes came home, what would be more appropriate than hosting them at a ball game, especially since baseball, it seemed, had been much on their minds all through the war.

Sergeant Dale Bordner made news when he was rescued by Australian forces after hiding for ten months in Japanese-held jungles on New Britain island following the crash of his bomber. Sent back to the States for his trouble, the Chillicothe, Ohio, native and his girlfriend were guests of the Cincinnati club at a Sunday doubleheader in May

'43. A display of gratitude from the team was certainly forthcoming, since Bordner's first words upon being found had reportedly been, "How did the Reds come out in 1942?"

Captain R. K. Morgan and his crew, veterans of twenty-five bombing missions in their Flying Fortress "Memphis Belle," were invited by the Tigers to a 1943 Independence Day doubleheader. Addressing the Briggs Stadium crowd from home plate, Morgan revealed, "All the time we were over Germany, we were thinking we want to get back and see a ball game."

The Senators had a special attraction at their 1945 home opener with the Yankees. The public address operator announced, "Ladies and gentlemen, you've all seen the pictures of six Americans raising our flag on Iwo Jima. Three of them survived. These are the three."

Pfc. Rene Gagnon, Pfc. Ira Hayes, and Pharmacist's Mate John Bradley, the latter on crutches, were escorted by Clark Griffith from their box seat to take a bow before the 24,494 fans.

Iwo Jima war bond poster is displayed at Griffith Stadium by House Speaker Sam Rayburn and Clark Griffith as flag-raisers (left to right) Pharmacist's Mate John Bradley, Pfc. Rene Gagnon, and Pfc. Ira Hayes look on.

"The acclaim was thunderous, sincere, and touching," reported the *New York Times.*

The trio was topping off a day that had included a visit to the Senate and a White House ceremony at which Harry Truman, in but the eighth day of his presidency, accepted a painting of the Mount Surabachi flag raising to be used for a poster promoting the Seventh War Loan drive.

Many a Medal of Honor winner graced a ballpark. Sergeant Jake W. Lindsey, who as the 100th infantryman in the nation's history to be so honored had received the commendation personally from Truman, sat behind the Dodger dugout at Ebbets Field for a June '45 game with the Giants. His introduction brought a grand cheer from the crowd.

Wounded servicemen like Jimmy Spillane were especially welcomed at ball games. The young man had once attended a Cardinal tryout camp, hoping to become a major league shortstop someday, but the war came along and he joined the Marines. There was a beachhead to be assaulted on an island called Tarawa. Spillane's amphibious tractor was peppered with grenades. He managed to toss five of them back, but the sixth exploded, tearing off his right hand. In the fall of 1944, the Marine corporal—winner of the Navy Cross and recipient of a commendation from Admiral Chester W. Nimitz, Pacific fleet commander—was convalescing in a Philadelphia naval hospital. His most ardent desire at that moment, he said, was to attend the World Series and see the Cardinal team he had once hoped to play for. The Skouras theater chain was only too happy to help and paid the marine's expenses to St. Louis.

Pfc. Donald Murray of Roxbury, Massachusetts, who had lost a leg fighting in Germany, was recuperating during the summer of 1945 at the Percy Jones military hospital in Battle Creek, Michigan. Murray was a great fan of Dave "Boo" Ferriss, the Red Sox's rookie pitcher en route to a twenty-one-victory season. When he noticed that Boston would be playing a series at Briggs Stadium, Murray phoned Red Sox officials to see if they could help him obtain a brief leave to watch Ferriss pitch. Manager Joe Cronin, aided by the Red Cross, got Murray a pass, arranged for his transportation into Detroit and a box seat, and then pitched Ferriss out of his regular rotation so he'd be on the mound the day the GI was at the ballpark.

"Am I happy? You can have all those camp shows. There's nothing like baseball to me," exclaimed Murray after seeing his idol outpitch the Tigers' Dizzy Trout, 4–3.

When it was not preoccupied with grand strategy, the military brass turned its thoughts to baseball. Arthur "Red" Patterson, the National League's public relations director, received a letter in the spring of 1945 from an officer stationed in China who boasted he had pitched a one-hit shutout for his softball team and was batting .667.

"I wonder if the Dodgers are not losing a good bet in not signing me up. Judging from the general situation on the fronts, it appears the war should be over soon and I am looking for a place to settle down in my old age," wrote General Claire L. Chennault, commander of the Fourteenth Air Force.

Much as they needed help, the Dodgers passed on the offer, but Chennault did make it to Ebbets Field as a spectator in September.

Four days after his return to the United States, General Jonathan M. Wainwright, commander in the doomed defense of Corregidor, turned up in the presidential box at Griffith Stadium to watch the Senators take on the Indians. Wainwright had told reporters follow-

Gen. Claire L. Chennault (right) confers with battery-mate Gen. Edgar E. Glenn on a softball field somewhere in China.

ing V-J Day, "After three years in a Japanese prison camp, I am particularly happy to be on the pitching end of a surrender rather than the catching end."

Now, after the obligatory hot dog and bottle of pop, Wainwright did a little hurling himself, throwing out the first ball—twice. When George Case caught what was to be the sole ceremonial toss, the Indians asked Wainwright to do it again so that one of them might get a souvenir. Cleveland's Elmer Weingartner, blocking teammate Stan Benjamin, dove on the general's second pitch.

Case, who still has a niche in his den for the Wainwright baseball, appropriately autographed, recalls, "He came in the clubhouse later and shook hands. We were awestruck. Here was this great gentleman and soldier."

Griffith Stadium would often be visited by military and political figures.

"At one game we had two or three generals and Secretary of State Stettinius in the clubhouse at the same time," says Case. "General Bradley once came by to shake hands with Cecil Travis, who was just back from the service, he'd gotten frozen feet in the Battle of the Bulge. The others were just baseball fans. The brass missed baseball, too. And Happy Chandler would be in the clubhouse every damned night."

Baseball reaped a public relations bonanza on a rainy Wednesday afternoon in June 1945 when a convertible came through the center-field gates at the Polo Grounds carrying a beaming Dwight D. Eisenhower. Making a triumphal return home, the Allied commander had begun his day riding through thirty-seven miles of New York City streets, cheered by millions. After receiving New York's Gold Medal in a ceremony at City Hall, it was off to the ballpark with Mayor Fiorello LaGuardia. The crowd of 27,062, willing to suffer through a game between the lackluster Giants and Braves in order to see Ike, returned his wave and salutes with a mighty roar as the car circled the field.

Managers Ott of the Giants and Bob Coleman of the Braves presented Eisenhower with a bat and two autographed baseballs, then each of the players lined up to have his picture taken with the general.

The Giants' first baseman that day was Phil Weintraub, making a comeback in the late war years. Weintraub had played with the Giants, Reds, and Phillies in the 1930s, retired for a brief period, then went to the minors and worked his way back to the big leagues. Until Ike's visit, the ballplayer figured the biggest thrill in his career would be the time he drove in eleven runs in a single game—the spree against the

Eisenhower gets some souvenirs from managers Bob Coleman of the Braves (left) and Mel Ott of the Giants. Mayor LaGuardia helps inspect the merchandise.

Dodgers in April '44 leaving him one shy of the record set by the Cards' Sunny Jim Bottomley—but this was a greater moment.

"He sat in a front box with the Giants' owner, Horace Stoneham, and other dignitaries and we were all brought over and introduced to him," Weintraub recalls. "You got near this guy, it was really something. He had a fantastic personality, was just as nice as could be. We talked and he was very knowledgeable about the game. Of course, he had been a baseball player at West Point and loved baseball all through his life. It was a bigger thrill for me than the eleven runs."

The glorious occasion was, however, later tempered by disappointment. Weintraub continues:

"We all took individual pictures with him and they were sent to Washington for personal autographs later and of all things, mine was mislaid or something, the only one that didn't come back. I never did get it. I don't have to tell you my feelings, because he was my hero, too."

But there was a happy ending. When his playing days were over,

Weintraub settled in Palm Springs, California, where he still lives, selling real estate and finding time for plenty of golf. He tells of a second chat during Ike's post–White House days:

"It was around 1961. I was a member of the Indian Wells Country Club in Palm Springs and as I was driving into the club, there was Eisenhower in a golf cart with a couple of his friends. I walked over and I was stopped by one of his Secret Service men and he asked me, 'What is it you would like?' I told him who I was and that I wanted to talk with the president. I shook hands with Eisenhower and told him about the incident and he sent me a picture with his autograph. I still have it hanging in my den."

Turning back to that wartime game, Weintraub notes how Eisenhower braved the elements, recalling: "It was the worst day you had ever seen. It rained so hard you couldn't see across from first base to third base. We'd never have played the game if Eisenhower wasn't there."

Servicemen admitted free to April '42 Dodger-Giant game at Polo Grounds are appropriately enthusiastic. Air raid sign on pillar reads: "Patrons. If alert is sounded, walk to place of safety. Don't run or shout. Obey the warden. Play your part in the 'defense game.' "

Servicemen's canteen at Polo Grounds does brisk business.

After meeting with the players, the general had settled down in a box seat draped with his personal flag and attempted to keep score amid the raindrops and the press of well-wishers seeking an autograph or just a handshake. In the fourth inning he retreated to watch from the center field clubhouse, sticking around until the end of the sixth when, with the Giants trailing, 6–2, other engagements beckoned. Ike's parting comment to Horace Stoneham: "What the hell has happened to the pitching since I went away to the war?"

Baseball's welcome mat wasn't confined to war heroes; the everyday GI Joe was also encouraged to see a game while on leave. At some ballparks, servicemen could obtain a seat merely by appearing in uniform at a special gate; in cities attracting large numbers of military personnel, blocks of tickets were made available at YMCAs or USO clubs. At Ebbets Field, the Polo Grounds, and Yankee Stadium, the Harry M. Stevens concession firm set up servicemen's canteens where hot dogs, peanuts, and soda were marked down from ten cents to a nickel.

There were some visitors from the ranks of the military that baseball could have done without.

Pilot of B-17 Flying Fortress bomber treats himself to an unauthorized bird's-eye view of Yanks-Cards '43 Series game.

During the first game of the 1943 World Series, a Flying Fortress buzzed Yankee Stadium three times within a seven-minute span, clearing the roof by only ten feet on one swoop and virtually drowning out the radio broadcast. Mayor LaGuardia fumed, "That pilot should be properly disciplined, endangering the lives of the citizenry of New York in that manner."

The airman, Lieutenant Jack Watson, was unrepentant. By the following July he had transferred his attention to German convoys. Upon returning to his British base after a mission in which all other members of his crippled bomber "Meat Hound" had been forced to bail out, Watson remarked, "I wonder whether Mayor LaGuardia will forgive me now."

Hizzoner sent a cable to the airman, "All is forgiven. I hope you never run out of altitude."

Just before one of the 1944 World Series games was to get under way, umpire Tom Dunn noticed a figure curled up inside the Sportsman's Park tarpaulin. It was a sailor all set for a ground's eye view of the proceedings. He was advised to find an alternate vantage point.

Then there was the battle of Ebbets Field. John Christian, a twenty-one-year-old ex-glider corps trooper discharged from the service for a knee injury, was loudly berating the Dodgers at a June '45 Saturday night game with the Phils. The young man's voice carried well beyond his upper-tier box behind third base. At the end of the sixth inning, ballpark policeman Joseph Moore invited Christian to accompany him beneath the stands. What transpired next became a matter of dispute. But Christian, seemingly no weakling at 5-feet 11-inches and 200 pounds, wound up his evening at Kings County Hospital with a broken jaw. The veteran told city police that Moore hit him with a blunt instrument on the dirt runway between the Dodger dugout and clubhouse and that when he got up, there was Leo Durocher to continue the clobbering. Moore and Durocher were arrested the next day on assault charges, then released on $1,000 bail.

The conclusion to the episode came the following April in a Brooklyn courtroom jammed with two hundred Dodger supporters. An all-male jury, after deliberating for thirty-eight minutes, returned a verdict of not guilty for both defendants.

Judge Louis Goldstein felt the jury's conclusion was "a fair and just one," declaring, "I am glad for the sake of the Brooklyn baseball team that their manager has been vindicated, that no discredit has been placed on the great American game of baseball."

Ex-GI John Christian tells Brooklyn Assistant District Attorney Louis Andreozzi how he went from a seat at Ebbets Field to a bed in Kings County Hospital.

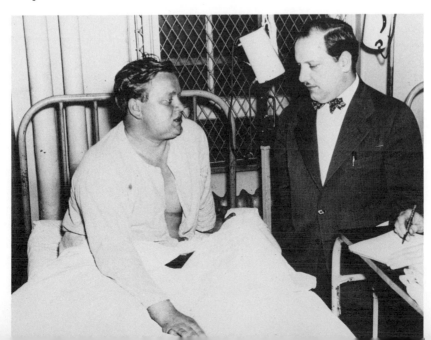

Durocher, who had made a payment of $6,750 to Christian prior to the trial in settlement of a civil suit, declined comment.

To what extent did the general public and servicemen in particular favor continuation of baseball during the war? If polls are an indication, professional athletics enjoyed solid support.

A Gallup Poll taken in May '41 provided baseball with early encouragement, finding 84 percent of the public agreeing with Larry MacPhail's proposal that ballplayers be deferred from the draft until the end of that season.

An April '42 survey by Gallup asked: "Do you think professional sports should be continued during the war or should they be stopped until after the war?" The response was 66 percent to 24 percent in favor of carrying on; 10 percent were undecided. A Gallup inquiry in April '43 asking whether baseball, specifically, should remain alive during the war found 59 percent in favor, 28 percent opposed, and the rest not sure.

Those who would be doing the fighting were especially strong in their support of athletics. A survey by *Esquire* magazine reported 88 percent of the soldiers at Jefferson Barracks outside St. Louis wanted wartime baseball.

Although hardly a neutral observer, the *Sporting News* reported a "thundering yes" for baseball in a poll of servicemen which it commissioned four months after Pearl Harbor. The winner of a ten-dollar prize for the best letter on the subject was Pfc. William Ashworth of Fort Benning, who wrote of his hunger for the game:

"Would you like to discontinue the use of salt and pepper on your eggs, dressing on your salad, icing on your cakes, catsup or mustard on your hot dogs? Baseball is THE American game."

Air Corps Sergeant Louis Eanes ventured, "Without baseball we would step back to the dark ages. Without baseball we are a lost people and all joy is gone from life."

Late in the war, informal surveys among wounded servicemen indicated little resentment over professional sports having been allowed to carry on. An April '44 poll taken in the recreation hall at Walter Reed Army Hospital in Washington, D.C., yielded a vote of 300–3 in support of baseball, with one of the convalescents declaring, "We're fighting for a lot of things in this war and baseball is one of them."

Sailors queried in February '45 at the Bainbridge, Maryland, Naval Training Station hospital were almost unanimous in wanting baseball to struggle through another wartime season.

There were, of course, those who felt differently. A poll taken by the Associated Press in early 1945 among GIs at a central Pacific base found a division of opinion on sports. Sergeant W.A. Justice, a twenty-four-year-old paratrooper who had been wounded at Leyte Gulf, believed "if those gridiron and diamond stars are husky enough to win games, they should come here to help us win this one."

Secretary of War Stimson doubted that servicemen had much use for ballplayers. A group of major league stars was to have visited Army bases in Australia and the South Pacific following the 1943 season, but at the last moment the War Department canceled the trip. The official explanation was that unforeseen difficulties in making travel arrangements had arisen, but Drew Pearson reported in his "Washington Merry-Go-Round" column that Stimson personally vetoed the trip because he "felt the troops would resent the sight of apparently healthy all-stars not in uniform, would not realize that each ballplayer of military age had been exempted from the draft because of some physical infirmity."

Stimson's fears may have had some justification since even ballplayers who did join the military faced occasional razzing from GIs when putting their skills to use.

Tex Hughson was breezing along with an 18–5 record for the Red Sox when the military beckoned in August '44. By the time the war was over, the tall right-hander had pitched for touring Army Air Corps teams before thousands of servicemen at bases on Guam, Saipan, and Tinian. Now a real estate developer and breeder of registered cattle on a spread outside San Marcos, Texas, thirty miles east of the LBJ Ranch, Hughson recalls his days playing baseball for Uncle Sam. The reception was cordial, but not without barbs.

"In most instances we were well received, but there's always some that would criticize us because we weren't carrying a gun, this type of thing, we heard some of that," he says. "Most of the criticism, the ones that got on us a bit, was—the way some of the older troopers over there described it—from those that had just been interrupted from their hideouts and sent over there. GIs that had been there a couple of years were glad to see us. Even for those who were not particularly baseball fans, it was something for them to do."

After dropping his *New York Post* sports column for a stint as a war correspondent, Stanley Frank became persuaded from talks with soldiers that baseball should pass up its 1945 season. Participating in a March '45 debate on baseball on the "America's Town Meeting" radio program, Frank reported that when he was in France he heard few comments from combat troops about sports, their drive "to keep alive and come home" preempting most other concerns. The newsman added that on visits to stateside military hospitals, he found servicemen listening to sports broadcasts mainly because "they are bored."

Also turning against baseball following a visit to the European front was *New York HeraldTribune* sports editor Stanley Woodward. Woodward joined Frank in urging that baseball suffer the same fate as racing, which was banned by the federal government in January '45 as a drain on hard-pressed transportation facilities and a suspected culprit in war plant absenteeism.

He wrote in a March '45 column:

"The clamor raised by the baseball people has been deafening during the winter months and they have won for themselves more radio time and newspaper space than ever before in the history of the game. Each day one or more persons gives an interview in which he tells how dependent the boys overseas are on baseball . . .

"This department is unable to convince itself that the efforts of the racing and baseball people are not prompted by the desire to preserve the ingress of easy money."

Similar suspicions had previously been expressed from within baseball's own family. When the Texas League decided early in 1943 to suspend operations for the duration of the war, its president, J. Alvin Gardner, contended that other minor league circuits planning to continue play were mainly concerned with "protection of investments."

Gardner said his club owners "believed it was more important that men build planes and tanks and work on the farms" than play baseball, adding, "We would have taken up space in hotels, used transportation facilities needed in other lines, and added to the food-rationing problem."

Morever, Gardner felt "many people who love baseball wouldn't want us to continue to play while their sons were risking everything in foreign fields."

Major league management, well aware that public opinion could sour on the game, let it be known that while baseball would try to carry on, there would be no place in its ranks for slackers.

Warren Giles, who had been a captain in the artillery corps during World War I, sent a letter to his ballplayers prior to their 1942 spring training camp. Its subject was not the importance of reporting in good physical condition. The Reds' general manager wrote:

"I urge every player on the Cincinnati club to take stock of his personal situation, analyze it carefully and ask himself this question: Can I stand at the bar of public opinion in wartime and conscientiously justify good and sufficient reasons for not being in government service? If you cannot answer that question in the affirmative, look men straight in the eye and justify in your heart and mind that you have justifiable reasons . . . you should not be playing on a professional team during wartime."

While pleased to comply with Roosevelt's wish that baseball continue operations to provide the public with needed recreation, Giles added, "We would rather finish last or not operate at all . . . and have all our players who should be in the service enter [it] than win the pennant, World Series, and make great profit with even one player . . . who could not justify his reasons for not being in the service."

Following the first wartime season, Cleveland's Alva Bradley told reporters, "I would rather not open the ballpark next spring than go out there and hear the wolves yelling 'why aren't you in the Army, you big lug?' The members of the Indians will have a very good reason for not being in the Army. They'll have wives and children to support. I don't want any men on my club who aren't heads of families."

And far from grumbling at the prospect of losing their star players to the armed forces, baseball officialdom seemed almost thrilled. When Tommy Henrich's dependency deferment was revoked in January '42, Yankee President Barrow commented, "If Henrich is called up, I think he'll make a good soldier. In our scheme of things, everything is subordinate to the prosecution of the war. I'm only too sorry I'm too old to get in there myself." (Henrich joined the Coast Guard late in the 1942 season.)

Pirate manager Frankie Frisch, when asked about his club's outlook for the 1942 season, responded, "I intend to play my youngsters as long as I can and when Uncle Sam calls them, I'll hope they bat .400 against the Japs and the Nazis alike."

Baseball was wary, meanwhile, of having its image tarnished by off-season frivolity.

Prior to the fifth game of the 1942 World Series, Cardinal manager Billy Southworth, anticipating a championship-clinching victory over the Yankees (he was right), made a little clubhouse speech.

"I'm prouder of you than words can express," Southworth told his players. "I have only this advice for the winter. I want every man to do what his conscience dictates about the war, but I want every man to do something. If you haven't a war job for the winter, line one up."

The *Sporting News* warned ballplayers of the need to be circum-

Pearl Harbor is still two months away as Giant pitcher Bill Lohrman (right) puts rivalry aside to hunt pheasants near New Paltz, New York, with Dodger infielders (left to right) Cookie Lavagetto, Lew Riggs, and Dolph Camilli. Soon a low profile would be deemed advisable when it came to off-season frivolity.

spect, cautioning against a repetition of the mistake made by Joe Gordon, who allowed himself to be photographed in the autumn of 1943 with a necklace of wild ducks bagged on a hunting trip. The picture had spurred angry letters to the War Department inquiring why the Yankee second baseman wasn't hunting down the enemy instead. (Gordon later joined the Army Air Corps.) Also disturbing, according to the *Sporting News*, were gag shots such as the stock photo depicting a ballplayer at some northern spring training camp sticking his head out the window, sadly eyeing raindrops. Things were a lot worse for the men peering out from foxholes.

While the game worked on its image, America's enemies were using baseball to score a few propaganda points for themselves.

Broadcasting to occupied territories in the fall of 1943, Joseph Goebbels found the World Series perfect grist for his Nazi propaganda mill.

"There are fresh atrocities in the United States," he announced. "The Yankees, not content with their pious interference all over the world, are beating up their own cardinals in St. Louis."

Wartime ballplayers were counseled to occupy themselves during the winter with endeavors other than hunting and fishing. More likely to keep a sports figure in the public's good graces was a defense job such as that held by Yankee outfielder Johnny Lindell, employed during the 1943–44 off-season at the Western Pipe and Steel shipyard in Wilmington, California.

The following autumn, baseball's annual extravaganza would provide an analogy for the Japanese radio, which likened the battle of the Philippines to "the final game of the World Series," the clash pitting General Tomoyuki Yamashita against General Douglas MacArthur, "the choice of the American League." American troops who might be listening were informed "the fate of the whole world hinges on the outcome and Yamashita is ready to lead East Asia to victory in the big game."

Japanese baseball, which continued through the early war years, did away with imported lingo such as strike and ball. "Yoshi" and "dam," translating into good and bad, would have to do. A shortstop became a "yugeki" or free-lancer, and when a runner slid into home, he was "ikita" or "shinda"—alive or dead—instead of safe or out. To encourage a properly militaristic spirit, the Hanshin Tigers were renamed "Moko Gun," roughly meaning Fiery Tiger Troop.

But it was all for naught. Not only did Yamashita lose the big game, he would be hanged by U.S. authorities. And perhaps proving the *Sporting News* hypothesis that the "treacherous Asiatic land was never really converted to baseball," the Japanese decided midway through their 1944 professional season to bid sayonara to the game for the duration of the war.

3

Blood Drives, Scrap Drives, and the War Bond League

The baseball hierarchy was due for a bit of a tongue-lashing decided Larry MacPhail, and the hot-tempered Dodger president was just the man to administer it. Here it was, the first day of February 1942, and apart from earmarking a few thousand dollars to buy athletic equipment for servicemen, baseball's support of the war effort had largely been confined to patriotic posturing.

Invited to address the New York baseball writers' annual dinner at the Hotel Commodore on the eve of the big league owners' first gathering since Pearl Harbor week, the man who brought night baseball to the majors would use the forum to call for new displays of imagination.

He was hardly a stranger to war era theatrics. Following the World War I armistice, Captain Larry MacPhail and seven fellow members of an artillery battery had staged an unauthorized foray aimed at snatching the Kaiser from a Dutch castle where he had taken sanctuary. The kidnap attempt failed, but MacPhail managed to swipe the German monarch's ashtray, which still occupied a prominent spot on his desk.

While he didn't envision anything quite as dramatic for baseball to undertake, MacPhail was ready with a few proposals at the writers' affair:

● Everyone in the game "from Commissioner Landis to the peanut vendor" should take part of his pay in war bonds.

● A second all-star game, matching the winner of the traditional contest against a military team comprised of former big leaguers, should be held to raise additional funds for the servicemen's ball and bat fund.

● A few cents should be taken out of every ticket sold during the season and placed in a fund for purchase of a $300,000 Flying Fortress bomber.

In outlining the program two weeks after Roosevelt had put his stamp of approval on wartime baseball, MacPhail told the gathering, "There will be some who will interpret the president's Green Light signal to go ahead as relieving baseball from some of its duties and obligations in the greatest crisis our country has ever faced."

But, warned MacPhail, "We can't adopt any 'business as usual' slogan for baseball. There is no business in this country so dependent upon the goodwill of the public as baseball. We are expected to do more than provide recreation for twenty million workers. We are expected to work out a definite program of unselfish cooperation with agencies of government needing help. If we keep the faith, the workers will agree with the president that baseball has its place in an all-out effort to win the war."

MacPhail concluded, "No club that doesn't sign up one hundred percent with this program should be allowed to open its gates."

Gathering at the Hotel New Yorker, the baseball owners adopted two of MacPhail's three proposals. Officials of all sixteen clubs announced they would set aside 10 percent of their salaries for purchase of war bonds and urged players to do the same. Before the week was out, Freddie Fitzsimmons, the Dodgers' forty-year-old knuckleballer, who had just signed for a reported $12,000, became the first big league player to enlist in the bond-buying plan. Fitzsimmons posed with MacPhail in front of a war bond drive poster, contract papers in hand, presumably to provide inspiration for his colleagues. MacPhail's proposal for a second 1942 all-star game to benefit the servicemen's athletic fund was also implemented. Ford Frick himself observed that the $24,000 allocated by baseball the previous December could purchase only one ball and half a bat for every 750 men in the armed forces. MacPhail's suggestion that baseball put up money for an Army bomber—it would be called the "Kenesaw Mountain Landis" and be flown by a crew of ex–big leaguers "to carry our compliments overseas"—never came up for discussion.

Two weeks after the baseball meetings, MacPhail decided there was still more to be done. He announced the Dodgers would turn over the receipts from a specially designated home game to a serviceman's welfare agency. "Baseball cannot content itself merely with giving paraphernalia to the soldiers and sailors of our country," MacPhail declared. "Something more substantial must be done and this may be a beginning. I hope the other clubs will follow suit."

They did. In mid-April, Landis, Frick, Harridge, and minor league officials met with Colonel John Taylor, head of the Army

Emergency Relief Fund, and Lieutenant William Huggins, Jr., director of the Navy Relief Society. Both agencies provided financial aid to servicemen's dependents in cases of special need. Out of the session came a plan under which each major league team would donate proceeds from one home game to servicemen's relief, with the minor leagues also promising to help out.

And so baseball was letting it be known the game would find concrete ways to pitch in with the rest of America in backing the boys overseas.

In the troubled times ahead, hardly a day would go by without a reminder that the "national pastime" was a national resource, making itself useful to the war effort beyond serving as a morale booster through its mere presence.

Gate receipts from selected exhibition and regular season games, all-star contests, and the World Series would be funneled to war-related charities or defense bonds. The ball clubs would schedule a bizarre mix of starting times for their games in order to accommodate war workers on varying shifts. Individual players would promote bond sales, watch the skies for enemy planes on off nights, pick apples to relieve a farm labor shortage, donate blood, go on USO-sponsored trips to the war fronts, and visit defense plants to spur productivity. Fans would be called upon to haul commodities such as scrap metal to the ballpark for conversion to war material—their reward a free seat —and would forsake the privilege of keeping foul pops, instead tossing the baseballs back onto the field for shipment to the armed forces, to supplement the official equipment fund.

Just as the idea of purchasing sporting goods for military camps had its origin in World War I, so, too, was there precedent for baseball aiding wartime welfare agencies. One of the first such charity events was staged back in 1917 and was intertwined with the controversy over Sunday baseball in New York City. Dodger owner Charles Ebbets arranged a game with the Phillies for Sunday, July 1, 1917, and announced a portion of the proceeds would go to an organization called the Militia of Mercy. The problem was the state legislature had outlawed Sunday ball games at which admission fees were collected. Ebbets figured he could get around the prohibition by staging a band concert before the game—the patrons ostensibly were buying tickets for the musical entertainment and then could stick around and watch the baseball game for free. The police didn't go for the maneuver, however, and arrested Ebbets and Dodger manager Wilbert Robinson. They both paid a small fine the next morning. But the game was

The men of the U.S.S. Prairie State *pass in review at Ebbets Field.*

played, and Ebbets turned over $5,000 to the Militia of Mercy while making a few bucks for himself and scoring some points for the idea of Sunday baseball. The ban was, in fact, lifted soon after World War I had ended.

As promised by Larry MacPhail, Ebbets Field was also the site of the first World War II ball game for servicemen's relief. The Giants furnished the opposition and the affair was quite a spectacle. Sailors from the U.S.S. *Prairie State* marched around the field, Army and American Legion bands played martial tunes, and Mayor LaGuardia joined the overflow crowd of more than thirty-four thousand in singing "God Bless America." The May 8, 1942, extravaganza—the first twilight game in the majors in 24 years—was a financial triumph, raising $59,859 for the Navy Relief Society. And the Dodger fans were sent home happy by a 7–6 victory over the hated foe; Dolph Camilli's seventh-inning homer into Bedford Avenue was the key blow.

The baseball hierarchy was elated at the huge success of the MacPhail promotion. The joy was to fade, however, as returns came in from the other ballparks.

The Phillies had provided all the trappings for their war charity effort, a midweek twilight game with the Pirates on May 19. Hugh Mulcahy, brought down from Camp Edwards on furlough, pitched batting practice, threw out the first ball, was presented with $250 worth of war bonds by his old teammates, and received a silver platter from the American Legion. Soldiers, sailors, and marines marched to the flagpole. A pair of bands provided stirring music. Governors Arthur James of Pennsylvania, Charles Edison of New Jersey, and Walter Bacon of Delaware were invited. The Phillie players, who savored victory on rare occasions in those days, did their best, beating the Pirates, 5–4. But none of the governors and precious few fans–3,366 in all—showed up. Stan Baumgartner, covering the game for the *Philadelphia Inquirer,* noted, "The Phils came to the relief of manager Hans Lobert although other Philadelphians were a bit shy about coming to the aid of the Army and Navy relief funds."

Four days later, only 12,216 spectators turned out to see the Red Sox host the Athletics in a benefit affair despite a mound duel between Mulcahy and Feller in an Army–Navy preliminary game.

Will Harridge had predicted the eight American League benefit games would bring in $375,000, but when the first four contests were over, only 37,991 fans had gone through the turnstiles, contributing a mere $41,000. With the exception of the Dodger–Giant game, attendance at the first few National League war relief games had also been disappointing.

Baseball had reaped some wonderful publicity back in April with announcement of plans for the benefit games. But the owners, seeking to minimize revenue losses to charity, had spoiled it all—none of the contests was held at night or on a Sunday when the biggest crowds could be anticipated.

Harridge, obviously embarrassed, decreed that three American League afternoon relief games scheduled for later in the '42 season be made part of Sunday doubleheaders, and he shifted the fourth remaining affair to a night game. Similar revisions were ordered in the National League.

While defending the original scheduling arrangement with the explanation "the only chance most of our owners have of finishing out of the red this year is to cash in on Sunday, holiday, or night games," Harridge told reporters, "We'll try to do something to make a stronger finish."

Attendance did pick up later. During 1942, a total of $506,000 from receipts at sixteen designated games was eventually earmarked for servicemen's relief agencies. Over the four war years, the majors would raise $2.5 million for the Army and Navy benefit organizations, the USO, and the Red Cross.

Perhaps the most spectacular charitable event was the second 1942 all-star game, held in early July under the lights at Cleveland's huge Municipal Stadium.

The crowd of 62,094 was awed by a display of military pageantry, then watched a collection of former big league players who had gone into the armed forces take on the American League stars. The AL squad had been victorious over the National League in the traditional all-star game, played the previous evening at the Polo Grounds. As for the preliminaries, tanks and jeeps from Camp Custer rolled over the ballpark terrain, marines from the Navy Pier in Chicago put on an exhibition of precision drilling, and sailors from the Great Lakes Naval Training Station joined with coast guardsmen to form a giant white "V for Victory," its apex at home plate. The hoopla, reviewed by Ohio Governor John Bricker and Cleveland Mayor Frank Lausche, drew wild cheers from the stands and touched the emotions of at least one press corps observer. Fred Lieb wrote in the *Sporting News*, "As though it were a contagion, one could feel the patriotic fervor. . . . It sent needles shooting down one's spine. . . . It started honest tears trickling down the cheeks and made one murmur to oneself, 'Thank God I am an American.'"

The way Lou Boudreau tells it, however, the American League stars were considerably less enthralled.

"It was quite a letdown from the original all-star game," says the former Indians' playing manager and AL shortstop in the two contests. "The fellas would have had three days off and even though it was for a good cause, they thought that another all-star team should have been represented, not the one that played in the first all-star game."

Tex Hughson, who pitched the last three innings for the American League against the servicemen, remembers otherwise.

"I don't recall anyone being unhappy," he says. "I know definitely that I wasn't. I was very happy and considered myself fortunate to be on the ball club and I thought this was a very minor sacrifice as far as myself personally was concerned. I thought it was the least thing we could do."

Whatever the level of their enthusiasm, the American League stars were able to handle the military team, knocking out the Navy's Bob Feller in the third inning and going on to a 5–0 victory.

The two 1942 all-star contests raised $100,000 to purchase balls and bats for servicemen and another $60,000 for the Army and Navy welfare agencies. In addition, fans at the Cleveland spectacle bought $60,000 worth of war stamps.

By time the war was over, baseball had provided military camps with $328,000 worth of athletic equipment, mostly from receipts at all-star games.

Service teams often were brought to the ballparks to boost attendance at the regular season games aiding war charities.

It was the Cloudbursters against the Yank-Lands in the second game of a July '43 Red Cross benefit doubleheader at Yankee Stadium. The Cloudbursters, representing the Chapel Hill naval pre-flight school, based at the University of North Carolina campus, had an outfielder considered something of a gate attraction: Ted Williams. The Yank-Lands were a hybrid of Yankee and Indian ballplayers managed by Babe Ruth. Their encounter helped bring out 27,281 fans who had the privilege of watching the wartime versions of the Yanks and Indians do battle in the first contest. Williams got a single in four trips to the plate. Ruth pinch hit and drew a walk off Johnny Sain, who had joined the Navy after his rookie season on the mound for the Boston Braves.

Ruth and fellow old-timers were trotted out periodically to hype the gate at benefit affairs. Having hit 10 of his 714 homers off Walter Johnson, the Babe got an opportunity during the war to blast a few more off the Senator great. Johnson came up from his Maryland farm to pitch against Ruth in an encounter that kicked off a New York–Washington doubleheader at Yankee Stadium raising funds for servicemen's welfare agencies. Crouching behind the plate was Benny Bengough, a catcher on the Yankee teams of the 1920s. The honor of calling balls and strikes was given to Billy Evans, the home plate umpire for both Johnson's first major league outing and the 1927 game in which Ruth hit his 60th home run. Looking at 20 pitches from Johnson, Ruth managed one make-believe homer, a drive landing in the lower right-field seats. After narrowly missing a second home run on his last cut, the Babe ambled around the bases, doffing his cap to cheers from the crowd of 69,136. James Dawson of the *New York Times* told his readers the next day, "Babe Ruth hit one of his greatest home runs yesterday at the Stadium, a typical Ruthian wallop in the interests of freedom and the democratic way of living."

Ballplayers competed in pregame running, batting, and throwing contests to amuse the fans attending the benefit games. Cardinal pitcher Ernie White had the fastest time in a baserunning event at the

Walter Johnson, Benny Bengough, Billy Evans, and Babe Ruth relive old times.

Polo Grounds in which participants picked up a pipe at first base, a tobacco pouch at second, and matches at third, then raced home to light up. Rube Fischer of the Giants took the pitchers' fungo-hitting contest with a clout of 446 feet while his catcher, Gus Mancuso, won a throwing-for-accuracy event which involved squatting at home plate and aiming a baseball at the mouth of barrel placed over second base.

It was said that the players, coaches, and managers paid their own way in at the benefit games. Well, they usually did. Leo Durocher, arriving at the Polo Grounds for a charity contest, discovered the ticket sellers had refused to accept any money from his men. The Dodger manager promptly took up a collection in the clubhouse, snarling, "They're not going to say we got in for nothing."

White Sox manager Jimmy Dykes, a practiced umpire baiter, was delighted to put up the price of admission. Displaying a yellow ticket stub in the dugout before a June '42 benefit game with the Indians, Dykes explained, "This is the first time I've got it over those umpires. They can't throw a guy out of the ballpark when he pays his way in. Today I'm just a spectator like everyone else and entitled to howl my head off."

Show business personalities were glad to lend baseball a hand. One April day in 1944, bobby-soxers began lining up outside the Ebbets Field gates at seven o'clock in the morning, seven and one-half hours before the start of a Dodger–Phillie exhibition benefiting the Red Cross. The girls weren't there to see Frenchy Bordagaray. Red Barber, who headed the Brooklyn Red Cross' fund-raising drive, had prevailed upon Frank Sinatra to deliver a few songs as the highlight

Like everyone else at May 1942 Dodger-Giant game benefiting sailors' relief fund, Brooklyn pitchers Kirby Higbe (left) and Whitlow Wyatt pay their way in to Ebbets Field.

Frank Sinatra gets set to croon for the Red Cross as Dodger coach Charlie Dressen takes a seat bobby-soxers would envy.

of pregame festivities. With Dodger organist Gladys Gooding providing accompaniment on a piano rolled out to home plate, Frankie seranaded with "Let Me Call You Sweetheart," "People Will Say We're in Love" and the less romantic "Take Me Out to the Ball Game." The teenagers shrieked with delight and the Red Cross, which collected $14,000 in gate receipts, wasn't unhappy either. There was even something for the males in the crowd of 13,314—an appearance by Flo Ziegfeld's follies girls.

Fiorello LaGuardia, something of a showman himself, became a baseball announcer for one inning during an April '43 exhibition doubleheader at Yankee Stadium raising funds for civil defense efforts. All three New York teams were involved. The Dodgers beat the Yankees, 6–1, in the first game, thereby earning the right to take on the Giants, whom they also defeated, 1–0. LaGuardia, who in addition to his mayoral duties was the first director of the federal Office of Civilian Defense, gave municipal workers a half-day off so that they could attend the games and was so enthused by a turnout of 35,301 despite snow flurries and temperatures in the 30s that he took over the play-by-play chores from Bill Stern. If the radio listeners were a bit confused by the participation of three ball clubs in a doubleheader, the mayor did nothing to clear up matters during his one-inning stint behind the microphone. A partial transcript reads:

"You must bear with me, and what I don't know you do. Here it comes, it's a ball. I don't know about that but I'll take the umpire's word. . . Now he's warming up and in she comes and he hits it. The shortstop gets it, throws it to second, second is out, first is out, two men out, three men out. That's a triple play. [It was a double play.] The weather is a little—oh, I can't talk about that. Here it comes and it's a hit. It goes to second base, he throws it to first, and that's out, and I'm through. If we didn't need the money so bad, I wouldn't have gone through with this. I'm sorry."

For those fans who got their kicks out of watching other people

Mayor LaGuardia turns baseball announcer for a worthy cause.

enter the service, mass enlistments were staged on ballfields before war charity games. One day in June '42, two hundred men were sworn into the Army, Navy, and Marines at Braves Field.

One of the World War II benefit games almost fell victim to a strike. The Phils were scheduled to play the Cardinals at Sportsman's Park in a July '43 night contest whose proceeds were earmarked for the Red Cross. But the Phillie players threatened a walkout over the firing that day of manager Bucky Harris by owner Bill Cox, a thirty-three-year-old lumber executive and sportsman who had bought the club the previous February.

Upset because they liked Harris and particularly angered that word of his dismissal was in the newspapers before he was notified personally, the ballplayers reported to their clubhouse but announced they wouldn't go on the field unless the manager was given a face-saving chance to resign.

"We feel because of his background and experience, he is entitled to just that decency," they declared in a statement.

Cox averted a strike by taking Harris into the clubhouse and telling him in front of the players that his ouster in favor of Freddie Fitzsimmons, who had come over from the Dodgers, "was not intended to reflect in any way on your ability as a manager."

The Phils took the field and proceeded to snap an eleven-game Cardinal winning streak while helping add to the Red Cross coffers.

Matters were, however, just in the warm-up stage. A few days later, Cox told reporters he fired the manager because Harris had given up on the team and had privately referred to the players as "those jerks." Harris denied making the remark and, in response, called Cox "an All-American jerk." The owner, determined to get in the last word, shot back that Harris "must have been looking in the mirror when he made that statement."

Bucky Harris eventually got his revenge by informing reporters that Cox had been betting on games. Landis launched an investigation and although finding that the young owner had only bet on the Phils to win, tossed him out of baseball for violating the game's anti-gambling regulations. The team was taken over by the Carpenter family, which still runs it.

Baseball made its biggest dollars-and-cents contribution to the war effort through promotion of bond sales.

If Betty Grable's stockings, Jack Benny's violin, and Man o' War's horseshoes could be auctioned at bond rallies to pay for $330 billion in war expenditures, why not peddle a few ballplayers?

Besides the American and National Leagues, there was the War Bond League, comprised of Dodger, Giant, and Yankee players "auctioned" at a June '43 rally at the Waldorf-Astoria. Business and civic organizations bid, through enormous war bond pledges, for the right to sponsor individual players. Once gaining title, the sponsors agreed to buy additional bonds based on their man's performance: a home run was worth a $10,000 bond, a shutout would require purchase of $50,000 in bonds.

The auction yielded $123,850,000 in initial war bond pledges. The most expensive of the thirty-seven players selected was Dixie Walker, who went for $11,250,000 in bonds to the Brooklyn Club, a social organization. At the other end of the scale, when a trio of Giant players appeared on the dais to be auctioned off, a member of the Brooklyn Chamber of Commerce shouted, "We bid twenty-five cents for the entire Giant team."

The Borden Company got Dodger hurler Bobo Newsom for $3.75 million in bonds, then came up with an awful pun to publicize the

Red Barber auctions off (left to right) Dixie Walker, Bobo Newsom, and Arky Vaughan of the Dodgers at war bond rally. Jimmy Walker, seated beside Barber, lends his charm to the proceedings.

acquisition. A telegram was sent to Newsom reading, "It is nice to have won you. For years I have been giving plenty of milk and cream for others and now for the first time I have a pitcher of my own. May I come over to Ebbets Field some day to see you play?" Signed: "Elsie the Cow."

Elsie did grace a big league ballfield during the war. In April 1944 at the Polo Grounds, a real-life Borden cow, wearing a green blanket and hat, was presented with a citation from the Treasury Department in recognition of the dairy firm's war bond purchases.

The most exciting moment at the auction came when former New York Mayor Jimmy Walker, helping to run things, announced one bid for $350 million. Quickly realizing he meant to say $3,500,000, Walker explained, "I've made a mistake with people's money before."

In the weeks following the auction, the press kept a running tally of additional war bond purchases that each sponsored player was accounting for by his hitting or pitching prowess. When the Giants beat the Dodgers, 8–5, on June 17, the *New York Times* noted that the victors also outpointed their rivals $45,000 to $25,000 in war bond achievements. A total of $7.3 million worth of bonds was sold via the gimmick.

The promotion's grand finale came on August 26, when a War Bond League all-star team composed of the players who had raised the most bond money through their performance took on an Army team featuring Hank Greenberg, Enos Slaughter, and Johnny Beazley. The Polo Grounds game brought in the staggering sum of $816 million worth of bond sales through program advertisements and seat purchases; "Golden Horseshoe" boxes went for $1 million in bonds apiece.

That same season, the Dodgers staged their own "spring offensive" war bond campaign, kicked off with Ebbets Field ceremonies at which Brooklyn Borough President John Cashmore swore in team members as "special agents" of the Treasury Department. The ballplayers visited seventy-five of the largest industrial plants in Brooklyn, urging employees to put part of their salary into war bonds. On one day alone, Freddie Fitzsimmons and Paul Waner visited the Vulcan Proofing Company, Billy Herman and Kirby Higbe went to the Todd Shipyards, and Dixie Walker and Joe Medwick spoke at the Brooklyn Union Gas Company. The appearances were credited with bringing in $77 million in bond sales.

Branch Rickey, who as a young man had promised his mother he would never appear at a ballfield on the sabbath, broke the vow to

Billy Herman (left) and Kirby Higbe make war bond pitch to a pair of women workers at Todd Shipyards as their male colleagues lend an ear.

accept a Treasury Department commendation for the "spring offensive" in ceremonies prior to a Sunday game with the Phillies. Dodger pitchers later moved through the crowd, soliciting even more bond pledges.

Red Barber recalls, "I asked Mr. Rickey, 'Will you come to home plate and say a few words?' He said, 'For this occasion and for this reason, because its's worthy. I will speak and then leave the ballpark.' It was the only time in his career since he made the promise to his mother that he went in a ballpark on a Sunday."

Barber himself promoted bond sales over the radio.

"We were divided in Vietnam, but World War II was such a tremendous event, the whole country was united in the rightness of that war," he points out. "There were so many things to be done, every broadcaster did everything he could.

"In 1942, the general manager at WHN and two or three others there came up with the idea that we'd go on the air. People would call in pledges for war bonds and we'd give their name. Then for every person who pledged, there was an acknowledgment card personally signed by me. I signed thousands. It was so successful the Treasury

Department in Washington asked me to come down and tell them how we'd done it."

While the New York clubs took the lead, there was plenty of bond sale promotional activity all over the major league map.

In Philadelphia, where they were auctioning baseballs instead of ballplayers—understandable in view of the talent on hand—it developed that a ball autographed by Connie Mack was of considerably greater value than one signed by Winston Churchill. A baseball bearing the signatures of both the Athletics' venerable manager and President Roosevelt was bought by a Philadelphia brewery in April '43 for $15,000 in bonds. Five months later, a Shibe Park auction yielded a bond pledge of only $10,000 for a ball containing the autographs of Churchill (substituting for Mack) and FDR.

· Jimmy Dykes auctioned off a hen for $1,150 in bonds at a Chicago hotel where a poultry exposition was being held. Dykes would make a financial contribution of his own elsewhere. When Will Harridge fined the White Sox manager $50 for a run-in with an umpire, he paid off by dumping a flock of 10-cent defense stamps at home plate the next day.

A month after guiding the Cardinals to their 1942 World Series title, Billy Southworth awarded the Treasury Department's "Minute Man" banner to employees of a Curtiss–Wright plant in his hometown of Columbus, Ohio, for their exemplary record of bond purchases. He told the workers, "It takes a great team to win a championship. It takes a unified effort to win this war. We're all members of a great big team."

Personalities ranging from British Field Marshal Sir Archibald Wavell, who made a little speech, to Kate Smith, singing the national anthem, appeared at Griffith Stadium in May '43 for a game between the Senators and Norfolk Naval Training Station netting $2.1 million in bond purchases by spectators.

Some twenty-five thousand youngsters who had been particularly zealous volunteer bond salesmen were rewarded with free seats to a White Sox–Cubs exhibition game at Wrigley Field.

An elderly Forbes Field vendor named Bill Flowers spent the 1942 season in an Uncle Sam suit, hawking war bonds instead of peanuts to the customers. He chalked up $15,000 in sales.

Although baseball took its bond-selling work seriously, there was room for comic relief. Bill Veeck, running the Milwaukee Brewers of the American Association during the war, decided the team would present manager Charlie Grimm with a $1,000 bond as a token of appreciation for his services.

"He knew we were practically broke so he thought we were losing our minds until he discovered the bond was one which he himself had bought by payroll deductions," Veeck later explained.

While helping to raise money to pay for munitions, baseball also sought to lift the spirits of those actually turning out the weapons. A May '43 survey by the Reds on starting time preference found 60 percent of the fans who were working in war plants—round the clock operations—favoring morning games. And so, many big league contests would begin in midmorning to give night-shift workers a chance to get to the park, a move hailed by War Manpower Commissioner Paul McNutt as "adding to the efficiency and morale of America's industrial army."

Even the lowly Phillies could draw an early turnout, attracting 11,129 fans for an August '43 doubleheader with the Pirates starting at 10:30 A.M.

Beginning to earn his reputation as the Barnum of baseball, Bill Veeck got lots of publicity from a Saturday game at Milwaukee's

War plant workers stopping off at Wrigley Field after the night shift oblige photographer by yawning through 11:00 A.M. game.

Borchert Field scheduled for 10:00 A.M. As the 3,500 fans filed in, ushers dressed in gaudy pajamas handed out cereal, coffee, and donuts. A seven-piece band wearing nightclothes and stocking caps helped keep the crowd awake. The only problem was that the visiting St. Paul Saints had missed train connections and didn't show up until noon. By then more than half the fans had left. But Veeck gave refunds to those departing and rewarded the more patient spectators with a 20–0 victory over the travel-weary opponents. Later Veeck made a more personal contribution to the war effort by enlisting in the Marines. He would lose a leg from wounds received in combat on Bougainville.

Ballplayers undertook a variety of chores, besides promoting bond sales, to show they could be useful to the war effort.

Since Fenway Park and Braves Field were still without lights during the war years, Red Sox and Braves players had time during home stands to scan the night skies as aircraft spotters, reporting to an American Legion lookout post atop Corey Hill in suburban Brookline.

"We were signed up and we would go, as volunteers of course, maybe once or twice a week," remembers Tex Hughson. "We'd go out to this tower. We were supposed to watch and be able to alert for planes."

Did he ever see anything suspicious?

"No, but I don't know whether at night I could have recognized an enemy plane or not," Hughson chuckles.

Actually, all that the Boston players and 600,000 fellow members of the Ground Observer Corps were asked to do was report the presence of every plane flying over their area to the local Army Filter Center. The military would sort out friend from foe.

Draft calls and the prospect of lucrative jobs in munitions plants brought about a farm labor shortage during the war. Urban teenagers, POWs, interned Japanese-Americans, and even soldiers were pressed into service to help with the crops at harvest time. So, too, were the Washington Senators. On an off day in September '43, Senator manager Ossie Bluege, his coaches, and three ballplayers trooped down to the Chilcott orchards near Vienna, Virginia, to pick apples, depositing the produce in sacks tied to their waists.

A number of baseball people went on overseas trips sponsored by the USO, entertaining servicemen with stories and showings of World Series films.

The first troupe, comprised of Danny Litwhiler, Stan Musial,

Enjoying the fruits of their labor are (left to right) Senators' coach Benny Bengough, manager Ossie Bluege, coach Nick Altrock, outfielder Jake Powell, pitcher Dutch Leonard, coach Clyde Milan, and pitcher Mickey Haefner.

Hank Borowy, Dixie Walker, and Frankie Frisch, visited Alaska and the Aleutian islands during the winter of 1943–44.

Rounding up a group of volunteers was no easy feat. Litwhiler recalls, "Ford Frick said to me, 'I've asked lots of guys to go but they refused and you'd be doing me and baseball a personal favor if you'd go.'"

At times, the honor may have seemed a dubious one.

The unit found itself stranded during Christmas just as it was preparing to descend from a mountaintop to the Aleutian base at Dutch Harbor where a boat was waiting for a trip to Adak Island in the Aleutians.

Litwhiler recounts the predicament:

"A storm came out and we got marooned up there. I guess we were there a day and a half and finally decided, well, the ship is leaving so we'd better get out. There was a kind of road they had built, but the vehicles had broken down, so we walked. The blizzard was blowing, you'd walk down at a forty-five-degree angle against the wind. We just pulled our knit caps over our eyes. You had an idea where you were going though you weren't too sure. But we were able to get down in time to get the ship out."

There was more awful weather ahead on the sea voyage. Litwhiler continues, "We got into a terrific storm in the Bering Sea. We were prepared then for submarine attacks by the Japanese. About the second day of the storm, we were hoping they'd hit us, it was that bad. Everybody was sick."

But looking back, Litwhiler feels that slogging through the snows and braving the storms—sometimes just to visit a handful of GIs at a lonely outpost—was made worthwhile by the enthusiasm with which the unit was received.

"We had great receptions, just fantastic, every place we went," he says. "We'd split up sometimes and go to a lookout post where there might be four or five people, and two of them are busy and three of them are in. So we'd go and talk to those fellas. And they'd have really good questions, they knew baseball real good."

Particularly fresh in Litwhiler's mind is what turned out to be a one-way chat:

"We went to a hospital and there was a guy who wouldn't talk; he looked like he was spaced out. They had him in the psychiatry ward. But they said he was crazy about baseball and if we'd get in there and talk baseball to him, he might come around. So we went and told him about different things and his eyes would kind of lighten up a bit. We thought maybe we were getting to him. And finally we left.

"Sometime later, it was in 1944, I saw this guy, maybe it was at a ball game. He'd got out and he was in great shape, he was perfectly normal.

" 'Yeah, everything's fine, I got out,' he said. It looked to me like he was bucking for a Section Eight and he got it. But he loved baseball like they said."

By all accounts the visit was, as Litwhiler indicates, a huge success. In a letter to the Yankees thanking them for allowing pitcher Borowy to make the trip, Pfc. Howard Kosbau, sports editor of the servicemen's newspaper *Sourdough Sentinel,* went so far as to report "one soldier said he'd rather talk to a major league ballplayer than Betty Grable."

The note touched off the curiosity of the *Sporting News,* which decided to offer fifty dollars for the best letter from a serviceman on the subject of ballplayers versus beauty queens. The contest winner was Major Alfred Brown of the Nineteenth Air Depot Group in North Africa, who wrote: "For over a year we've had nothing feminine to observe but Arab women, their heads and faces covered with possibly just one eye peeking out. Compare this constant view to that of one squint at Betty's gams. Brother, let's exchange places."

USO troopers (left to right) Stan Musial, Dixie Walker, Frankie Frisch, Danny Litwhiler, and Hank Borowy are fitted with Army-issue apparel on visit to Alaska and the Aleutians.

Apparently convinced it was at least running a strong second to pinup stars, baseball intensified its tour activities during the winter of 1944–45, sending five USO contingents abroad.

Frankie Frisch, Mel Ott, Bucky Walters, Dutch Leonard, and St. Louis sportswriter J. Roy Stockton spent six weeks visiting troops in Belgium, France, Holland, and Germany. Decked out in steel helmets, they rode on a converted weapons carrier along highways strewn with Nazi armor, the whistle of artillery shells occasionally heard overhead. Should the baseball emissaries wander into enemy lines—these were the days of the Battle of the Bulge—identification cards were issued requesting they be given the privileges afforded Army captains.

The unit visited rest camps for the 82nd and 101st Airborne Divisions in the French towns of Mourmelon-le-Ground and Sissonne, appearing before as many as three thousand GIs at a time. Its smallest audience was a group of forty-five infantrymen—five apiece selected from nine front-line companies—entertained with baseball stories in a ramshackle German barn two miles from a stretch of river being guarded.

Patton and Bradley took a break from strategy sessions at their headquarters in a Luxembourg hotel to view World Series films. Frisch later told how Patton, living up to his image, wore his pearl-handled revolvers while sitting through the showing and then ended the evening by rising and informing the baseball visitors, "Gentlemen, I'm sorry but I have to retire now. I have to get some rest. I've got a lot of killing to do in the morning."

Another USO contingent touring Italy and North Africa planned to show the 1944 World Series film one evening in a tent near the front lines, but never got the action rolling—the projector and generating equipment had been stolen during the day by German infiltrators.

But the enemy was not always at hand. A baseball unit visiting the Middle East found time to hunt gazelles in the Iranian desert, taking aim from a jeep speeding along at seventy miles an hour to keep up with the herds.

A USO-sponsored trip to Southwest Pacific bases by a group including umpire Beans Reardon yielded dividends at home. Upon his return, Reardon delivered pep talks at Chicago area war plants exhorting workers to reduce absenteeism and step up production. Reardon explained, "The morale of our soldiers is of the best, but they want equipment to get this job done in a hurry."

Howard Reineman, the general manager of Industrial Metal Fabricators' four huge Chicago factories, credited Reardon's visits with reducing absentee rates by 80 percent. The industrialist reported that workers didn't pay much attention to lectures by soldiers returning from the front, believing the GIs were merely repeating what their commanders had told them to say, but "they will listen to sports figures."

Baseball comedian Al Schacht made a series of one-man visits to the war theaters and estimated he entertained some two million servicemen. Schacht had a close call in September '43 when his plane was

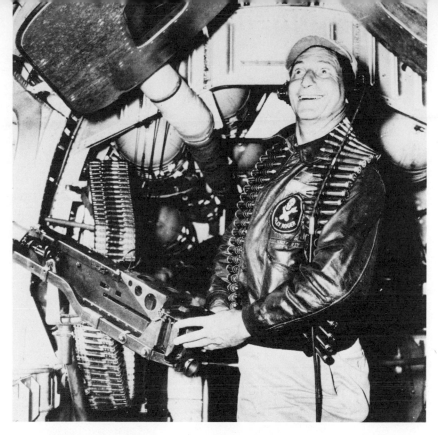

Baseball clown Al Schacht, on 1945 tour of South Pacific bases, seems ready to win the war by himself from gunner's spot on B-24 Liberator bomber.

strafed upon touching down at an airstrip in Catania, Sicily. The craft caught fire, but he dove for cover and was unhurt.

The fans could support the war effort in a variety of ways. Besides attending ball games at which the price of admission was a bond purchase or a donation to servicemen's welfare agencies, they were called upon to contribute a host of precious commodities—among the most important, their blood.

In New York City, the man doing the asking on behalf of the Red Cross was Red Barber.

"I was the best-known fella in Brooklyn then, so somebody said Red is the fella to be chairman, he's a natural," Barber recalls. "I worked full time on it during the off season. I had an office in Brooklyn and one in Manhattan. I worked day and night. People wanted to work for the war effort, this was our national survival."

When the baseball season was on, Barber appealed for blood donations at the start of Dodger broadcasts.

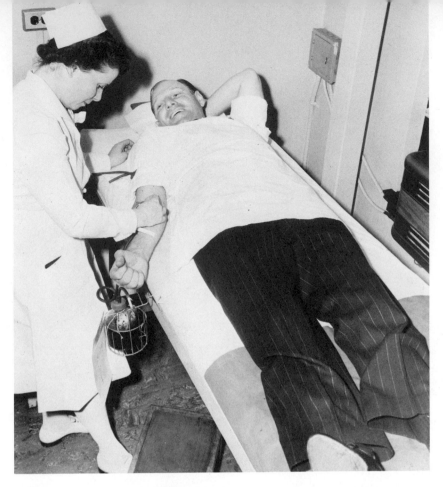

Leo Durocher, assisted by nurse Gladys Collins, parts with a pint of blood.

Red Cross worker Babe Ruth finds time for a few autographs.

"I would come into the booth a half-hour before the game. I'd call the Brooklyn Red Cross chapter and ask how many donors they needed and at what hour," he remembers. "On the air I'd say 'here's the phone number and their needs.' And by the fifth or sixth inning, the center would call and say 'we have all our appointments set for tomorrow.' "

Barber says he had the Dodger players set an example for the fainthearted:

"I made arrangements with Mr. Rickey, and one morning around nine o'clock Durocher took the entire squad—including the starting pitcher—down to the Red Cross center. And they won that day. You can imagine the sales force this had."

One afternoon at Forbes Field, eight Pirate players who had given blood were called out to home plate, presumably none the worse for wear. Women volunteers in Red Cross uniforms then went through the stands, signing up seven hundred fans as prospective donors.

Many ball clubs offered a free seat in return for a pint of blood and the newspapers reported the number of donors on hand at each game. Warren Giles received an unexpected bonus when he gave blood at the Cincinnati Red Cross headquarters—an attendant who didn't recognize him handed the Reds' executive a pass to Crosley Field.

Youngsters couldn't give blood, but there were other ways to help out. According to the government, the iron in an old shovel could be used to make 4 hand grenades, and 30,000 razor blades contained enough steel for 50 machine guns. And so, when the Dodgers announced in September '42 that anyone bringing ten pounds or more of scrap metal to Ebbets Field would be admitted free, the response was overwhelming. Over a four-day period, 520 tons of junk were heaped outside the park for eventual conversion into war material. The *New York Times* reported, "Thousand of youngsters brought everything metallic they could lay their hands on. One presented his mother's new toaster and another came with mom's meat grinder. The pile of metal back of the left-field stands has grown to a small mountain."

The Giants, running their own scrap drive, lost a ball game to the youthful scavengers' exuberance. They were leading the Braves, 5–2, in the eighth inning of a doubleheader finale near the end of the 1942 season when many of the 11,205 kids who had been let in free in reward for dumping junk outside the Polo Grounds gates started to swarm onto the field and couldn't be coaxed off. The umpires or-

Enthusiastic response to scrap iron appeal leaves sidewalk outside Ebbets Field looking like a junkyard.

dered the game be forfeited to Boston. Horace Stoneham promised continued participation in the scrap drive but announced the youngsters would be confined in the future to special grandstand sections where they could be kept under surveillance.

Baseball also joined in nationwide community drives to round up wastepaper—old newspapers, cardboard boxes, and envelopes—suitable for conversion into containers that would package items ranging from artillery shells to blood plasma. The youngsters were zealous in this campaign as well. Boy Scouts who collected one thousand pounds of paper were promised the General Eisenhower War Service Medal for Extraordinary Patriotic Achievement—when metal could be spared. The ball clubs couldn't come up with anything that glamorous, but did promise free seats in exchange for the deposit of paper products tied neatly into bundles.

The sport was profligate, however, in its own use of paper. A dispute between Landis and the *Sporting News* resulted in the printing of two 1943 baseball guides, running to a total of nearly 1,100 pages.

The *Sporting News* had taken over publication of organized baseball's official record book in 1942, its 574-page volume replacing the traditional Spalding-Reach guides, which were no longer being printed. But the following year Landis had a falling out with the *Sporting News* publisher Spink and denied him permission to put out another official guidebook. Spink went ahead and printed an unofficial record book for 1943, although shrinking the guide to 357 pages (minor league batting averages were condensed) in view of impending paper shortages. Landis' office waited until August to print an "official" guide, but it was a whopper—736 pages. In 1944, the commissioner's office had to forego a guidebook because it couldn't get another allocation of paper from the government.

The ladies made a contribution by bringing cans filled with kitchen fats to the ballpark. It was said a pound of the stuff yielded enough glycerin to produce black powder for six 75-millimeter shells. On a Saturday afternoon in July '43 designated by the Dodgers as "Kitchen Fat Day," a total of 4,512 women arrived at Ebbets Field with 5,002 pounds of grease. They got in without having to buy tickets, but for a time it appeared there would be no ball game to see. Like the Red Cross benefit between the Phillies and Cardinals, the day's scheduled game between the Dodgers and Pirates nearly fell victim to a

Actresses from show Early to Bed *gain free admission to July 1943 game at Ebbets Field—not to mention some free publicity—by depositing containers of fat for conversion to explosives.*

strike. The Brooklyn players briefly threatened a walkout over Leo Durocher's suspension of Bobo Newsom, a free spirit whom the manager had accused of disobeying pitching instructions. Finally persuaded to get into uniform, the team let loose its aggressions with a 23–6 trouncing of Pittsburgh. The support from his teammates didn't do Bobo much good. Although he was the club's leading pitcher with nine victories, he was traded a few days later to the Browns.

The fans were also asked to help Europe's civilian war victims. The Giants offered free admission at an April '45 game with the Phils to anyone bringing seven pounds of clothing, bedding, or shoes wrapped for shipment overseas.

Tiger rooters gave up precious 1945 World Series seats to wounded veterans. Convalescents at the Percy Jones Hospital had expected to receive complimentary tickets, but at the last moment were told nothing was available. Responding to a public appeal launched by a Detroit drug firm, 716 fans sent in tickets to the third game at Briggs Stadium for use by the servicemen.

Spectators were expected to relinquish foul balls they had been lucky enough to snare. It wasn't that the clubs wanted to put the baseballs back into play to save money. These balls were being sent off to military camps to supplement those in the official equipment kits. At Ebbets Field, a soldier was stationed by one dugout and a sailor by the other to retrieve foul balls tossed back from the stands and place them in large wire baskets. During the first three wartime seasons, a total of 148,644 balls were returned at the various big league parks, an average of about 40 per game.

There were, however, two schools of thought on the matter. More than happy to give up any pops that might come his way was Fred Wertenbach, who expressed his sentiments in "Foul Ball," a poem he mailed to the *Sporting News.* It went:

> I landed almost within the lap
> Of a man, a wife and a little chap.
> The tiny fellow, a lad of ten
> Tossed me back over the wall again,
> Knowing a baseball returned enjoys
> Giving delight to the soldier boys.
> I'm proud am I that a boy that size
> Should make for him such a sacrifice.
> A foul ball I, yet when all is done
> The proudest foul ball 'neath the April sun.

Another view was presented by *New York Times* reader Lester Thorpe, who asserted in an April '42 letter to the editor: "When one considers the staggering sums of money appropriated for the Army and Navy, the problem of buying a supply of baseballs is quite insignificant. The truth is, as every intelligent person ought to know, this present policy is just another scheme to regiment the American people."

Some teams offered bribes to get baseballs back. The Tigers came up with twenty-five-cent war stamps for every foul ball turned in.

Mel Ott and Leo Durocher preside over receptacle holding foul balls returned from the stands for shipment to the armed forces.

Considerably more generous were the Atlanta Crackers of the Southern Association, who stamped each ball put into play with a designated reward for its return; the jackpot was a fifty dollar war bond.

Most of the fans sided with the theme of Fred Wertenbach's "Foul Ball." When umpire Bill Summers inadvertently pocketed a baseball thrown back from the stands during the Yankees' 1942 home opener, he was roundly booed.

But Lester Thorpe had his supporters too.

Reds' manager Bill McKechnie told of an incident at a game in May '43. "I saw a woman fan in the park scramble for a foul ball hit into a field box, get it, reach into her purse, take out a very old ball, toss it to a sailor, put the new ball into the purse, and then settle back in her seat with a satisfied smile all over her face."

An amazed McKechnie observed, "What some persons won't do to get a ball in a big league park is beyond all comprehension."

A dispute erupted at Ebbets Field when a fan in the upper stands behind third base caught a ball fouled off the bat of Phillie Ron Northey and refused to throw it back. The *New York Times* reported, "Another pugnacious patriot threatened to punch him. Eventually the ball was returned after several ushers had kept the would-be combatants apart."

The following drama unfolded in the Polo Grounds: A spectator grabbed a foul ball and put it in his pocket. A fan sitting nearby offered two dollars for the baseball, with the intention of tossing it back. When the man who caught the ball still refused to give it up, the other fan disgustedly dropped two dollars in his lap and turned away. Now thoroughly ashamed, the man decided to return the baseball and handed the money to a soldier. When the GI refused it, the penitent fan sought out the donor and returned the bills while the crowd cheered.

For those fans who otherwise might have been reluctant to part with a foul ball, there was the opportunity to turn it into a weapon, as umpire Art Passarella discovered. Soon after ejecting Athletics' third base coach Al Simmons from a game at Shibe Park, Passarella watched a ball hurled from the stands sail in the general direction of his head.

Even when intentions were the best, the men on the field might be in peril. Giants' pitcher Jack Brewer was struck below the left eye with a wild heave from a patriotic fan during an exhibition game in Lakewood, New Jersey. He went around with a shiner for several days.

Some baseballs sent to servicemen found their way into the hands of the Japanese, but not in a manner they appreciated. Tiger fastballer Virgil "Fire" Trucks, who joined the Navy after the 1943 season, spent part of the war touring Pacific bases with military baseball teams. Now the director of a youth center in Leeds, Alabama, outside his native Birmingham, Trucks recalls how the servicemen-ballplayers passed their free time:

"We took rides, we took one in a B-29 and some in B-24s. We didn't go along on any bombing runs, we'd just fly around the islands with the pilots and come back in and land. But we signed some baseballs they would take out and drop on their bombing missions. We had some on a B-29 that went to Japan. The balls were completely filled with autographs."

Trucks says that alongside the signatures was inscribed a personal message for the Japanese prime minister: "To Tojo With Love."

III

Home Front Headaches

4

Spring Training in the Snow

Pirate pitcher Rip Sewell relaxed under the palms, enjoying a breeze created by manager Frankie Frisch, who stood over him waving a towel converted into a fan. True, baseball was beginning to feel a manpower pinch. But it was not every day the boss provided such personal services for his charges.

Sewell and Frisch were merely teaming up for a gag photo—posing beside a potted palm inside the lobby of the Hotel Roberts in Muncie, Indiana, to display their longing for the warm weather of springtimes past. It was March 1943 and spring training, wartime style, had arrived.

With the railroads jammed by soldiers reporting to camps or embarkation points and civilians journeying to war plant jobs near the big cities, federal authorities looked for ways to cut nonessential travel. Their eyes turned to baseball. The game, they pointed out, could make a contribution to travel conservation by shifting spring training to northern sites, thereby eliminating the traditional barnstorming trips home from Florida and California.

Although the movement of sixteen ball clubs could hardly have a major impact on scarce rail facilities, baseball would, of course, do its patriotic duty. And so, beginning in the spring of 1943 and continuing for the following two exhibition seasons, ballplayers would battle frigid temperatures, rain, and an occasional snowstorm at a string of training camps near their home parks.

Big league teams had been training in the South since well before the turn of the century. As far back as 1886, the Chicago White Stockings worked out in Hot Springs, Arkansas—a favorite sobering up spot for grog shop devotees—and the Phillies went to Charleston, South Carolina. The 1888 Washington club, whose roster included a catcher named Connie Mack, may have been the first ball club to train

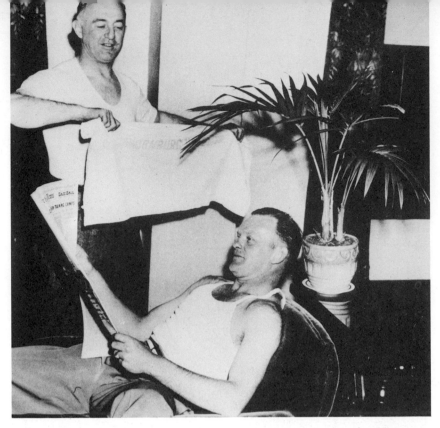

Frankie Frisch and Rip Sewell bring a touch of Florida to Muncie, Indiana, hotel serving as Pirates' wartime spring training headquarters.

Red Sox pitcher Tex Hughson warms up before spring exhibition game at Ebbets Field.

in Florida, going to Jacksonville. Prior to World War I, most of the major league camps were in Texas or Georgia. But by the spring of 1942, twelve teams were training in Florida and the other four in California.

Baseball was advised to begin looking elsewhere via a letter from Joseph Eastman, director of the Office of Defense Transportation, one of the numerous federal agencies created to oversee the war effort. Writing to Landis, Frick, and Harridge on November 30, 1942, Eastman asked that the major league meetings scheduled for the first week in December "give careful consideration to the problem of how your basic travel requirements can be met without a waste in space or mileage."

The official had a few thoughts of his own, suggesting "the elimination or drastic curtailment of preseason exhibition schedules requiring travel."

An obvious way to accomplish this, Eastman pointed out, would be "the selection of a training site as near as possible to the permanent headquarters of the team."

The club owners announced at their December session that they would cut rail mileage during the regular season by scheduling only three intersectional trips instead of the normal four, but they took no immediate action on shifting the spring camps.

There were faint hopes that the government might permit training along the South Atlantic Coast. The Senators envisioned a move from Orlando to their minor league park in Charlotte and the Giants, who had trained in Miami, received an invitation from Statesville, North Carolina. The Browns and Pirates, who had been spending their springs in California, looked, meanwhile, into the possibility of resurrecting Hot Springs as a training camp. A more realistic Branch Rickey conferred during December with Yale University officials on use of their field house, but was advised it might be needed for servicemen's physical training programs. Ed Barrow had a simple solution: the clubs could train in their own ballparks, waiting until early April to get under way, with the start of the regular season to be pushed back by two weeks.

As December moved along, Landis sent a letter to the ball clubs advising that they abandon Florida and California, then followed up with a note telling them to forget about relocating anywhere in the Southeast. Just before the end of the year, the commissioner went to Washington to thrash out the 1943 spring training boundaries with Eastman.

"Nobody needs to enter any orders on us," Landis told reporters covering the meeting, asserting the majors would be "happy to cooperate" with transportation authorities as "a very small contribution to the war effort on our part."

Eastman publicly confined himself to the hope that baseball "would serve as a guide for others" in cutting back on unnecessary travel, saying he had no specific proposals beyond those in his letter.

But definite ground rules there would be. Landis called an emergency session of the club owners for Chicago's Palmer House, where on January 5, 1943, what would be known as the Eastman–Landis line

Pitcher George Munger tries on his new suit of long underwear at Cardinals' spring camp in Cairo, Illinois.

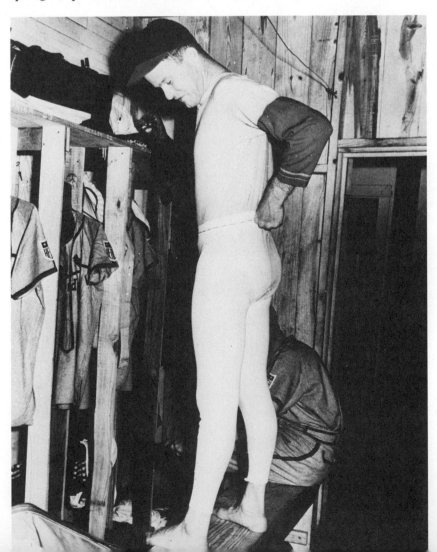

Getting in a little batting practice on Bear Mountain ski slope are (left to right) Dodgers Howie Schultz, Carden Gillenwater, Tommy Warren, and Howie Wafer. The make-believe pitcher is ski champion Hans Strand.

was drawn up. With the exception of the two St. Louis teams, who of course could hold their camps in Missouri, training would be confined to an area east of the Mississippi River and north of the Ohio and Potomac rivers. Eastman was pleased, commenting, "The example which such an important national industry as this has set will have, I am sure, a most beneficial influence throughout the nation. I hope and believe there will be many who will follow this fine example."

The Red Sox were the first team to settle on a northern camp, announcing even a week before the Chicago meeting that they would go to Tufts College in Medford, Massachusetts, and use an indoor batting cage. The following day the White Sox and Cubs reported they would both train at French Lick, Indiana, 278 miles south of Chicago. Soon the other clubs moved into line, creating a 1943 spring training map showing camps in Connecticut, New York, New Jersey, Pennsylvania, Delaware, Maryland, Illinois, and Missouri, as well as Massachusetts and Indiana.

The players coped, having no other choice, but it wasn't easy.

Though there would be some stretches of mild weather, long underwear quickly became a part of the training camp attire. The Athletics would ride sleighs to an indoor workout at their Frederick,

Maryland, training site, and the Dodgers would try out skis at their Bear Mountain, New York, camp—a snowstorm blanketing the East Coast in March '44. The French Lick ballfields and the Cardinals' training field in Cairo, Illinois, would be hit by floods.

Some clubs were fortunate to have good indoor facilities for days when the weather was too frosty to practice outside. The Dodgers were allowed to use the spacious batting cage at the U.S. Military Academy, down the road from Bear Mountain. But the Yankees at one point had to make do with an abandoned Navy aircraft hangar, and the Cubs and White Sox limbered up in what had once been a stable.

Could the ballplayers get into a semblance of reasonably decent shape? This depended to a large degree on the individual. A youngster would require less conditioning than an old-timer and anyone who had done some exercising through the winter was that much better off.

Pitchers could always find a place to warm up in. One day, the White Sox hurlers threw inside their hotel ballroom. But with travel curbs and poor weather cutting the spring training schedule, the batters—especially those on clubs unable to obtain an indoor cage—were hard pressed to get their timing down.

There were some baseball people who felt workouts in a field house or gymnasium, where there could be no sunlight or wind, would never be of much value.

"The sport is essentially an outdoor one and indoor training is of little help," Joe McCarthy told reporters at the Yankees' 1943 camp in Asbury Park, New Jersey. The manager was, however, quick to add, "We are willing to do all in our power to cooperate with the war effort, and do not let this be analyzed in the slightest as any sort of beef. It is just a technical diagnosis of training."

A few clubs tried to gain an edge by stepping up physical conditioning programs.

The Reds hired a $100-a-day muscle relaxation specialist named Bill Miller for their spring camp at Indiana University. Miller had helped train the Tulsa University football team that went undefeated in 1942 before losing to Tennessee in the Sugar Bowl and taught body control to Army aviation cadets so that they would not freeze up in an emergency.

"We called him Yogi Miller, he was what I'd call the relaxer, he tried to teach you how to relax," remembers Frank McCormick, an outstanding first baseman for the Reds from 1934 through the end of the war.

Seated at his desk in Yankee Stadium, where he directs group ticket sales, McCormick picked up a paper cup and let it fall to the floor.

"Miller would tell you, if you dropped this, don't grab for it, pick it up slowly," he explained, reaching down easily to retrieve the cup.

"We went through exercises sort of limp, with no tension," McCormick added, slowly flapping his arms.

Besides the repertoire of slow motion exercises, Miller had the players do an occasional rhumba in the Indiana field house to loosen up. On one occasion the team put on a production number of sorts for the benefit of newsreels. The chief choreographer was Tommy de la Cruz, a Cuban pitcher whose brother sang with Xavier Cugat's band. Nancy Uland, a local high school student, provided accompaniment on an accordion. As the players shook their hips, soldiers passing by en route to physical training programs in the field house couldn't resist a snicker or two.

As for whether all this helped round the players into shape, McCormick says, "The field house was acceptable, but of course we preferred sunny Florida. I didn't feel like I was getting in condition inside, I just didn't feel it."

The Bloomington, Indiana, camps did produce one major dividend, McCormick recalls. "We got Ted Kluszewski because of training there. The college groundskeeper recommended him so we took a look."

The muscular first baseman, an Indiana student at the time, would make his debut with the Reds in 1947.

Ill-fated Phillie owner Bill Cox brought Harold Bruce, his prep school track coach and later a trainer of Olympic runners, to the club's 1943 spring camp in Hershey, Pennsylvania.

"He was a good man, our ball club was well conditioned," says Danny Litwhiler. "We were probably in as good a shape as any team as far as conditioning is concerned. The main thing was run, run, run."

Remembering the abbreviated exhibition schedule, Litwhiler adds, chuckling, "We didn't get a chance to play ball, but we sure ran a lot."

Bruce also had some definite ideas about the training table menu. Litwhiler recalls, "He liked fruits, he thought that was one of the good things in a diet."

It was this penchant that gave Bucky Harris the pretext for firing the trainer, a move which angered Cox and led to the ousting of the manager himself. Harris, a member of the old school who didn't have much use for conditioning programs, finally decided to get rid of

Cox's mentor when, it was said, Bruce fell asleep on the bench amid a mess of sliced orange quarters.

Another traditionalist was Cub manager Jimmy Wilson, who told reporters at his 1944 training camp, "Calisthenics stink as a baseball conditioner. A player goes through all of those monotonous drills and when he gets through he's sore all over. He has exercised muscles he never knew he had, muscles that won't help him one bit when he's out there in a game."

Whatever alternative the manager had in mind for getting his players ready for the season didn't work out too well, however. The Cubs went on to lose nine of their first ten games, at which point Wilson was fired.

A few older ballplayers who lived in the South were excused from the first weeks of camp on the theory they could better limber up their bones working out near home.

Bobo Newsom, who joined the Athletics in 1944 at age thirty-six after making the rounds of the Dodgers, Browns, and Senators the previous season—he would be traded sixteen times in a twenty-year career—was permitted by Connie Mack to remain at his Hartsville, South Carolina, home while the rest of the team drilled in Frederick, Maryland.

Among the ballplayers in the Frederick camp was a twenty-one-year-old rookie who would win the third baseman's job and go on to play fifteen seasons in the American League. Now behind the microphone for the Tigers, George Kell chatted about Bobo Newsom one afternoon over a cup of coffee before telecasting a game at Yankee Stadium that featured a latter-day pitching flake—Mark Fidrych.

"Bobo would not report," Kell recalled. "He told Mr. Mack he could get in better shape at home. Everybody was horrified that Mr. Mack agreed to it. But when Bobo finally got there, he did pitch.

"He was some kind of character," Kell added with a smile. "I don't remember anybody talking back to Mr. Mack—except Bobo Newsom."

Newsom stayed home during the first few weeks of both the 1944 and 1945 A's camps. One Wednesday afternoon well into the last wartime spring, the pitcher telephoned Mack long distance and was reported to have told his patient manager, "I read in the papers that your men haven't been doing so good so far. I guess I'd better come up and help you out. I'll be in Baltimore to pitch Sunday and I'll win twenty games for you this year. I've been running over the hills and pitching to the high school kids."

On Sunday, a big car carrying Newsom, his wife, and their three dogs pulled into the parking lot outside the Baltimore Orioles' ballpark. The late arrival pitched three innings against the International League club, giving up two runs. Newsom did attain a twenty-game milestone that year, but not the way he had envisioned: he won eight games and *lost* twenty.

Perhaps Bobo would have fared even worse had he reported in chilly March. The Dodgers' thirty-five-year-old Whitlow Wyatt, coming off a 19–7 record, sought permission to work out near his Buchanan, Georgia, home during the spring of 1943, but was turned down by Branch Rickey. So Wyatt went to Bear Mountain, and promptly developed a sore arm. The veteran right-hander wasn't back in the groove until July, when he began a ten-game winning streak, finishing out the year 14–5. The following training season, Rickey allowed Wyatt to stay at home and permitted Paul Waner and Johnny Cooney, his forty-year-old-plus outfielders, to try getting into shape in the Sarasota area.

With federal authorities frowning on side trips between major league training camps, one way to get an exhibition game was to visit an Army or Navy installation, since the military was happy to provide bus or plane transportation. Bizarre as training generally was in the North, there was a special aura of absurdity in the military posts when it came to baseball.

An April '43 game at Camp Kilmer, New Jersey, between the Giants and their Jersey City farm team was declared off limits to reporters. Because the installation was a point of embarkation, the Army feared some tidbits on troop movements might be divulged inadvertently in the sportswriters' stories. A post public relations officer transmitted a play-by-play summary for the press, providing such gems as: "Poland, batting for Mancuso, cleared the bases when his single into left went by Brack for a homer." The *New York Herald Tribune* headlined its secondhand story, "Giants Belabor Jersey City 17–7 in Secret Game."

Fortunately, reporters were not barred from an exhibition between the same teams a few days later at the Lakehurst Naval Air Station in New Jersey, else they would have missed perhaps the longest home run in baseball history. A ball hit by the Giants' Babe Barna over the head of Jersey City outfielder Howie Moss came to a stop out of sight—the field was a vast, dirt landing terrain without fences. Barna could have circled the bases several times, since the ball landed 450 feet from home plate and then rolled another 200 feet before

Moss caught up with it. The game was delayed while a jeep retrieved the out-of-breath fielder.

Lakehurst provided a variety of challenges. On a windy, cold day in April '44, the Navy dropped baseballs from a blimp four hundred feet in the air to Giant players poised on the landing terrain. First baseman Phil Weintraub and Danny Gardella, an eccentric outfielder who had trouble with routine flies, were the only ones to make a catch.

While northern spring training games often would be curtailed by bad weather, an exhibition the Pirates played at Fort Benjamin Harrison, Indiana, was halted after the seventh inning for a different reason—the crowd of two thousand GIs had been summoned to mess call.

The Fort Meade, Maryland, Army base was the site of particularly strange doings.

The Washington Senators and Philadelphia Athletics, arriving there for a game in April '43, were treated by the post mess to a delightful ration-free spread: a main course of steak along with hard-to-get trimmings such as genuine coffee, sugar, and butter. But a vital ingredient was missing so far as the ballfield was concerned.

George Case recalls, "We were gonna cancel out because of bad weather, but they were expecting a huge crowd. The commander called Mr. Griffith and said, 'If you could bring the ball club down, it would mean a lot to the boys.' So we got there and the field was rimmed with soldiers. But there were no bases. They couldn't find the bases. So they put down towels. Well, we didn't slide anyway because it was too wet."

The game stands out in Case's memory for another reason. While it was an occasion where the spectators—ten thousand GIs—should have been properly appreciative, "There were some soldiers in the crowd who yelled 'get a gun' and all that. The MPs got them away or shut them up."

"You know," Case continues, "that was the only time we had trouble at a camp. There was very little resentment otherwise."

When the Senators played the Baltimore Orioles at Fort Meade, the ball clubs weren't the only source of entertainment. A band composed of Italian prisoners of war tooted away on the sidelines.

Two Wacs helped warm the Athletics' bench during a Fort Meade game with the International League's Buffalo Bisons and a male lieutenant served as home plate umpire. Italian POWs were on hand again, this time in a different role. Four of them were used as groundskeepers, raking the infield.

"We were told they were POWs, but I didn't know from where," says George Kell. "They didn't look like soldiers, but you knew they weren't civilians. They wore what looked like denim prison garb so you figured what they told you was true."

An umpire became a prisoner of sorts during an April '43 exhibition game in the Midwest. American League ump Art Passarella, having almost been beaned the previous spring by that irate fan throwing back a foul, found himself in another unhappy situation while calling balls and strikes at Vincennes, Indiana, in a game between the White Sox and the host Camp George air base team.

The shortstop for the service team got into a heated argument with Passarella in the bottom of the eighth and naturally lost. But his mates obtained their revenge. A group of MPs pulled up at home plate in a jeep, bundled the umpire inside, and drive him off to the guardhouse. By the time Passarella was given his liberty, the game was over.

When the White Sox later visited Camp Grant, Illinois, Passarella was behind the plate again, but this time his sympathies lay with the Army team—he had been drafted and was stationed at the post, umpiring in his spare time. Now he could turn the MPs loose for his own purposes, getting even with Jimmy Dykes for past tirades. The Sox manager later recounted his ordeal:

"My personal Gestapo agents tip me off that Passarella is all set to have me thrown into the clink if I open my trap even once so I keep nice and quiet. I won't even talk to him. But by the ninth inning I begin to get curious. So I tell Mike Tresh, my catcher, to object to a decision. As soon as he does, I rush over to the plate and raise Cain, kick dirt all over Art and everything. Before I know what's happening, the MPs whisk me out of there and bring me before a major.

"'What's the charge?' he asks. Then he adds, 'Oh, never mind, leave the charge open. Into the guardhouse with him.' I'm in there awhile and Passarella comes to see me. 'Get me out of here,' I tell him. 'Sorry Jimmy,' he says, 'I'm just a private in this man's Army. I haven't any influence.'

"They left me in there at least half an hour before releasing me. I sweated so much I was wringing wet. It taught me that the Four Freedoms are not enough. There should be a fifth one—guaranteeing that Dykes will be kept out in the open air."

The individual major league camps had their own share of oddities. In the East, the ball clubs were housed, among other places, at a New England prep school, a ski lodge, and a mansion once owned by John D. Rockefeller.

The Braves settled in at the exclusive Choate School in Wallingford, Connecticut. Since students were away for spring recess, the team bedded down in vacant dormitory rooms and a wing of the infirmary. Casey Stengel, who wasn't the "Ol' Professor" for nothing, made the photographers happy by lecturing to his players in an academic cap and gown. While the atmosphere was pleasant, the weather wasn't. After two springs at Choate, the club switched to Georgetown University in Washington, D.C., for the final wartime camp. Medical students attending classes in a building along the campus ballfield's left field foul line would wander over to take in workouts when tired of their cadavers.

The Red Sox stayed close to home the first two wartime springs, drilling in the batting cage at Tufts College, which was a six-mile trolley ride from the Hotel Kenmore in downtown Boston, where the players were housed. The team headed south—relatively speaking— for the 1945 camp, going to Atlantic City. The ballplayers were put up at the popular Claridge Hotel, doing their outdoor drills on a high school field in the nearby town of Pleasantville. The Army Air Corps was kind enough to let the club hold an occasional calisthenics session or pepper game inside the Atlantic City Convention Hall, which had been taken over to house servicemen awaiting reassignment.

One warm, sunny day in March '43, a middle-aged lady carrying the cowbell that had become her trademark arrived at the ferry slip

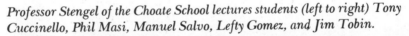

Professor Stengel of the Choate School lectures students (left to right) Tony Cuccinello, Phil Masi, Manuel Salvo, Lefty Gomez, and Jim Tobin.

With bats taking the place of rifles, Red Sox go through Army-style "daily dozen" exercises at Tufts College gym.

off Manhattan's West Forty-Second Street. Hilda Chester, most zealous of all Dodger rooters, the personification of Ebbets Field fanaticism, was seeing her heroes off for their first wartime spring training camp. She tinkled her bell good-bye to an advance party of eight players who boarded the ferry "Catskill" for a brief trip across the Hudson River and then transferred to the West Shore Rail Road for a forty-five mile ride northward. The contingent would have been wise to soak up the sun that afternoon. It wouldn't be shining very often over the next three springs at Bear Mountain.

The Dodgers arrived at the resort complex to find a caretaker hard at work on their ballfield, which happened to be laid out near the foot of a ski jump and toboggan slide. The groundskeeper was building a fire over first base, trying to take the frost out of the ground.

There would not be too many days when the diamond could be used, but Branch Rickey had planned well, obtaining one of the best indoor facilities of any training camp—the spacious, steam-heated West Point field house, complete with batting cage and dirt floor. The club practiced at the well-lit field house—a five-mile bus ride from Bear Mountain—for the first nine days of the 1943 camp and could count on it whenever the weather was frosty. The workouts had to be scheduled, however, around cadet activities. During the 1944 camp, the Dodgers drilled in the field house from noon to 1:00 P.M., then returned at 5:45 P.M. (A surveying class occupied the facility during the afternoons.) Leo Durocher returned the hospitality by serving as adviser to the military academy baseball team.

Home was a rustic lodge called the Bear Mountain Inn, whose proprietors were anxious to keep the players as happy as possible, providing game rooms with pool tables and roaring log fires. At dinnertime, the dessert menu featured Jelly Roll a la Higbe, Stewed Mixed Fruits Fitzsimmons, and Ice Cream Puff Medwick.

The Dodgers weren't the only distinguished visitors. The day the 1943 camp opened, Mme. Chiang Kai-shek and party arrived for lunch at Stone Cottage, next door to Hessian Lodge, the section of the inn where the players were housed. The public relations man for the Palisades Interstate Park Commission, which ran the Bear Mountain facilities, tried to get Mme. Chiang to pose with the team, but she declined the honor.

The Giants found spring training headquarters with an elegant past: the grounds of the old John D. Rockefeller estate in Lakewood, New Jersey. The Meadow Brook Country Club in Westbury, Long Island, and the Westchester County Club in Rye, New York, also wanted the team, but a nine-hole golf course where the oil baron played daily while in residence at an adjoining forty-seven-room mansion would be the Giants' springtime ballfield.

The complex, which had become public parkland after Rockefeller's death in 1937, was not chosen for any residual snob appeal. Although Lakewood was only sixty-five miles south of New York City, temperatures were said to be, on the average, ten degrees warmer than in the city. The golf course diamond drained well and sections surrounded by thick pines provided some shelter from brisk March winds. It was also a homecoming after almost five decades, the Giants having trained at Lakewood in 1895 and 1896 when they were owned by Andrew Freedman. An active member of Tammany Hall, Freedman had chosen the Jersey resort town because the Democratic bigwigs held their annual spring meetings there—he could attend to politics and baseball at the same time.

Lakewood was thrilled to have the ball club back. The two dozen Giants arriving as advance guard for the first camp were met at the railroad station by a crowd of 1,200, headed by Mayor William Curtis, and given a ride to their hotel in horse-drawn victorias, a mode of transportation revived in the war era to symbolize gasoline conservation efforts. When the Rockefellers and the Goulds (Georgian Court, the former estate of financier George Gould, was also in town) played an intrasquad game, some twenty-five hundred school children were given a half-day off to watch.

*Townspeople provide horse-drawn carriage for Giants arriving at 1943
Lakewood, New Jersey, spring camp. Mel Ott greets veteran pitching star
Carl Hubbell, who settles in alongside catcher Gus Mancuso for ride from
train station to hotel. The local folks were a bit overly optimistic. Giants did
not exactly go on to win the World Series—they would, in fact, finish the '43
season in last place.*

What the town fathers couldn't produce was a decent facility for
indoor workouts. The Giants had to settle for a YMCA gym so small
that no more than ten players could toss a ball around at the same
time. The 1944 team, able to play a total of 8 exhibition games in a
snow-plagued spring training season, was described by Mel Ott as
"the worst conditioned club in Giant history."

During their first two springs at Lakewood, the Giants stayed in
hotels, but no space was available for 1945. Declaring "anything the
Giants want in Lakewood they can have," Ocean County Freeholder
Alfred Brown solved the problem by helping to arrange for the team
to take over the county-owned Rockefeller mansion. The three-story
estate, containing seventeen baths to go with the forty-seven rooms,
had been kept much as the Rockefeller family left it. Rich oriental
rugs and plush chairs abounded. There were bedrooms done up in

Their arms may be cold, but Giants' pitchers (left to right) Cliff Melton, Van Lingle Mungo, and Carl Hubbell at least have a bonfire to keep their feet warm on first day of '43 Lakewood camp.

yellow, and if that wasn't his favorite color, a ballplayer could select buff or lavender quarters. Meals were taken on glassed-in porches. They may not have rounded into shape, but the Giants sure were comfortable.

The Yankees held their first camp 17 miles from Lakewood, choosing the New Jersey shore community of Asbury Park, which boasted a summer population of 100,000. Only 14,000 people, however, found the community attractive enough to live in on days like those of the chilly early spring. The winds were blowing and the mercury was flirting with the forty-degree mark when the Yanks held their first workout on the local high school field. Five hundred hardy souls looked on. The *New York Times* reported, "The athletes were red and purple and blue by turns, but all thawed out in the clubhouse, where scout Paul Krichell's pot-bellied, wood-burning stove did overtime duty."

The ballplayers might have done well to sleep in their stove-heated clubhouse. A fuel shortage made for nippy nights in their rooms at the Hotel Albion. As for indoor drilling, there was but a high school gym best suited for calisthenics and basketball.

Though the locals were anxious to please—a candy firm supplied the players with saltwater taffy—the Yankees decided, not surprisingly, that one spring in Asbury Park was enough. The team shoved on to Atlantic City, sixty miles farther south, for its last two wartime camps.

Some twelve thousand cubic yards of rich, imported sod were transplanted from the $500,000 beachfront mansion of the late Mrs. Isabelle Fishblatt to the Yankees' Atlantic City practice diamond, a municipal field formerly used for football. A few thousand portable seats were added. They weren't put to much use in the spring of 1944, however, since the weather permitted only six days of outdoor work.

The indoor facility, something of an improvement over the Asbury Park gym, was the larger 112th Field Artillery Armory, whose floor was covered with a layer of soil taken from Convention Hall, where football had been played prior to the Air Corps' arrival. But the team was still without an indoor batting cage, and confined its activity at the armory to pepper games, except for the day Joe McCarthy broke up the monotony with a potato race. In the last wartime spring, the armory was requisitioned by the military to house wounded servicemen. The Yanks would hold their final indoor drills on the concrete floor of an abandoned Navy aircraft hangar behind the left-field fence of the Atlantic City ballpark.

Club headquarters was the modern, 300-room Senator Hotel, whose management was every bit as generous as the folks in Asbury Park—here, too, the players were stuffed with saltwater taffy.

The Athletics pitched their initial wartime camp at Wilmington, Delaware, limbering up with a snowball fight the first day of training. Wilmington produced what must have been the smallest turnout in history for a game involving a big league team—the A's defeated the University of Delaware, 2–0, one day in a contest that attracted six spectators.

Anticipating better weather and perhaps even larger turnouts, Connie Mack took his men to Frederick, Maryland, in the Blue Ridge Mountains for the following two spring camps. The right-field fence at McCurdy Field, the local ballpark, was 506 feet from home plate, and the only indoor facilities were an armory and a YMCA. But at least the players could pick up an education. If nothing else, Frederick was historic.

The 200-room hotel housing the team was named the Francis Scott Key. The man responsible for the lyrics being sung before every game had been born on the outskirts of Frederick, practiced law there, and was buried in the community's Mount Olivet Cemetery.

Another headstone was that of the old lady whose supposed courage had inspired John Greenleaf Whittier's poem "Barbara Frietchie."

According to legend, as Stonewall Jackson was passing through Frederick with his troops in 1862, he noticed a Union flag flying from the second-story window of Mrs. Frietchie's home and ordered that it be fired upon. Moments later, the ninety-six-year-old woman seized the riddled banner and waved it defiantly. Rather than seek retribution, Jackson, touched by the old woman's spirit, decreed death to any Confederate soldier who might harm her.

The tale made an impression on the Athletics, who lined up for intrasquad games as the Stonewall Jacksons versus the Barbara Frietchies. It was, however, apparently apocryphal. Jackson's staff and Mrs. Frietchie's family subsequently reported that the two had never laid eyes on each other. She is conceded to have feebly waved a small American flag at Union soldiers passing through Frederick six days after Jackson left town.

At any rate, a reconstructed version of the Frietchie home at 156 West Patrick Street in downtown Frederick was a tourist attraction.

"My wife, who was a schoolteacher, was very much interested, she took me to all these places," recalls George Kell. "She had a ball, it was a very historic town."

Less attractive was the weather. But Connie Mack, who by now had presumably seen everything, was undeterred. During a 1944 snowstorm, he ordered sleighs to transport the players to an indoor workout. When the weather was good enough for drills at McCurdy Field, Mack dispensed with the horses.

"Mr. Mack would lead us out of the hotel," Kell remembers. "He'd say, 'Hey, we're gonna walk.' It was about a mile to the ballpark. There were no buses and we had no cars, so we walked. He led the way."

At times there wasn't much competition around, even by the lowly Athletics' standards. The A's beat the Martin Bombers, a semipro aircraft plant team, 20–0, in a game halted by cold after seven innings. On another occasion, they took on the Frederick Hustlers, an outfit described by the *Philadelphia Inquirer* as "made up of the grocery clerk, baggage man, a salesman, two schoolboys, a serviceman on furlough, and four young, married men." That made ten players, but the Athletics triumphed nonetheless, 7–1.

The Phillies tried Hershey, Pennsylvania, for their first northern camp, playing on a field not too much larger than latter-day Little League parks. Any ball well hit to left field would land in Cocoa Creek. When the team visited Yale, owner Bill Cox was behind the plate while the university's athletic director, Ogden Miller, switched allegiance to start on the mound. The pair didn't fare badly. Cox drew a base on balls in his one time at bat while Miller pitched a scoreless inning. The battery-mates were then relieved by catcher Tom Padden and hurler Al Gerheauser.

With the Wilmington-based Carpenter family taking over before the 1944 season, the Phillies spent the last two wartime springs in the Delaware city, abandoned by the Athletics in favor of Barbara Frietchieland.

The 1944 camp didn't begin very auspiciously. Snow fell as the ballplayers, bundled up in overcoats, scarves, and hats, left Philadelphia's Thirtieth Street Station for a twenty-eight-mile rail trip south. The first four days at Wilmington were spent inside a state armory, where manager Freddie Fitzsimmons kept the boys puffing by having them run up twenty-five steps of a corner staircase, then hustle along a fifty-yard balcony, and scamper down another twenty-five steps at the opposite end. One such session lasted for three-quarters of an hour. Not called Fat Freddie for nothing, the skipper just supervised. The players finally got outdoors on the fifth day but their ballfield was still too damp for full-scale workouts, so they contented themselves with bunting practice on the cinder surface of a parking lot.

When the weather relented sufficiently to allow for some baseball, the attendance was up sharply from the turnout of a half-dozen at the A's–University of Delaware game in Wilmington during the spring of 1943. A crowd of ninety-seven showed up to watch the Phils battle the Martin Bombers.

The Senators stayed at the University of Maryland in College Park, ten miles outside the District of Columbia. " 'Curley' Byrd, the president of the university, was an avid baseball fan and he offered the facilities," says George Case. "We'd take over a whole dorm, there weren't too many students during the war. We ate in the guest house.

Mr. Griffith hired his own cook and he managed to get pretty good steaks for us occasionally."

Case continues, "The first year the weather was nice, but the second year it was miserable. We were playing in bad weather all that spring."

Latin ballplayers (most of them Cubans), whom the Senators had made a specialty of signing, particularly suffered during the frigid spring of 1944.

Among more than a dozen recruits experiencing wintry weather for the first time was a twenty-year-old shortstop who would have a brief playing career in the big leagues but would return to the majors many years after the war to manage and coach.

Reached at his Santa Monica home one day during the Dodgers' dismal 1979 season, Preston Gomez—then the Los Angeles third base coach and later to be named manager of the Cubs—thought back to hard times of a different sort thirty-five years before. He remembered how it was when he arrived at College Park fresh from amateur ball in Havana.

"We got a little snow in March and it was very cold. I liked to keep inside. When I had to go outside, I would suffer," Gomez recalled. "I'll never forget, I tried to go out one day to take ground balls and hit wearing my big jacket, and the manager, Ossie Bluege, called me over and said 'you cannot do things like that.' I didn't know how to explain to him I was too cold. Finally, Gil Torres [a Cuban infielder with experience in organized ball] came over and explained that if I trained this way, I wouldn't be able to move. And he was right. That's the problem we had most, getting used to the climate."

While half the clubs trained along the eastern seaboard, the other eight teams were in the Midwest. The Cardinals chose the town of Cairo, Illinois, on the east bank of the Mississippi River; their Sportsman's Park colleagues, the Browns, went to Cape Girardeau, Missouri, forty miles upstream on the west bank. The Reds, Indians, Pirates, Tigers, Cubs, and White Sox were spread out over Indiana.

In the months before the Cardinals arrived at Cairo, what passed for the local ballpark, a place called Cotter Field, had become pretty much a municipal dump, strewn with tin cans and broken glass. But the townspeople cleaned things up, put down fresh sod, and transferred seven hundred portable seats from the high school gym. They hardly need have bothered. Isolated from the other major league camps—at least by the standards of wartime travel—the Cards could do little more than stage intrasquad contests. During their entire time at Cairo, they played only two real games, both against the Army's Fourth Ferrying Group from Memphis.

Although the team was able to drill outdoors most days during the first two springs, the weather was far from accommodating. Danny Litwhiler, traded from the Phils to the Cards during the 1943 season, has chilly memories of the 1944 camp.

"An awful lot of us got sick there," he recalls. "Colds, you know, real bad colds. Everybody, the ballplayers, the wives, the kids. You'd call it flu today, but we called it colds. It was just so damp and so cold there."

When the ballplayers arrived for their 1945 camp, they found Cotter Field under four feet of water, the runoff from a rain-swollen Ohio River, which meets the Mississippi at Cairo. A fire department pump was pressed into service, but the waters kept rising as fast as they could be channeled into sewers and drainage ditches. Photographers got a rookie named Red Schoendienst to pose with two teammates on swings. The caption read, "It's about the only baseball training, even in name, the Cards have been able to do."

After five days of futile efforts to dry out the field, the Cardinals packed up and went to St. Louis, working out for the rest of the spring at Sportsman's Park.

The only indoor facility at Cairo had been a high school gym. The locals tried hard, installing four extra showers—making a grand total of eight—and building a large wooden locker for drying uniforms, but it hardly would do. Billy Southworth commented after watching his players run relay races one day, "We're making the best of it, but a wooden gymnasium floor is no place to prepare to play baseball. I admit I'm relieved each time we get out of a crowded gym with all the players intact."

Up at Cape Girardeau, the Browns played on a municipal ballfield and also set up mounds for pitching drills in a wind-sheltered natural amphitheater belonging to Southeast Missouri State Teachers College. Providing competition for exhibition games were the Toledo Mud Hens, the Brownies' American Association farm team, which shared the complex.

Indoor workouts were held at the Arena, a building on the edge of town built for horse shows and livestock exhibits. The facility had a six-inch soil base and was large enough to hold a batting cage.

Here, too, the townspeople were eager to help out, furnishing Browns' officials with unrationed gasoline from fire department pumps when club affairs required a 240-mile round trip to St. Louis.

The Cards and Browns had each other for a brief period at the end of each spring, playing a city series in Sportsman's Park for their only big league training season competition.

Of the six ball clubs training in Indiana, the Indians and Reds were best off, enjoying the use of Big Ten field houses during bad weather.

The Cleveland club originally eyed Marietta College in Ohio, where a field house had been built with funds donated by alumnus Ban Johnson. The college expressed reluctance, however, to pack the floor with soil, so the Indians went, instead, to the West Lafayette, Indiana, campus of Purdue University, which had a 300×160-foot field house already covered with dirt.

The facility boasted a cage to accommodate batting and pitching drills, but hurler Vern Kennedy was particularly interested in the equipment belonging to the Purdue track and field team. Finding its pole vault unattended one day, Kennedy lifted himself over the bar at the nine-foot mark and came up smiling. Asked if he recalls the feat, Kennedy's old manager, Lou Boudreau, says, "If he did that, he did it without my noticing it."

The Reds quickly realized how lucky they were to have the dirt-surfaced Indiana University field house—five inches of rain hit Bloomington the first week of the 1943 camp. Track team equipment was a lure there, too, with unhappy consequences for pitcher Bucky Walters. On the first day of training, Walters tried to leap over a hurdle, caught a spike, and sprained his left ankle. He didn't get into form until mid-season. In an authorized exercise, the players studied batting stance flaws by gazing into a large mirror used by the Indiana track team to examine starting-block form.

The team dressed in locker rooms underneath the football stadium and held outdoor workouts at Jordan Field, the university's baseball diamond. There were those who displayed something less than the hospitality afforded big league clubs elsewhere. Three of the Reds' windbreakers were stolen one day while the club drilled on the ballfield.

Both the Indians and Reds stayed in downtown hotels not far from their respective campuses.

The Pirates did without a field house at their Muncie, Indiana, camp—a small gym was the only available indoor facility—but the local officialdom certainly was nice. Honus Wagner, brought back by the team as a coach, was given a silver badge by Mayor John Hampton designating the Hall of Famer an honorary policeman. In return,

Hizzoner got to umpire at home plate in an intrasquad game. Housed in town at the Hotel Roberts, the club worked out on the Ball State Teachers College field when the weather permitted. Manager Frankie Frisch ordered long hikes when it didn't.

The Tigers, training in a minor league park at Evansville, Indiana, at one point faced the prospect of having their entire 1945 exhibition schedule wiped out by toughened travel curbs. It appeared that no games could be played without running afoul of the ban on side trips instituted by the Office of Defense Transportation. But general manager Jack Zeller had an idea. The players could get in a series by walking to the White Sox camp at Terre Haute—it was only 112 miles away.

"Have them carry their uniforms, bats, and toilet articles on their backs," Zeller told manager Steve O'Neill. "The players are supposed to be athletes in good condition. There are a few million boys who aren't athletes and are walking from ten to twenty miles a day in training camps in this country and they're carrying something heavier than uniforms and bats. They're carrying packs of from forty-five to sixty pounds on their backs. You could take five or six days to get there, stopping along the way."

O'Neill responded, "If they walk, they'll have to go without the manager. I can't foot it that far."

Dizzy Trout, once an Indiana farm boy, volunteered, "All I got to do is speak to some of my farm friends around here. They'll drive us over in hayracks paced by a hillbilly band. We'll each take a basket of lunch."

A compromise was suggested by second baseman Eddie Mayo: "Why should we do all the walking, why can't we meet the Sox halfway and play them on the most convenient hayfield?"

The idea for the stroll was dropped, but the Tigers did get to Terre Haute. They took a train to the White Sox camp and instead of returning to Evansville after the series, stayed around for a few practice sessions, then continued on to St. Louis when time came for the season's opener.

The White Sox had repaired to Terre Haute after two unhappy exhibition seasons elsewhere. The Sox and Cubs had trained together during the springs of 1943 and 1944 in the resort community of French Lick, Indiana, but they were not, it developed, very neighborly. For the better part of the two springs, the clubs argued over use of a golf course that turned out to be the only available playing field in sight.

Both teams were housed in the seven-hundred-room French Lick Springs Hotel, centerpiece of a resort area known for its natural springs and baths. The Cubs laid out their diamond on a golf course outside the hotel while the White Sox made arrangements to use a semipro park down the road at West Baden. But they were thrown together in both '43 and '44 by heavy spring rains swelling the Lost River, its overflow flooding both ballfields. The Cubs' turf drained well and would be playable only a few days after being inundated. The White Sox field, however, became a muddy mess. And so, with nowhere else to go, Jimmy Dykes moved in on his rivals. The squabbling over practice time on the golf greens made for lively newspaper copy. Cub general manager Jimmy Gallagher put up an arch proclaiming the golf course his club's exclusive territory. Jimmy Dykes in turn called the Cubs a "bush league outfit." And one day in April '44, the GIs became involved. The White Sox scheduled a 2:30 P.M. game on the golf course with the 820th Tank Destroyer Batallion from Camp Breckenridge, Kentucky. But the Cubs, having previously planned a workout for 2:00 P.M., invoked a veto. A saddened Jimmy Dykes told reporters, "I have been forced to cancel the game with the soldier boys."

At this point, White Sox five-mile hike at 1944 French Lick, Indiana, spring camp doesn't seem like such a good idea.

It's raining outside, but in the ballroom of French Lick Springs Hotel spirits are high as Charlie Grimm provides accompaniment for calisthenics by (left to right) Roy Johnson, George Hennessey, Al Nusser, Andy Pafko, Paul Derringer, and Len Merullo.

Indoor training put a premium on improvisation, there being nary a YMCA in town. The White Sox pitchers, working out in the ballroom of their hotel, propped mattresses against the walls as backstops. In the spring of 1945, the Cub players did their calisthenics in the ballroom to a piano accompaniment by manager Charlie Grimm, Jimmy Wilson's successor. Also available to provide some shelter from the elements was an abandoned stable.

One ballplayer may have had a premonition that French Lick was a place to stay away from. Cub pitcher Vallie Eaves went out to California in the spring of 1943 to report as usual for training on Catalina Island. Traveling secretary Bob Lewis sent him word there was a war on and provided a bus ticket to Indiana.

Len Merullo, the Cubs' shortstop through the war years and now a talent hunter for the Major League Scouting Bureau—a consortium of seventeen clubs—has some rather fond memories of French Lick. He reminisced one day upon returning to his Reading, Massachusetts, home after a busy '79 spring preparing reports for the free agent draft.

"The French Lick Springs Hotel had the finest of everything; the wealthy people, businessmen, used to go there. The leading bands were still coming in, fellows like Glen Gray," he recalls. "Of course, it was a health spa, with the natural springs. It's famous for steam baths, hot baths and all that bit. The players were allowed to go through this procedure and it was great; it was something we had never experienced before. The big fellas, especially, went down there to lose weight."

"You know what I remember most about French Lick?" Merullo continues. "These old-timers that would come down there. It was the home of Pluto water, very famous for cleaning your body out. They would have this path through the woods and it was just beautiful, but every so many yards there would be these little outhouses. The old-timers got up before breakfast and they'd give them the Pluto water. Then they would hand them a cane and they'd take a walk through the woods. Well, when they got the urge, they'd just put their cane on the outhouse door, that meant it was occupied. Then they would come back and have their breakfast. This was the first step, in other words, back to good health."

At times, however, there was just too much water around.

"The river would come up every spring and the golf course would be just flooded over," Merullo remembers. "Don Johnson and myself and Phil Cavarretta and Peanuts Lowrey posed for a group photo supposedly fishing in our baseball uniforms."

In the spring of 1945, not only did the Lost River overflow for the third time in three years, but the train to French Lick was taken out of

It wasn't always raining at French Lick. Sometimes it snowed. The setting seems more appropriate for a snowball fight than a pepper game as Cub coach Roy Johnson works out with (left to right) pitchers John Burrows and Paul Erickson and infielder Eddie Stanky at '44 camp.

service by the government. Coach Red Smith had to drive eighteen miles to Orleans, Indiana, which had become the end of the line, to pick up arriving ballplayers.

The White Sox by then were off to Terre Haute, where they found themselves more than welcome for a change. When Jimmy Dykes complained about having to walk twenty-six blocks every day from his hotel to the training field, Mayor Vern McMillan had the police pick him up in a Model T paddy wagon. (Despite all good intentions, the thing broke down en route to the ballpark.)

Did the bizarre conditions provoke grumbling? Ballplayers looking back on the wartime camps say they were resigned to the situation and, give or take a field house or two, knew everyone was experiencing the same hardships.

Virgil Trucks, talking about the Tiger base at Evansville, Indiana, says, "It was quite cool, it was always wet, it wasn't anywhere near like Florida weather, but you could train, you could do running. It wasn't an ideal area for spring training, but since the circumstances called for that, nobody complained about it, we all went about our jobs."

Then, turning his thoughts to the modern-day ballplayer, Trucks adds with a chuckle, "I don't know what they would do if they had to go through that today. Probably all rebel, pay their own way and go to Florida."

5

Dimouts and Dead Balls

Having thawed out from spring training, ballplayers would be confronted during the regular season with a series of restrictions and irritants imposed on home front life by the demands of war.

In New York, night baseball would be banned during the first two wartime seasons. Elsewhere, practice blackouts might interrupt everything in midgame. A new baseball, put together with materials unessential for the war effort, would turn out to be "dead." The jammed rail network would convert road trips, leisurely journeys in days past, into a trying experience. Finding a decent meal and even an apartment could no longer be taken for granted. And overshadowing a player's annual salary battle with the front office would be government wage curbs and the inevitable comparison with what an infantryman was earning in a somewhat more demanding job.

An early casualty of the war was night baseball at Ebbets Field and the Polo Grounds. (The Yankees didn't get around to installing lights until 1946.) Neither the Dodgers nor the Giants were playing at home the evening of May 12, 1942, but their ballpark lights had been turned on—for a test. A boatload of Army officers and baseball representatives had gone several miles out into the Atlantic to determine whether the lighting systems could silhouette ships, making them easy targets for German submarines.

Nazi U-boats were on the prowl in the war's early days, preying on the oil tankers bound for Eastern ports and freighters headed for Britain with war supplies. The menace had been so great that when Churchill returned home in January of '42 after a three-week visit to Washington, he chose to fly rather than travel on the British battleship that brought him here. In the first six months of 1942, some 300 ships would be sunk along U.S. coastlines.

A week after testing of the ballpark lights had been completed,

124

New York City Police Commissoner Lewis Valentine announced that the Army had found the glare unacceptable and wanted cancellation of the fourteen night games scheduled for 1942 by both the Dodgers and Giants.

The whole city was, in fact, being "dimmed out"—there could be no lighting that might give enemy subs a fix on shipping lanes. A ban on neon advertising signs left Times Square theatergoers to grope their way to performances. Black paint was daubed over the gold leaf roof of the United States Courthouse in lower Manhattan so that it would not gleam in the moonlight. Coney Island went dark. Streetlights along the ocean were shielded. The Statue of Liberty's beacon was snuffed out, remaining dark until D-Day, when it would shine for fifteen minutes at sunset.

New York was the only major league city to lose night baseball. The Army also carried out tests in the waters around Philadelphia, but determined the Shibe Park lights did not threaten shipping. The minors, heavily dependent on night ball, would, however, suffer a blow. Night games were out for a string of minor league ballparks along the East and Gulf coasts and in the Pacific Coast League.

By the time night baseball returned during the 1944 season, the prohibition had given rise to ludicrous complications.

Since ballpark lights could be left on until an hour after sunset, when their intensity would first become noticeable, the Dodgers and Giants, along with the latter's Jersey City farm club of the International League, shifted their 1942 night games to twilight contests. The teams would play against a deadline, the games to be called at the moment set for lights out with the final score reverting to that at the end of the last completed inning.

While they seemed like a good idea at the time, the twilight affairs brought nothing but trouble. The first dispute broke out on June 12, when Jersey City hosted the Montreal Royals in a game that was to be stopped at 9:24 P.M., the moment designated for dousing the lights. Montreal trailed, 3–2, going into the top of the ninth inning, but rallied to take the lead. Once his club fell behind, Jersey City reliever Hugh East began stalling, hoping the ninth inning would drag on until the game was halted by the curfew. Jersey City would then be the winner based on the score at the end of the eighth. East walked four men in a row, making no effort to get the ball over. Soon the Royals began swinging at anything in reach. Finally the top of the ninth ended with Montreal ahead, 10–3. A few moments later, with one on and one out in the bottom of the ninth, the game was called—9:24

P.M. had arrived—and Jersey City was declared an eight inning, 3–2 victor. The ploy had seemingly worked. But not quite. The following day, International League President Frank Shaughnessy fined Jersey City manager Frank Snyder $100 for turning the game "into a farce" and ordered that play be resumed from the point of interruption on Montreal's next visit, in July.

The next complication occurred following the 1942 all-star game at the Polo Grounds, which had barely been completed when everything went black. Trusting that Jersey City–type shenanigans wouldn't be repeated in a setting attracting nationwide attention, the majors scheduled the July 6 all-star affair as a twilight contest. The game was to get under way at 6:30 P.M. and conclude by 9:10, an hour after sunset. When a shower (or, as Rud Rennie had put it, a "military secret") held up the start of play, permission was granted to go until 9:30 P.M., the moment set for a citywide practice blackout. The timing was just right; only two minutes before the lights were to be shut off, Ernie Lombardi of the Braves hit a fly to the Yanks' Tommy Henrich in right for the game-ending out.

The American League squad, 3–1 victors, was in a mood for celebrating, but had to hold off for a while. The center field clubhouse, along with the rest of the Polo Grounds and the whole city of New York, was plunged into darkness as soon as the game concluded.

Lou Boudreau, the AL shortshop, had been a happy man that evening, helping to account for a big inning that wrapped things up early.

"I led off the ball game with a home run off Mort Cooper and then there was a single and Rudy York hit the second home run in that inning," he recalls.

Boudreau, York, and company were ready to whoop it up after the game, but couldn't do much of anything until the lights came back on.

"You just had to sit around and wait," Boudreau remembers. "There were quite a few ballplayers that sat right in the dugout afterward. I went to the clubhouse and just sat there in the dark. There was not too much talking. And the people were asked to remain in their seats."

Winning manager Joe McCarthy did give an interview in the darkness, surrounded by players waiting out the blackout drill in their wet uniforms. Over in the National League clubhouse someone lit a cigarette. An air raid warden stationed outside shouted a command to put it out. After twenty minutes, the lights came back on, the players gave

The Polo Grounds and vicinity before and after citywide blackout called at conclusion of 1942 twilight all-star game. Lights still twinkling after blackout are said to be generally beyond city limits.

their full post mortems to reporters, and the crowd was allowed to go home.

The Polo Grounds was the scene of blackout controversies two consecutive evenings during August. Appropriately enough, the visitors were the Dodgers.

The largest single-game crowd in Polo Grounds history—57,305—was on hand to see the Giants host Brooklyn in a twilight game August 3 for the benefit of the Army Emergency Relief Fund. Going into the last of the ninth, the Giants were trailing, 7–4, but then came a rally. Bill Werber got a leadoff single against Whitlow Wyatt, and Mel Ott drew a walk. And that was it. Suddenly the ball game was over. The moment designated for lights out—9:10 P.M.—had arrived. The umpires declared the Dodgers the winner based on the score after eight innings.

Giant fans were furious. When the Fred Waring Orchestra and a 150-member choral group went out to second base to conclude the evening with the national anthem, their rendition was drowned out by boos. The jeering stopped only when a spotlight was shined on the American flag atop the center field roof.

Horace Stoneham promptly announced that all remaining twilight games, except for the one with the Dodgers scheduled for the following evening, would be shifted to the afternoon.

"The game was a heartbreaker for the Giants and their fans," he lamented.

Mayor LaGuardia later blamed the police for the sour note on which the game ended, declaring, "Had I been there I would have seen to it that any inning started before the dimout also should have been finished, no matter how many minutes it ran over. There would not have been the squawks and confusion which followed the sudden calling of the game."

A less sympathetic view was expressed by "A Dodger Fan" who wrote to the *New York Times,* "Every Brooklyn fan regretted winning the game, but it was the Giant adherents who booed while 'The Star Spangled Banner' was being played and no Giant fan can ever live down the disgrace embodied in that episode."

The very next evening after the fiasco, Dodger rooters did a little jeering of their own. This time the Giants benefited from the clock. Pee Wee Reese had apparently clinched a Brooklyn victory in the second twilight game with a bases-loaded, inside-the-park homer off the Giants' "Fiddler" Bill McGee, breaking a 1–1 tie in the top of the tenth inning. But moments later, with the Dodgers' Joe Medwick at the plate, dimout time arrived and the game was ruled a nine-inning tie that would have to be replayed in its entirety. Dodger fans, seeing their lead wiped out, let loose with a torrent of boos. They could, however, hoot with a clear conscience, there being no patriotic music arranged this time.

The two blackouts, while abrupt, weren't nearly so sudden as the one that came during a minor league game in Florida. As described by John Kieran in his *New York Times* sports column, "Down in Jacksonville, a twilight game ran into blackout time and the switchman pulled off the lights just as the pitcher let fly with a fastball. Nobody was killed. The catcher later claimed it was a perfect strike whereas the batter said it was a foot outside. The umpire said nothing. He went home to bed."

The ban on night baseball in New York lasted until May 23, 1944, when the Dodgers—decked out in new satin uniforms said to be particularly attractive under the lights—celebrated the rekindling of Ebbets Field with a 3–2 victory over the Giants.

In cities where night baseball was permitted throughout the war, players and fans had to put up with test blackouts that could interrupt a game at any point.

A two-minute blackout coming in the sixth inning of the 1942 all-star benefit game at Cleveland left the *Sporting News'* Fred Lieb awestruck.

"One's neighbor disappeared into the inky darkness and only the grim outlines of the wings of the great stand were visible on a moonless night. It made one feel alone with one's God," he wrote.

Not enough neighbors were disappearing to satisfy Shibe Park public address announcer Babe O'Rourke when a 30-minute practice blackout halted an August '42 game between the Phils and Dodgers. Noticing a clump of smokers along right field, he admonished, "You gentlemen who are lighting cigarettes and cigars, if you are Americans, you won't do it."

O'Rourke later figured out a way to keep the fans occupied during a blackout so they would be less likely to produce unwanted sparks. When the lights went out for sixty-five minutes during a June '43 game between the Athletics and Red Sox, the PA announcer led 8,053 spectators in a songfest.

Of more immediate consequence than the transgressions of a few smokers was an incident that occurred in Lancaster, Pennsylvania. While the Lancaster Red Roses and York White Roses waited out a blackout coming in the midst of their September '43 Interstate League championship game, one of the bases was swiped.

George Kell, then the Lancaster third baseman, recalls:

"They had a blackout in the fifth inning of the final game of the playoffs. Somebody came out of the stands, I think. When the lights came on they had no second base. It created quite a stir until they found another bag."

Fans were assured, meanwhile, that if an air raid ever occurred, the safest place to be in was probably a ballpark.

Soon after Pearl Harbor, Fiorello LaGuardia—this time wearing his civil defense director's hat—warned that the Nazis "will send over suicide squads for token blastings."

But baseball rooters needn't be alarmed, he counseled, for "if we are to be hit, I'd just as soon get hit in the Yankee Stadium, the Polo Grounds, or Ebbets Field as I would in my apartment. It seems to me under the stands of the Stadium is as safe a place as any in the city."

Instructions were printed on every Yankee Stadium seat advising what to do in the event of a bombing attack. Fans in the upper stands were to follow green or red lines to shelter areas below,while those in the lower tier were to stay put. Yankee President Barrow noted that the shelter corridors below the stands were "protected by concrete three decks deep." And just in case, fire extinguishers, red barrels filled with water, and bins containing sand were placed around the ballpark.

Even inland, precautions were taken. Air raid wardens stood by during night games in Cincinnati and the electrical system at Crosley Field was rewired so that the lights could be shut off quickly by two master switches.

Harry Prince, a civil defense official in New York, suggested that if a raid came during a ballgame, the best thing might be to continue play.

"The ballplayers will be the soldiers in that situation," he explained. "They must stay right there and take it, if it comes, up to a certain point. The show must go on. Otherwise, it would be the actors rushing off a stage. If they show panic, you can see what might happen."

The players might be "soldiers," but they would have trouble obtaining ammunition. The war effort gobbled up materials needed for balls and bats.

A ton of rubber went into construction of a tank, and a half-ton was required for a B-17 bomber. So when Japan's seizure of Malaya and the Dutch East Indies cut off almost all of the nation's rubber supplies at the war's outset, the federal government banned use of both crude and scrap rubber in nonessential items. Baseballs—their heart a combination of high-grade cork and crude rubber—were not deemed essential to the war effort, however uplifting to GI morale the major league servicemen's equipment fund might appear.

A.G. Spalding & Brothers, manufacturer of both the American and National League balls, got by during 1942 on inventories, but a new type of baseball had to be found for the 1943 season. The commissioner's office told Spalding to come up with a ball which, while containing materials unessential to the war effort, would have the same resiliency as the one used in 1939, an outstanding season for slugging.

The Spalding people devised sixteen variations for testing by the U.S. Bureau of Standards, then selected what seemed the best of all possible baseballs. A committee consisting of Commissioner Landis, AL President Harridge, and Reds' general manager Giles looked over the concoction and on March 13, 1943, announced approval of what would be known as the "balata ball."

Replacing high-grade cork in the center of the ball would be ground cork with a binder of balata, a nonstrategic material obtained from the milky juice of tropical trees and most commonly used for golf ball covers and telephone cable insulation. Substituting for the traditional layer of rubber surrounding the cork center would be red

Examining the "balata ball" approved for 1943 season are (left to right) American League president Will Harridge, baseball commissioner Kenesaw Mountain Landis, commissioner's aide Leslie O'Connor, and Reds' general manager Warren Giles.

Inside view of the "balata ball."

and black layers of balata. And the cover of the baseball would come from domestic horsehides; the more desirable Belgian hides were no longer available. Spalding acknowledged that balata was inferior to rubber, but hoped that a tighter winding of the yarn inside the ball would bring the resiliency up to acceptable standards.

It was a disaster.

"The ball wouldn't ride," recalls Frank McCormick. "If you hit it on the end of the bat, or even if you got good wood on it, it felt like you had a handful of bees. It stung. It was like hitting a piece of concrete. It reminded me of when I was a kid, I used to practice by swinging at stones."

Especially incensed was Warren Giles who, as a member of the three-man committee charged with approving a new baseball, felt personally hoodwinked. After watching the Reds and Indians roll up a total of one extra base hit in twenty-one innings of spring training play, Giles speculated that Spalding used "ground up bologna instead of balata and cork."

On the opening day of the season, Giles conducted a little test, dropping a dozen leftover '42 baseballs and a similar number of '43 balls from the Crosley Field roof to the street below. Groundskeeper Matty Schwab and his son Tommy, stationed on the sidewalk, reported that the '42 balls bounced an average of thirteen feet in the air compared with only nine and one-half feet for the new baseballs. A more scientific study produced the same conclusion. An analysis by technicians at Cooper Union undertaken at the request of *New York Daily News* sportswriter Hy Turkin found the "balata ball" was 25.9 percent less resilient than its predecessor.

As the season got under way, Giles threatened to put the remaining 1942 balls, or baseballs produced by another manufacturer, into play at Crosley Field "even if the games are forfeited" as a result.

"Asking big leaguers to play with the sort of ball with which we are opening the season would be like asking our soldiers, sailors, and marines to win the war with blanks instead of real ammunition," he argued.

Giles' disgust quickly proved well founded. Eleven of the season's first twenty-nine games ended in shutouts, with the clubs averaging 5.3 hits per contest. In their opening series, the Reds beat the Cards 1–0 twice, both extra-inning games, and then were nipped 2–1 and 1–0. After watching his team lose to the Indians, 1–0, on opening day, Tiger manager O'Neill, who had been a catcher during the 1920s, remarked, "Any ball club would be lucky to get two runs in a game with this new ball. It's deader than the one in use when I was playing."

Spalding at first defended its product. Company Vice-President Lou Coleman contended, "It has been too wet and too cold. In time the new ball will prove to be just as lively as the old one."

But on the fourth day of the season, Coleman acknowledged what everyone could see and promised that Spalding would come up with a better ball within two weeks. Admitting the '43 baseball was 25 percent less lively than its forerunner, Coleman said that the fault lay not with the new-found balata but in the rubber cement applied to the layers of wool between the core and cover. He reported that the glue, made from reprocessed rubber, was of inferior quality and had hardened, making the wool brittle and thereby deadening the ball. The problem would be solved, said Coleman, with use of a better grade of rubber cement that had been tested and accepted.

The American League decided to stick with the dead baseballs until the new and improved variety arrived, but Ford Frick immediately authorized National League teams to use leftover '42 balls during the interim.

"There is nothing in the book that requires the two major leagues to use the same ball," said Frick. "I am thinking of the fans. Baseball faces a tough enough year as it is, without continuing play with a dead ball and thus alienating the spectators. You can imagine the fans' reaction to going to a game and watching well-hit balls plop feebly into fielders' hands."

In the National League, at least, hitting quickly became a part of baseball again. The Dodgers beat the Phils, 11–4, the two clubs banging out twenty-three hits, in the first game using the '42 balls.

Exactly two weeks after the start of the 1943 season, Frick called reporters to his Rockefeller Center office to unveil the revised "balata ball," which, according to Spalding, contained rubber cement that remained soft and sticky. Bounced on an uncarpeted section of the office, the ball jumped twice as high as the original balata sphere and turned out to be even 50 percent livelier than the '42 baseballs.

Spalding had, in truth, made amends. American League batters had managed only nine home runs in the first seventy-two games of the season, but on Sunday, May 9, the first day the new balls were put into play in the circuit, six homers were struck during four doubleheaders.

The original "balata ball" made a comeback one day in Philadelphia. Steve O'Neill protested his Tigers' loss to the Athletics in the second game of a June 1 doubleheader at Shibe Park, contending the dead baseballs had been put into play and "it might or might not have been an accident."

Will Harridge disallowed the protest, finding that while the dead balls—recognizable by small, star-shaped markings—had indeed slipped into the day's allotment, they were also used in the first game of the doubleheader (a 7–0 Tiger victory), apparently through an oversight by the umpires.

By time the 1944 season arrived, Spalding had received government permission to replace the balata with synthetic rubber. Fifty-one factories built by the federal government and leased to private industry in a crash program to find an alternative to natural rubber were

Getting a good bat may have been a problem during the war, but things weren't quite as bad as Milton Berle would have Leo Durocher believe during get-together at Dodgers' Bear Mountain spring camp.

synthesizing 800,000 tons of rubber a year from petroleum, the equivalent of a harvest from 180 million rubber trees, and enough to have a little left over for baseballs.

Labor shortages in the great lumber fields of the Northwest, combined with heightened wartime demands for pulp, presented another problem for the hitters—it became difficult to get bats containing high-quality wood.

The ingenuity of big business was pressed into service to help the Washington Senators surmount the problem.

George Case recalls, "Glenn Martin of the Martin Bomber Company was an avid baseball fan, he was always at the games and he had one of the best semipro teams. He came into the clubhouse once and we told him, 'We're having a helluva time getting bats, the wood is terrible, we can't get the models we want.'

"Well, he had his engineers design a bat, he sent me two or three dozen. Where he got the wood I don't know. It wasn't good wood, but it was tapered a little on the end like an airplane wing. It had good wind resistance. Their theory was there's wind resistance when you're using a bat, just like with an airplane wing."

The Braves' Tommy Holmes wielded an ancient bat supplied by his third base coach (and later manager) Del Bissonette to complete a thirty-seven-game hitting streak during the 1945 season, setting a

Tommy Holmes and friend eye Rogers Hornsby's modern National League record for consecutive game hitting streak. The Boston outfielder, swinging a hand-me-down bat, will go on to break the mark by four games.

modern National League record that would remain unbroken until Pete Rose's forty-four-game mark in 1978.

Now community relations director for the New York Mets, Holmes talked one day about the bat he used to break Rogers Hornsby's thirty-three-game NL hitting streak, set back in 1922.

"We took care of our bats, I seldom broke a bat, I don't think I broke more than a bat or two a year," he says. "But I cracked my bat when the streak reached about twenty games. I had some others but none I liked particularly. We had an off day scheduled and Bissonette said, 'I'll get you a bat, I'm going up to my home in Maine, I'll bring you back a piece of concrete from my attic.'

"It was a like a rock, it had been aging. But I tried it in batting practice and I liked it."

There were problems away from the ballpark as well.

Late one evening during the 1944 Easter season, a Pennsylvania Railroad train stopped at the Terre Haute, Indiana, station and out came the Pittsburgh Pirates. The players walked down the platform to board another train taking them to Indianapolis for an exhibition game with the Indians. The train was there, but it was jammed with holiday travelers. Frankie Frisch tried to persuade a conductor to make some coach seats available, but for the satisfaction he got, the manager might as well have been arguing with an umpire. Then he spotted a small truck unloading its wares into one of the cars. The problem had been solved.

"Get into the baggage car," Frisch shouted to the entourage.

The ballplayers piled in with their luggage and the team made its seventy-mile journey amid stacks of mail.

Riding the rails in wartime wasn't always that tough, but leisurely trips were a thing of the past. Soldiers were en route to southern camps, trailed perhaps by their wives; troops journeyed to points of embarkation; men and women left farms and small towns for war plant jobs in the big cities—everyone, it seemed, was on the move. They traveled, of course, via train. By 1944, the railroads were logging three times as many passenger miles as in 1941, bringing old locomotives and coach cars out of retirement to meet the crush.

"It's only fair to tell you the trains are crowded these days. You'll be more comfortable at home," declared the Atlantic Coast Line Railroad, so overburdened that it undertook a public campaign to discourage nonessential travel.

The first signs of the times to come were evident at the 1942 World Series.

Mel Ott set out with Horace Stoneham on a plane bound for St. Louis, but the Giants' manager never got there. He was bumped for a higher priority passenger at a stopover in Dayton, Ohio, could not make a westward train connection, and finally returned to New York.

In prewar days, four special trains were hired for World Series travel—two for the teams, a third for the press, and a fourth for the commissioner and his guests. But only one special train was available for the trip from St. Louis to New York after the second game of the 1942 Series. To avoid fraternization, the Cardinals and Yankees were berthed at opposite ends of the nineteen-car luxury special. Even that train was no longer around for the Cards' trip back to St. Louis after their five-game Series triumph, the federal government having taken special trains out of service on October 4, the day of the fourth game.

The Cardinal players returned on a regularly scheduled train, most of them managing to get seats in the same car despite their purchase of individual tickets.

Baseball gradually reduced its travel mileage by shifting spring training to the North, cutting intersectional trips from four to three per season, and even revising the World Series home-and-away sequence from 2-3-2 to 3–4 to save one potential rail trip. But the situation became progressively worse. Space was so tight that in early 1945 there were rumors the government would ask the sixteen major league clubs to regroup into two "victory leagues" based on an East–West alignment. Such a proposal was never presented formally, but the majors did eliminate the '45 all-star game at the request of the Office of Defense Transportation and for a time were faced with the prospect that the '45 World Series would be canceled. The Tigers were refused government permission to make a sixty-six mile rail detour on a July '45 eastern swing so that they could play an exhibition in Pittsburgh for the benefit of servicemen's welfare agencies.

By the late war days, ball clubs might might find it difficult to travel as a unit. Giant players traveled on four different trains for a trip from Chicago to Pittsburgh in July '45.

The best laid plans of road secretaries could fall victim to equipment shortages. The Braves arrived at the Cincinnati railroad station one evening during a 1945 road trip, got aboard a waiting train, and promptly went to bed in their Pullman cars, expecting to awaken in St. Louis. But when the players arose the next morning, they were still in Cincinnati. Nobody had bothered to attach a locomotive to the train.

The Braves could have been thankful, at least, for having Pullman berths on that occasion. Such was not always the case. Before the war, each ball club would have two railroad cars set aside for road trips, assuring every man a lower bunk. "But," explains George Case, "when the war came, you might be in a car with ten businessmen and four or five ladies and have an upper berth. There was no privacy. In some cases, there were no berths at all, the guys had to sit up at night.

"I remember a trip from Washington to Boston. There were no seats. The cars were crowded, mostly with servicemen. We sat on our bags."

When a few Pullman berths were available, recalls Danny Litwhiler, "The guys that were playing regular, they'd have lowers, and the guys who weren't would have uppers."

"But it never bothered me," he says, "because I liked the uppers so

I always took an upper. I didn't like people climbing over me and stepping on the bed while I'm trying to sleep."

There were others whose egos didn't take kindly to an upper bunk. Hank Wyse, a rookie pitcher with the 1943 Cubs, was dismayed to find he was still sleeping upstairs after blanking the Reds, 7–0, for his third straight victory.

"How come I win a shutout and I have to sleep on a shelf. What do I have to do to get a lower?" he asked road secretary Bob Lewis. The reply: "You get a lower after you have won two shutouts in one day."

With flexibility in making travel arrangements limited, a visiting team might request that the starting time of a getaway game be moved up so that it could make a train out of town. But the home club was not always accommodating.

The Dodgers, playing a series in St. Louis two weeks before the close of the 1945 season, asked the Cardinals to reschedule a twilight doubleheader for the daytime so that they could get aboard the regular night Pullman for Chicago and be rested for a date with the Cubs the next afternoon.

Figuring he could draw more people during the evening, Cardinal owner Sam Breadon refused to make the switch. His obstinacy backfired, however, and at the same time almost resulted in some Dodger players losing their lives.

The evening came up chilly and foggy, holding the crowd down to 2,378, a smaller turnout than would have been on hand had the doubleheader been played during the afternoon. And Breadon was to take a beating on the field as well as at the box office. Leo Durocher had been saving Hal Gregg and Vic Lombardi, two of his best pitchers, for the league-leading Cubs, but angered by Breadon's refusal to play in the daytime, threw them against the second place Cardinals instead. The Dodgers got their revenge, topping the Redbirds 7–3 and 6–1 and pushing them two and one-half games out of first.

Then, scrambling for train space because of the late hour at which the doubleheader concluded, the team split up into two groups. The regulars boarded one train while Durocher, his coaches, the reserves, and pitchers were herded aboard a night freight, crowding into an antique parlor car attached at the rear. The freight train travelers dozed fitfully—some of the players curled up in overstuffed velvet chairs from a bygone era while others stretched out on a frayed carpet —as the train sped along through the predawn hours. Suddenly, there was an explosion. The windows of the parlor car shattered. Flames licked at the train. A lumber plant, a coal yard, and the dawn skies over Manhattan, Illinois, were ablaze. The freight had collided with a gasoline tanker truck attempting to get across the tracks.

Panic momentarily erupted in the parlor car, but Durocher calmed the players and everybody leaped to safety. The contingent escaped with nothing worse than a bruised right knee suffered by coach Charlie Dressen and a cut on the right arm received by outfielder Luis Olmo. But the engineer and fireman were not so fortunate—they died of massive burns.

On a number of occasions, games would be suspended so that the visiting team could catch a train. Since the contests would be resumed at a later date from the point where they were stopped, neither club gained an unfair advantage. But the fans, who had paid to see a full ball game, understandably felt cheated.

Here, too, Sam Breadon was at the center of controversy. The Phillies and Cardinals agreed that no inning of their May '44 getaway night game in Sportsman's Park would start after 10:15 P.M., so that the visitors could make train connections. But there was no announcement of the arrangement until moments before the game started. The 10,159 fans bought tickets expecting to see a complete game. When play was suspended after seven innings to enable the Phils to board an 11:15 train, many of the spectators were furious and let their feelings be known in letters to the St. Louis newspapers. Breadon conceded that the Cardinals "may have made a mistake" by not moving up the 8:30 P.M. starting time.

Travel conditions being what they were, the most valuable man on a team might be the road secretary.

"We had difficulties with reservations. At times it was very annoying and very trying because you were never sure of your accommodations," says Phil Weintraub. "But one thing that was in our favor, we had Eddie Brannick, who knew all the railroad agents. If anybody got any preferential treatment, certainly Eddie and the Giants got it because this guy really worked at it. We probably didn't suffer as much as some of the other ball clubs because he was just a fantastic road secretary and knew everybody. He stayed around for a zillion years."

An any rate, the wartime ballplayers reconciled themselves to home front hardships and were a hardy lot, according to Weintraub.

"You loved the game so much you didn't mind these things. I never objected to any of those things. It was a thrill just to be playing the game and be a part of it," he says. "You know the old saying, 'In those days we'd have played for nothing and most of us did.' Now you see all these guys with their injuries and sore arms and everything.

Every time I pick up the paper somebody else is going out of the lineup. When we got hurt in those days, they said 'stick it in the dirt.' You were afraid to say you were hurt. You had an entirely different breed."

And if the train situation wasn't vexing enough, there was the problem of finding decent accommodations on road trips. The club hotels were first class but often hopelessly overcrowded. In wartime Washington, where every available lodging seemed to be occupied by bureaucrats or military officialdom, visiting ballplayers were sometimes stacked four to a hotel room. After sitting up all night in railroad coach seats—Eddie Brannick's wizardry apparently having failed him on that occasion—the Giants arrived in Cincinnati one morning to find that their hotel rooms weren't ready. Ernie Lombardi, who didn't move very fast on the base paths, acted quickly. He grabbed a taxi, went to the Crosley Field clubhouse, and napped away the day on the trainer's table.

A clubhouse once served as sleeping quarters for an entire minor league team. The Pacific Coast League's San Diego Padres were unable to find hotel space on a May '45 visit to San Francisco. Delegates at the forty-six-nation conference drawing up the United Nations charter had preempted all the rooms. So the Padres turned for help to the host San Francisco Seals, who obtained twenty-five cots from a hotel that had the spares but no place to set them up. The cots were transported to the Seals Stadium visitors' clubhouse. Padre manager Pepper Martin provided a touch of home with an electric coffee pot.

During the 1945 World Series, hotel rooms were scarcer than a ballplayer without a draft deferment. When the Cubs arrived in Detroit for the first three games of the Series, nine ballplayers and their wives received an unpleasant surprise—management had arranged for them to sleep in tiny cabins aboard a Great Lakes steamship tied up in the Detroit River at the foot of Wayne Street. There wasn't enough hotel space to accommodate all the Chicago ballplayers plus their families.

The excess Cubbies were among one thousand souls to be distributed aboard a pair of D & C line boats leased by Detroit hotels to house their overflow.

One Series visitor who had come all the way from El Paso, Texas, only to find himself stuffed into a shipboard cubbyhole told a reporter, "I don't like it at all, but it's better than sleeping on a park bench."

Then, fearing he might indeed find himself under a tree, the man quickly added, "Don't tell the boat people I said that. They might kick me out."

The ballplayers were not as humble—they staged a rebellion. Len Merullo tells the story:

"The World Series, even during the war years, was still a big, big thing, and especially for the wives. It meant that they would go out and buy clothes and be entertained. It was a big thing just to be part of a winning ball club. And then they saw those rooms. I remember Bill Nicholson distinctly, because he really raised hell. His wife was a very nice-looking woman. He had bought her some furs and things like that. And she took one look at those little cabins where you couldn't turn left or right where we were gonna stay for the Series. Well, they just stormed right out of there and my wife and I just followed right with them. My wife wasn't too happy about it either; you wouldn't have been when you saw the size of the cabins. They wound up finally getting us rooms at the Book Cadillac. There was an awful lot of confusion. We were told there were no rooms to be gotten, but we just stayed around that lobby until they set us up. We spent most of the night waiting to get a room."

The hotel situation didn't improve much as far as the general public was concerned, when the Series moved on to Chicago for the last four games. A reservations clerk at Chicago's Hotel Sherman advised, "A fellow bringing his own cot can get space in the hallway."

While road trips could be an exhausting experience, the wartime ballplayer was confronted as well with difficulties at home. Among them was the ordeal of simply finding a place to live.

Players seeking an apartment for the season when they arrived from spring training had to compete with the hordes that had descended on the big cities, drawn by war plants or government jobs. "No Vacancy" signs sprouted on inner city apartment buildings while jerry-built housing developments and trailer colonies proliferated in the suburbs as almost 5.5 million people left rural areas for the great urban centers during the war.

Managers Luke Sewell of the Browns and Billy Southworth of the Cardinals thought they had surmounted the housing problem with a sharing arrangement. Since one of the St. Louis teams was always on the road when the other was at home, the two managers and their respective wives took turns living in the same apartment in the Lindell Towers development. Then the Browns did the seemingly impossible and finally captured a pennant, setting up the all-St. Louis 1944 "Streetcar Series." The prospect of an interleague foursome living under the same roof, sharing thoughts of Series strategy as well as the dishes, was averted when a neighbor who was going out of town loaned his apartment to Southworth.

With San Diego having become among the ten most congested areas of the nation by 1945, Pepper Martin had trouble finding living quarters for his family. The Padres' manager might put up with sleeping in a locker room on a road trip, but he wasn't about to stay with his wife and kids in the San Diego clubhouse during home stands. So Martin put an advertisement in the local papers offering a season's pass to anyone finding him a five-room apartment.

The hospitals were jammed, too, as a certain manager with a busted leg discovered. When Casey Stengel was run over by a taxi in Boston's Kenmore Square one night just before the start of the 1943 season, he was placed in traction in a maternity ward. There was no other space available at St. Elizabeth's Hospital. Two fans sent him Mother's Day cards.

Once having secured an apartment for the season, a ballplayer next faced the travail of getting to and from his job. The parks were easily reachable by subway, trolley, or bus; baseball's move to suburbia was still years away. But what of the player who wanted to take his car to work? He hardly merited an "E" windshield sticker exempting a driver from gasoline rationing (policemen and politicians, occasionally, so qualified). On the other hand, the low priority "A" sticker, at times good for as few as two gallons of gas a week, might seem niggardly for someone helping to sustain the nation's morale. It could come down to haggling for allocations with the local rationing authorities.

"To get my car from home to the ballpark I had to go before the gas rationing board," recalls George Case. "I told them I was a professional baseball player. Well, there was a hassle. But one member of the board was a Presbyterian minister who knew me. He gave the deciding vote."

When the fans weren't using public transit, they would have to settle for rather austere models of travel. The Elmira, New York, club of the Eastern League, anticipating a problem drawing crowds because its ballpark was a bit of a walk from the end of the transit line, provided free rides in a hay wagon drawn by a two-horse team. For those who favored pedal power, a bicycle rack was installed outside the park.

A ballplayer performing feebly at the plate could point to a dead baseball and brittle bat as mitigating circumstances, but the excuses

With gasoline and tires rationed, automobiles weren't of much use during the war. Finding an alternate method for getting from their Lakewood training camp hotel to the practice field are Giants' (front row, left to right) Gus Mancuso, Dick Bartell, and Tom Sunkel, along with (rear, left to right) Babe Barna and Carl Hubbell.

did not have to end there. The man might also be slightly undernourished. With the government earmarking 60 percent of the prime and choice cuts of meat for servicemen, the railroad dining cars and hotel restaurants were offering omelettes and fish concoctions in the menu spot formerly reserved for steak. As for home cooking, a shortstop's wife, like everyone else, had to watch ration points.

As early as the 1942 season, prospects of getting a decent meal in a train diner had become rather uncertain.

On one '42 road trip, a number of St. Louis Browns players took to their Pullman beds without supper, having been unable to squeeze into the crowded dining car. Manager Luke Sewell came up with a solution, however, by the time the next journey rolled around. He had the Sportsman's Park concessionaire pack box meals.

Chicago sportswriter Ed Burns told readers of his *Sporting News* column about a couple of hungry road trips he'd made with the Cubs.

Burns recounted how the team went to the Boston railroad station right after a day game without having had a chance to grab supper and boarded a coach for Philadelphia, hoping to have a meal en route. But as the six o'clock train pulled out, the players discovered to their dismay that there was no dining car aboard. Trainer Andy Lotshaw, unwilling to allow the men in his care to go hungry all night, got hold of four pineapple pies during a brief stop at the Trenton station at one-thirty in the morning and proudly offered the treat on reboarding the train.

"It broke our hearts to have to tell the good doctor that next to day coaches, we hate pineapple pies," wrote Burns.

On a rail trip from St. Louis to Philadelphia, the Cubs were served a dinner billed as fish cutlets, but described by Burns as "reminiscent of that dark, scummy stuff which comes out of a can of salmon."

He added, "Don't say it was good enough for a civilian. We ate with three soldiers fresh in from China and the same slop was shoved at them at one dollar and twenty cents a dose."

When a ballplayer got a crack at a first-class dinner on a road trip, he wouldn't hesitate to pay a little extra. But he exceeded the club's meal allowance at his own peril.

A floor show was in progress in the dining room of Philadelphia's Ben Franklin Hotel late one night during the summer of 1944 when Pirate outfielder Vince DiMaggio and a few teammates arrived for a meal following a long game at Shibe Park. In light of the entertainment, a 20 percent surcharge was added to the check. His dining mates paid the extra charge out of their own pockets, but DiMaggio signed his entire bill over to the Pittsburgh ballclub, reasoning the hotel was the only place where a decent meal could be found at such a late hour. The Pirate management reasoned otherwise. DiMaggio was incensed to find the overpayment deducted from his next paycheck

Recalling the affair years later, Frankie Frisch reported that DiMaggio, believing Pirate road secretary Sam Watters was responsible for his being docked, tried to have his teammates freeze the official out of a share of the World Series proceeds awarded the team that fall for finishing in second place. Only after the National League brought pressure on the players did Watters get his cut, according to Frisch. Just before the 1945 season got under way, Joe D's less famous brother found himself in a position to enjoy all the Ben Franklin floor shows he wanted—he was traded to the Phillies for pitcher Al Gerheauser.

Philadelphia's two doormats, in need of any edge they could find, were resourceful in finding ways to fortify themselves despite rationing.

Connie Mack turned to vitamins, ordering his ballplayers to take one capsule a day at their 1943 training camp.

"With meat rationing, the butter scarcity, and the possibility that other foods may go on the ration list, the vitamins may play some part in keeping my men at peak condition," he explained.

Thus bolstered, the club went out and lost 105 games.

Late in the war, the A's carried a ballplayer whose value was hardly reflected in the box scores. George Kell remembers: "We had a third string catcher, Tony Parisse. He and his father owned a meat market three blocks from Shibe Park. They took care of us. The wives would have a ball, it was the only place they could get all kinds of cuts."

The wives of four Phillie ballplayers—outfielders Danny Litwhiler and Ron Northey, third baseman Pinky May, and pitcher Si Johnson—announced during the spring of 1943 they were going on diets to free up ration coupons that they could redeem for steaks for their men. Says Litwhiler, "They kept fit and we ate good."

That year the Phils lost only ninety ballgames.

Charlie Grimm found an unlikely source of beef for his ballplayers—a Jesuit seminary down the road from the Cubs' French Lick training camp. Hearing that the Jesuits raised their own livestock and fortunately were baseball fans, the manager arranged for his men to pay a visit whenever a barbecue was scheduled. The players would swap baseball stories for steaks.

George Case tells how the entire Senators' ball club once went to Canada for the sole purpose of getting a square meal:

"We'd often get on the train late at night and all the food was gone. Or they'd say, 'The dining car is now open, servicemen will be served first.' You'd have to eat whatever they had left. It was really tough to get food.

"On one road trip, everywhere we went there were meatless days. You'd have substitutes—cheese and macaroni. So we go into Detroit. The road secretary, Eddie Eynon, came in after the first game of the series and he said, 'I've located you guys some meat. There's a private club in Windsor, Ontario.' After the game we climbed into a bus and we went across the river to the private club and we had our first meat in about a week."

The men keeping baseball alive experienced lean times in their pocketbooks as well. While war plant workers were bringing home fat paychecks, ballplayers felt a squeeze from two directions—the federal government and public opinion.

Under Treasury Department regulations enacted prior to the 1943 season and in effect throughout the war, no ballplayer could make more money than the top salary paid by his club during the 1942 season unless special permission was obtained. The bureaucrats

Ernie Lombardi thanks Connie Ryan (left) and Hugh Poland for their role in helping him get a raise.

would grant approval to exceed the '42 wage ceiling only if convinced there was a basis in "merit or service."

The restriction was said to have been a major factor in an April 1943 trade that sent slow-footed but heavy-hitting backstop Ernie Lombardi from the Braves to the Giants for two unknowns, catcher Hugh Poland and infielder Connie Ryan. Lombardi, the National League's leading hitter the previous year with a .330 average, reportedly had demanded a 1943 salary of $15,000, which happened to be $2,500 above the upper range of the Braves' wage scale. As a member of the Giants, Lombardi could, however, get his $15,000 without the need for government approval, that team's ceiling being $17,500, the 1942 salary of shortstop Billy Jurges.

Poland stuck around in the majors as a substitute catcher for parts of five seasons, getting into a grand total of eighty-three games. When his playing days were over, he returned to the Giants' organization. Now a scout based in his hometown of Guthrie, Kentucky—San Francisco shortstop Johnnie LeMaster his most recent find—Poland took time from talent-hunting chores one spring day to recall the Lombardi trade, with some amusement.

"The Braves got a lot of criticism," he remembers. "Lombardi led the league the year before and I think I wound up in '43 at about .189 or something and I don't think Ryan hit much more than that." (Poland batted .183 for the Braves as their third-string catcher while Ryan, playing regularly at either second or third base, swatted .212. Lombardi went on to hit .305 for the Giants.)

When Casey Stengel returned to the Braves in mid-June upon his release from the St. Elizabeth's maternity ward, he had trouble fathoming who his new catcher was.

Poland recalls Casey's bewilderment:

"Stengel had gotten run down in Kenmore Square, broke his leg. In the meantime, why, they made the deal for me and Connie Ryan, for Ernie Lombardi.

"The first day Stengel came back, it was at Braves Field. I was catching the ball game, we were playing Cincinnati. I kept hearing somebody whistle and whistle and whistle. Then I got to the bench and Lefty Gomez—this was about at the end of his time—said, 'Don't you hear Stengel whistling to you?' It seems he wanted to give me some pitching signs.

"I said, 'Well, I heard somebody whistling, I didn't know who it was.'

"So Gomez said, 'Well, Stengel kept whistling and whistling and says you wouldn't turn around and he finally asked me, by the way, who is that fella catching?' "

Poland says Gomez told him he had informed Stengel, 'That's Hugh Poland' to which Casey retorted, 'Who's Hugh Poland?'"

Government wage restrictions were also at issue in a 1945 salary dispute between the Cardinals' star brother battery—Mort and Walker Cooper—and owner Sam Breadon. Mort Cooper won sixty-five games during the first three wartime seasons while Walker Cooper was probably the best catcher in the National League. Yet their 1945 contracts called for only $12,000, the same money each had been making the three prior years. Since the Cards' top salary in 1942 had been $12,000, no one could make more than that figure without government sanction.

Soon complications developed. After signing the Coopers, Breadon offered shortstop Marty Marion, the NL's Most Valuable Player in 1944, a contract for $13,500, contingent upon approval from Washington. In fulfillment of a promise that nobody on the team would be paid more than the Cooper brothers, the owner then called them in to renegotiate, offering each the same $13,500, also subject to an okay from Treasury officials.

Instead of being pleased with long-delayed salary hikes, the Coopers were angry that Breadon had offered to exceed the wage ceiling for another player before coming to them, so they promptly demanded $15,000 apiece.

"You know you have to make your money over just a few years in baseball," Walker Cooper observed.

When Breadon wouldn't budge beyond $13,500, the brothers threatened to stay home. Finally they agreed to play while putting the dispute into the hands of Leslie O'Connor, Landis' former secretary, who, with Frick and Harridge, had been running baseball since the commissioner's death from a heart attack in November '44.

But before long, both of the brothers were gone from the Cardi-

Walker Cooper (left) and brother Mort reluctantly get into uniform for their 1945 season's opener at Wrigley Field as they await resolution of contract dispute.

nals. Walker Cooper found himself playing ball for a lot less money, going into the Navy on May 1 and crouching behind the plate for the Great Lakes Naval Training Station in a game against the University of Illinois soon thereafter. Mort Cooper, who was being paid on the basis of $13,500 per year while O'Connor mulled over the situation, jumped the Cardinals on May 16 and was promptly fined $500 and suspended. A week later he was traded to the Braves for pitcher Red Barrett and $60,000. The deal seemed like a steal for Boston, but luck was with Breadon. Cooper developed a sore elbow and won only seven games for the Braves before undergoing surgery. Barrett, who could manage only a 9–16 record with Boston in 1944, came through with twenty-one victories for the Cards.

In seeking a salary hike, a ballplayer had more than the government's anti-inflation policy to deal with. He also faced the proposition that he should be happy merely having the opportunity to participate in a sport while other men of the same age were dodging bullets.

Coming off his fabulous 1941 season, Joe DiMaggio felt a raise was in order the following spring. The Yankees, however, thought differently. DiMaggio said later that Ed Barrow initially told him he would have to take a $2,500 cut because "there's a war on," then offered a contract for the same $37,500 he had made in '41.

"Eventually I signed for $43,750; but while I was battling for it, the Yankee front office put out a lot of propaganda about boys being in the Army at $21 a month, the insinuation being that I was lucky to be playing ball. I don't think anything burned me up as much as that," the Yankee great subsequently told an interviewer in looking back on his relationship with management.

DiMaggio had, in fact, felt quite a bit of pressure while holding out during the spring of 1942, sunning himself on a beach ten miles from the Yankees' St. Petersburg training camp.

A group of soldiers from Camp Blanding, Florida, sent him a telegram—copies thoughtfully made available to the press—reading: "In event the Yankees don't kick in with more than $37,000, we cordially invite you to a tryout with the 143rd Infantry, 36th Division, the fightingest regiment in this man's Army. The pay is only $21 per month, but that is far better than nothing. Please advise. P.S. Would settle for last year's salary."

Time magazine observed that Britain, in "a closer approach to total war effort," had restricted horse racing, dog racing, and boxing "while a U.S. baseball star pouted on a Florida beach because he did not consider $40,000 enough for one season's harrowing toil."

Mort Cooper faced a similar response during the spring of 1944 when he sought $17,500 in a contract dispute with Sam Breadon which served as the warm-up for their salary battle the following year.

In laying out his justification for a pay hike, Cooper noted he had been classified 4F, explaining, "That leaves me a private citizen and businessman. Other businessmen are making the best deals they can without criticism and I think I have the same right."

Breadon responded, "It is unwise for players who have been excused from military service for some reason or another to publicize their dissatisfaction with the contracts which have been sent to them. I do not think it makes for very good reading for persons who have their boys on the fighting fronts."

One of those boys, *Stars and Stripes* sportswriter Bill McIlwain, was indeed unimpressed by Cooper's reasoning. Two weeks after the Cooper-Breadon argument flared in public, Corporal McIlwain wrote in his column, "For a baseball player, who isn't exactly a key production figure, to moan over his salary comes as a bit of a pain. There isn't a major leaguer who makes as little as the average serviceman. Keep baseball alive, but don't put up with any fancy holdouts. A lot of guys in other uniforms won't like it."

Cooper had to settle for $12,000. While impressing upon their employees the necessity of sacrifice, the owners, it developed, didn't exactly starve. Data provided by the ball clubs for 1951 congressional hearings on baseball's relationship to the antitrust laws showed that twelve teams turned a profit over the four war years; only the Athletics, Red Sox, Phillies, and Braves wound up in the red. The major leagues reported overall profit margins of 7.8 and 8 percent for the last two wartime seasons, the most impressive bottom line figures since 1930.

Attendance sagged early in the war, but rebounded in 1945 to a record 10,847,123 paid, more than 700,000 over the old mark set in 1930. And overhead apparently was being held in check. With most of the star players in the service and government wage restrictions holding down the pay of the ballplayers left behind, the average big league salary declined from $7,306 in 1939 to $6,423 during the 1943 season.

The biggest money-makers were the Tigers, who led the majors in attendance during '44 and '45, battling for pennants both seasons and drawing on a boom-town economy that boosted the population of Detroit and its environs by 200,000 during the war years. The club reported an overall profit during World War II of $532,810.

The most financially successful National League team of the era? Showing a ledger $410,587 in the black were Sam Breadon's St. Louis Cardinals.

IV

Help Wanted

6

Never Too Young, Never Too Old

Baseball's state of affairs was pretty much summed up in the help wanted ad's two-column headline: "Cardinal Organization Needs Players."

Readers of the *Sporting News'* edition of February 25, 1943, were advised: "If you are a free agent and have previous professional experience, we may be able to place you to your advantage on one of our clubs. We have positions open on our AA, B, and D classification clubs. If you believe you can qualify for one of these good baseball jobs, tell us about yourself."

The Cardinals asked applicants to list experience, position played, age, height, weight, marital status, and perhaps most important, selective service classification, ending their plea with the words "Write Today."

The champions of all baseball, once overseers of a vast farm chain comprising more than thirty clubs, were now desperate for minor league talent.

"These are unusual times," explained a sheepish Sam Breadon. An understatement, to be sure. The minor league universe that spanned forty-one leagues during the 1941 season would have but nine circuits as the 1943 campaign opened, the young ballplayers having been sent off to war. (Few more would be found through the advertisement, only about a half-dozen replies meriting any consideration.)

And while the big leagues were slower to feel the manpower pinch than the minors (major league ballplayers for the most part being married and thus not among the first to be called into military service), more and more familiar names were missing as the 1943 season approached. The Cardinals had already lost two-thirds of their outfield with Enos Slaughter, league leader in hits the previous year, and

155

fancy-fielding Terry Moore having donned khaki uniforms. Johnny Beazley, rookie winner of twenty-one games and twice conqueror of the Yankees in the World Series, would now be doing his pitching for the Army. Others less notable had gone off to the military as well, seven members of the 1942 Cardinal team in all.

It would get worse.

Eleven months after the Cardinals' plea for help in the *Sporting News,* the Yankees, now champs after beating St. Louis in the 1943 World Series, received a certain letter.

"I am ready to play left field for the Yankees," the note opened. "I am a fine fielder and a good hitter and could easily make good. I also am free from draft or war work call." The explanation: "I have a recent discharge from the state hospital for insane at West Haven, Connecticut."

Ed Barrow told reporters, "If this man still were at West Haven I would write him to move over. The situation in baseball is enough to drive anybody daffy."

If Barrow had visions of a fourth consecutive pennant in 1944, he knew it would be done without DiMaggio, Henrich, or Keller, without Gordon or Rizzuto, without Dickey, without Ruffing. In fact, peopled with forgettables such as shortstop Mike Milosevich, third baseman Oscar Grimes, and catcher Mike Garbak, the Yanks would finish third, behind the runner-up Tigers and the St. Louis Browns, who would win the only American League title in their history with a cast barely more distinguished.

The 1944 American League ball clubs and, of course, the National League squads as well, bore little resemblance to their prewar versions. And by the last year of the war era, it seemed that just about anybody in civilian clothes was a candidate to play professional baseball.

A survey by Cub general manager Jimmy Gallagher prior to the 1945 season found the sixteen big league clubs with 565 players on their reserve lists, but another 509—in large part the genuine big league talent—off to war. Gallagher reported that the minor leagues had only 1,188 men, having lost 3,576 to military service.

Managers didn't know from one day to the next who they would have in their lineup—today's ballplayer could turn into tomorrow's soldier or sailor.

When the Yankees opened their 1944 spring training camp, Joe McCarthy was asked by reporters if he could name his starting team for opening day. The exasperated manager replied, "How could I possibly do that? Why I couldn't tell you who will be here next Tuesday." Then he thought for a moment and went on, "Yes, I could give you an infield. Neun could play first, I could cover second, Schulte on short, Fletcher on third, Krichell catching, and Schreiber pitching, and some of you writers could fill in, too."

Johnny Neun, John Schulte, and Art Fletcher were the Yankee coaches, Krichell a scout, and Schreiber the batting practice pitcher. (In the latter case, McCarthy was prophetic, but a year off. Nearing age forty-three, Schreiber would be summoned to the mound for a pair of 1945 relief stints, twenty-two years after his last major league appearance.)

There would be no sympathy from the likes of Jimmy Dykes, who gloated over the Yankee manager finding himself with talent—or lack thereof—comparable, for a change, with the rest of the league.

"I feel sorry for that McCarthy," said his White Sox colleague, envisioning a mediocre 1944 Yankee team. "Now the poor guy will have to have a thought now and then instead of pressing a push-button every time he wants a DiMaggio or a Keller or a Gordon to hit a home run."

With the supply of talent thinned out, managers were particularly challenged to get the most out of what they had. Nowhere was there less room for mistake than on the Philadelphia Athletics, a team that had been floundering in the second division for years. Connie Mack, whose managerial career went back to 1894, was not, however, quite up to it, according to George Kell.

"He was in his eighties then —and that is OLD. He was bright, but he didn't run a ball game like a manager should run it," says Kell. "I remember several mistakes he made. We had two substitutes—Jo Jo White did most of the pinch hitting and Joe Berry was the reliever. One day Mr. Mack sent White out to be a pinch runner at second base. It was the ninth inning of a tie game. The pitcher was due up two batters later. Al Simmons was coaching at third base; he was the assistant manager, Mack delegated most of the authority to him.

"Simmons said to White, 'Where are you going?' and White told him. Simmons said, 'You're not running, you're going to bat for the pitcher.' And he told Mr. Mack they needed White as a pinch hitter. Mr. Mack said, 'My goodness, yes.' That was about the strongest language he used—'my goodness.'"

Adds Kell, "He never knew anybody's name. George Case was Chase. Case was fast. He'd say, 'You gotta play Chase in close.' I once had a list of ten names that he'd never had exactly right. And these were old-timers."

The 1944 season was not a very good one for Leo Durocher either.

Connie Mack imparts some wisdom to 1944 pitching staff.

With only Dixie Walker and Mickey Owen left from the starting lineup of his 1941 pennant winners, Durocher fielded a collection of youngsters, has-beens, and never-weres winding up in seventh place, forty-two games out. After one road trip on which the Dodgers lost ten games out of fourteen, Durocher thought about getting back into uniform, declaring, "I could swing with one hand and come closer to doing what ought to be done than some of these fellows. I can't possibly be any worse. He (the manager) wants to put on a hit-and-run, I'll know what to do and at least I'll get the sign. I can do better just standing out there than we've been doing." Durocher resisted the temptation, however, saving his comeback for the following season, when he played two games, then went back to the bench with a charley horse.

Whether they could figure out a sign or not, nine somebodies had to be out on the field every day. In the minors at least, the somebody might be almost anyone. The Salem (Oregon) Senators of the Western International League sought to borrow the state penitentiary team's star hurler, suggesting he be accompanied to the ballpark by a guard when his pitching turn was due and then return to his cell after the game. Governor Charles Sprague gave the Senators a polite no on behalf of the inmate, who was the property of the state of Oregon because he happened to have killed a policeman.

Although the big league clubs did not resort to such extremes, they were quite resourceful. Many ballplayers with dependency deferments remained in baseball uniforms through the first year or two of the war. But by the last two wartime seasons, the rosters were stocked largely with kids not ready for the draft, oldsters whom the Army and Navy could do without and, especially important, the 4Fs–men physically unfit for military service, but not so lame they couldn't play ball against others equally indisposed. There would be a smattering of part-timers, men available for night and weekend play while retaining deferments by working in defense plants on weekdays. The Washington Senators would corner the market on Latin players who, as aliens, were unlikely draft material.

The search for young talent became Branch Rickey's pet project. While others were cutting back on their scouting staffs because of the war, Rickey increased the Dodger corps fourfold and in the summer of 1943 sent letters to twenty thousand high school coaches asking for recommendations. The man who had built baseball's mightiest farm chain in his days with the Cardinals explained, "We're engaged in the development of a vast, expansive farm system. We are building for the future and if the war is over within two years, we expect wonderful results."

Armed with letters from high school coaches touting their top prospects, Dodger scouts journeyed to spots such as Lancaster, Pennsylvania; Janesville, Wisconsin, and San Mateo, California, to inspect two thousand hopefuls in tryout camps. About four hundred were signed. Most would not begin their professional careers until the war was over, but a few youngsters briefly donning Dodger uniforms during the war days provided a preview of the "wonderful results" Rickey envisioned.

A nineteen-year-old from Indiana who had been impressive at a tryout session was invited to Ebbets Field in late August 1943 and took some good cuts during practice batting. "This boy looks like a belter," concluded the *New York Herald Tribune*. The lad would get into one game at third base, striking out twice and drawing a walk, and then joined the Marines. In 1947, Gil Hodges would be back.

Three dozen tryout camp products who had not yet entered the armed forces were invited to the Dodgers' 1944 Bear Mountain sessions. Leroy Jarvis, a teenage catcher, had to return home soon for a tonsillectomy. A more auspicious debut was made by a California youngster who, put into the Dodger lineup for a game against the U.S. Military Academy, belted a three-run homer. The seventeen-year-old would be sent to the minors at the end of training camp, but when the war was over, more would be heard from the bat of Duke Snider.

At times it seemed the Dodgers were running a boys' camp at Bear Mountain instead of a major league training operation. Two evenings a week, traveling secretary Harold Parrott gave the youngsters fifty cents apiece and sent them off in a bus to see movies in the nearby town of Newburgh. The stipend was not, however, sufficient to cover all the needs of Donald Runge, a sixteen-year-old outfielder from Fort Wayne, Indiana. "Don't we get money for candy?" he asked Parrott.

When the team broke camp, most the the kids were placed in the custody of Jake Pitler, the manager of the Dodgers' Piedmont League farm club at Newport News, Virginia. Pitler would describe himself later as having been a "glorified babysitter," recalling, "When we took off in a bus on a road trip we were loaded with comic books and candy bars, but we carried practically no shaving cream."

Dealing with teenage tantrums was part of the job. One day a Pitler neophyte kicked a water bucket in a rage at being given the take sign. When the manager imposed a fine for his behavior, the boy wired the Dodger club with a plea to be sent elsewhere.

Eight of Pitler's prodigies would reach the major leagues. As first base coach for the great Dodger teams of the postwar era, he would be reunited with the bucket-kicking Duke Snider and fellow Newport News alumni Clem Labine and Tommy Brown.

While it turned out he would not be among the most talented of the youngsters, Tommy Brown took honors for precociousness, being summoned by the Dodgers after only three months at Newport News. Brown originally had been spotted by Brooklyn scouts only a few blocks from Ebbets Field, playing in the Parade Grounds league, a source of young talent whose most illustrious graduate was Hall of Fame pitcher Waite Hoyt. Brought up in late July 1944 as one of the Dodgers' numerous experiments in filling the gap left by Pee Wee Reese's entrance into the Navy, the Brooklyn boy made his shortstop debut at the age of sixteen years and seven months.

Brown got into forty-six games, but found the pitching too tough, batting only .164. The following season, appearing in fifty-seven games, he brought his average up to .245 and hit two home runs. His tender years, however, precluded the customary reward for batting prowess from the Dodgers' radio sponsor, Old Gold cigarettes.

Red Barber remembers, "We called homers 'Old Goldies.' We'd roll a carton of Old Golds down the screen whenever any ballplayer hit a home run. There was a hole in the screen and the batboy grabbed them for the player. When Tommy Brown hit one, Durocher said, 'Give me the cigarettes, he's too young to smoke.' "

The 1943 club for which Gil Hodges played one game also had an eighteen-year-old pitcher signed out of an Omaha, Nebraska, high school. Rex Barney hurled in nine games that year, compiling a 2–2 record. The young right-hander showed a blazing fast ball, but for every man he struck out, two would draw walks. Barney was in the Army by 1944. Returning to the Dodgers after the war, he enjoyed one outstanding season, but was deprived of stardom by control problems.

The 1944 Brooklyn ball club was hardly lacking in young pitchers. Though Barney was gone, teenagers Ralph Branca, Clyde King, and Cal McLish were on the mound. Branca was signed off the New York University campus while King came from the University of North Carolina. McLish had starred for an Oklahoma City American Legion team. Their wartime success was limited, but all would prove of major league caliber when they grew up. Then there was seventeen-year-old Charlie Osgood, who pitched in one game and was never heard from again. Osgood had been signed by veteran Dodger scout Clyde Suke-forth—his uncle.

Barely Tommy Brown's seniors in the infield were Eddie Miksis and Gene Mauch.

Miksis, whose experience at age seventeen consisted of playing for a Burlington, New Jersey, high school squad, saw action during the 1944 season at third base and shortstop. Although seldom a regular, he would remain in the majors for fourteen seasons.

Mauch was president of the student body at a Fremont, California, high school when he signed a professional contract. Envisioning him as a leader of the Dodger infield as well, Leo Durocher gave the eighteen-year-old first crack at the '44 shortstop job. By way of initial impressions, the youngster broke his manager's thumb. Putting himself in at second base for an exhibition game against the Red Sox just before the season began, Durocher suffered the injury taking a toss from Mauch on a force play. The teenager stuck around for five games, then was sent to the Montreal farm club. Following the war, Mauch knocked around with a half-dozen major league teams before finding his niche as a manager.

The Phillies had a few youngsters, too. There was Rogers Hornsby McKee, a left-handed pitcher with a reputation as a prodigious milk drinker. Spotted while starring for an American Legion team in

Granny Hamner (left) with big brother Wesley. Phils were also called Blue Jays during the war, thus accounting for creature on sleeve.

Shelby, North Carolina, McKee, not quite seventeen years old, joined the Phils late in the '43 season, and pitched a five-hitter against the Pirates. He fell somewhat short, however, of the success achieved by the original Hornsby. It was to be his only major league victory.

McKee was among a number of wartime Phillie youngsters who accomplished little except for getting their names in *The Baseball Encyclopedia.* But one genuine major leaguer did emerge from the Philadelphia kiddie corps—Granville Wilbur Hamner, not to be confused with Wesley Garvin Hamner, his older brother by three years.

The Hamners had played together at Benedictine High School in Richmond, Virginia, with Granny at second base and Wes the shortstop. In 1944, Wes joined the Richmond club of the Piedmont League, playing under Ben Chapman, the old American League outfielder. Things didn't look too bright at first for Granny, who went to Brooklyn at age seventeen for a tryout with the Dodgers, failed to impress, and returned home. But Chapman, having seen Granny work out with his older brother, recommended him to Phils' general manager Herb Pennock. Granny left his summer job as a camp counselor in Maine to try out before a Phils' scout and was signed in September '44 for a $6,500 bonus. Before the season was over, the teenager had played twenty-one games at shortstop, batting .247. Wes signed with the Phillies after the season for a smaller bonus. Both brothers saw some action with the Phils in 1945, but their double-play combination was to have a short run. Though Granny went on to play in the majors for seventeen seasons, Wes's big league career didn't outlast the war.

Granny Hamner was almost a senior citizen when compared with Joe Nuxhall, discovered by the Reds while pitching in a Hamilton, Ohio, amateur league at age fourteen. A trio of Cincinnati scouts were on hand one Sunday to look at Joe's father, who played first base and pitched in the same league as his son, but on a rival team. They happened to catch a glimpse of the youngster in action and decided he was a hotter prospect. But before turning professional, Joe had some unfinished business to complete. He was also a basketball player and in prospect was a third straight conference title for his junior high school five. After leading the squad to another championship, Joe signed with the Reds in February 1944 for $175 a month plus a $500 bonus. While continuing to attend classes, he would come to Crosley Field for night games and weekend contests, sitting on the bench and soaking up baseball wisdom from his elders.

One Saturday afternoon in June, manager Bill McKechnie took a chance on the young southpaw—the Reds were behind by a mere 13–0 in the ninth inning. In came Joe from the Crosley Field bullpen

Joe Nuxhall (left) and sixteen-year-old catcher Ray McLeod look over pitching machine at Reds' 1945 Bloomington, Indiana, spring camp with a couple of venerable moundsmen, forty-three-year-old Guy Bush (foreground) and forty-six-year-old Hod Lisenbee.

to face a Cardinal team en route to its third straight pennant. The result was about as expected. Before being mercifully yanked by Mc-Kechnie, the nervous youngster gave up two singles along with five walks and made a wild pitch, although he managed to get two men out. His earned run average at the end of the 18–0 debacle was 67.50. It was another statistic, however, that put Joe Nuxhall in the baseball trivia hall of fame—at the age of fifteen years, ten months, and eleven days, he had become the youngest big leaguer ever.

The shellacking did no permanent psychological damage. The teenager went to the minors, but returned to the Reds in 1952 at the ripe old age of twenty-three. Nuxhall would pitch in the big leagues for sixteen seasons, winning 135 games.

The youngest "man" in American League history was also a pitcher who got into his first box score during the war. Carl Scheib, a fastballing right-hander signed by the Athletics out of high school, made his debut late in the 1943 season, four months shy of his seventeenth birthday. Scheib got into fifteen games for the A's in 1944 and pitched for them briefly the following year before going into the Army. He returned to the club in 1947 and stayed around in the majors for another seven years.

Connie Mack took a skinny, 5-foot 10-inch first baseman barely past his sixteenth birthday to the Athletics' 1944 training camp.

Casimir Kwietniewski, now known as Cass Michaels, makes second base pivot in May 1945 game at Comiskey Park as Ben Steiner of the Red Sox is forced out. The umpire is Jim Boyer.

George Kell holds his arm out in describing the lad, remarking, "Scheib was a big fella, but he was about this high, it looked to me. I was always used to throwing to somebody tall. He was just a punk kid."

Earle Mack, his father's assistant, carried a work certificate for the youngster, who was known to wear a Boy Scout pin in his lapel. When training camp concluded, it was off to the Athletics' minor league club at Lancaster, Pennsylvania, and conversion into a second baseman. The switch worked. Two years after the war, Nelson Fox returned to the A's to begin a 2,663-hit, nineteen-year career.

Outbidding six other clubs, the White Sox signed a seventeen-year-old American Legion star from Detroit named Casimir Kwietniewski during the summer of 1943. The youth got into two games that season, played a bit in 1944, and was the regular shortstop in the last wartime year. But it wasn't so much his age as the dilemma surrounding the young man's name that made for good copy. Cass let it be known at the 1944 spring camp that his last name was a bit too long for his liking. But what to do? "If I cut it down to Kwiet, they'll call me quiet or quit and I don't think either of them are very good," he agonized. The youngster was taking correspondence courses that spring so he could graduate from high school, but it wasn't his only mail. A dozen letters with suggested name changes came from fans seeking to help resolve the plight.

At the end of spring training, White Sox general manager Harry Grabiner farmed the teenager out to the Little Rock club. In the following weeks, Grabiner perused box scores from the Southern Association to see how his boy was doing. Trouble was, he couldn't find any Kwietniewski—a fellow named Michaels was playing shortstop. An irritated Grabiner finally phoned the farm team to find out why the promising youngster was being benched. He then learned that Michaels was Kwietniewski. The young man had decided at last on a new name. By the time he retired, there would be twelve years of American League box scores containing Michaels instead of Kw't'ski.

For another hopeful at the White Sox's 1944 spring camp, it was a nickname that posed problems. Pitcher Al Wittmer had unfairly been dubbed "The Diaper Kid." The rookie was erroneously listed on the roster as having been born on May 1, 1927, making him not quite seventeen, but he was, in fact, a mature man of nineteen, his birthdate January 4, 1925. Wittmer was dispatched eventually to Little Rock along with Kwietniewski-Michaels, but there the similarity ended. He never made it back to the majors.

Eddie Yost, who by the end of his career seemed to have been around forever, drawing bases on balls, started out as a wartime teenager. Signed by the Senators off the Bushwicks, a well-known Brooklyn semipro team, Yost was seventeen years old when he got into his first game at Griffith Stadium one August night in 1944. Making a fine stop at third base and singling off the White Sox's Ed Lopat, he merited a good review from the *Washington Evening Star*, though sportswriter John Keller tempered his enthusiasm with a passing reference to the less than sparkling style of wartime play.

"One naturally would expect a youngster drafted from semipro ranks less than a month ago to be nervous when suddenly assigned to a job in a major league game, or what passes for a major league game these days, but if Eddie was shaky, he certainly didn't reveal it," wrote Keller.

Yost would play in the American League for eighteen seasons, mostly as a Senator, drawing 1,614 walks as his moderate claim to fame.

A pair of teenage pitchers for the wartime Tigers would also be around for quite a while. Art Houtteman, then a seventeen-year-old right-hander, and Billy Pierce, an eighteen-year-old southpaw, began their long careers with the 1945 American League pennant winners.

For those youngsters seeking advice, there would be no lack of

They're never too old or too young as far as the 1944 Dodgers are concerned. Leo Durocher welcomes his latest acquisitions, Ben Chapman and Tommy Brown.

experienced hands on the wartime clubs. When Tommy Brown arrived at Ebbets Field, he posed with another newly acquired Dodger: Ben Chapman, who was getting a new life in the majors as a pitcher at age thirty-five. Chapman was a top-notch base stealer and hitter on the Yankee teams of the early 1930s, playing in the same outfield with Babe Ruth. His big league days seemingly had come to an end in 1941 when he got into only eighty-five games with the Senators and White Sox. But he learned how to pitch while managing the minor league Richmond Colts and was summoned in August '44 by a desperate Branch Rickey. Chapman was good enough to post a 5–3 record through the end of the season on a team that, in addition to its complement of teenagers, had ten players at least thirty-five years of age, four of them past forty.

Baseball's oldsters, those pressing or already past the upper age limit for the draft — men from ages eighteen to thirty-eight could be taken—would help keep the sport alive during the war years, relying on guile to compensate for lost reflexes and aching legs.

Among the ballplayers who came out of retirement or extended their careers for just a few more years were some of the top gate attractions.

Pepper Martin had a mission to fulfill. "The Wild Hoss of the Osage," whose colorful, aggressive play personified the Gashouse Gang of the 1930s, returned to the Cardinals after three years managing in the minors because, he said, the game needed some familiar faces to retain fan interest. Reporting to the Cards' 1944 spring camp at Cairo to try a comeback at age forty, Martin told newsmen he was engaged "in serious business right now." There would be no time for the postgame hijinks of years past, which had ranged from racing midget autos to dropping water bags out of hotel windows.

"I don't want to give the impression of being a character," Martin said, portraying himself as "holding down the fort for the ballplayers who are soldiers so that when they come home the game will be alive and they can practically pick up where they left off."

Teammate Danny Litwhiler says Martin was as good as his word:

"He was a fine man on the ball club. He didn't go through any antics. He filled in, did a lot of pinch hitting and pinch running. He was one of those guys who was always in perfect health, in perfect condition. We had trunks that were three feet high and about three feet wide. He would jump over them without a run. Just to show what he could do."

Martin didn't fare badly, batting .279 in forty games. He then called it quits to manage at San Diego.

A still spry Pepper Martin, back with the Cardinals at age forty.

Slugging great Jimmie Foxx came out of retirement twice, convinced he could hit wartime pitching, and ended up as a pitcher himself. Foxx had announced he was packing it in after a disappointing 1942 season that saw him released by the Red Sox after thirty games and then picked up by the Cubs, to hit only a puny .205.

He stayed out of baseball in 1943, but got the urge to try it again and rejoined the Chicago club in '44. The comeback was short-lived, amounting to twenty times at bat with one hit to show for his efforts. In August, Foxx took a job as manager of the Portsmouth, Virginia, team in the Piedmont League.

Come 1945, there was another, more successful comeback at age thirty-seven, this time with the Phillies. Though plagued by bursitis, Foxx showed a flash of his glory days in spring training, belting a 405-foot pinch homer off the upper left-field tier at Shibe Park in a game against the Athletics. He would hit 7 more home runs during the season, bringing his lifetime total to 534. For most of the year, Foxx alternated among his accustomed first base position, third base and a pinch-hitting role, winding up with a .268 average. In a final flourish to his twenty-year career, he turned to the pitching mound late in the season.

Making his first start on August 19, relying on a fastball and screwball, he went six and two-thirds innings and was credited with a 4–2 victory over the Reds. A milestone achieved by the Phillies that day illustrated their desperate straits: Foxx's effort provided the team with its first three-game winning streak of the season. In all, Foxx made nine pitching appearances, turning in an impressive 1.59 earned run average in twenty-three innings.

Foxx was the most distinguished, but hardly the only old-timer on the 1945 Phils; eleven others admitted to at least thirty-five years of age. Gus Mancuso, concluding his seventeenth and last big league season two months shy of his fortieth birthday, was behind the plate for seventy games. John Drebinger of the *New York Times,* covering a game between the Phils and Giants at which clothing was collected from the fans for Europe's war victims, couldn't resist writing, "It was old clothes day at the Polo Grounds yesterday and what with the venerable Jimmie Foxx on third and the even more ancient Gus Mancuso behind the plate, it looked for a few moments as though some of the stuff the folks were leaving at the gate for admission had found its way onto the playing field."

The 1945 club managed to drop 108 games without being the worst Phillie team of the war era. That honor went to the '42 aggregation, which lost 109 times. In between, the 1943 Phils suffered only 90 defeats while the '44 version lost 92 times. The Phillie ball clubs of the 1930s had not done much better, with owner Gerry Nugent, always strapped for cash, making a habit of selling off just about any player rising above mediocrity.

By the spring of 1944, management decided steps were in order to boost the morale of player and fan alike. So a contest was dreamed up to select a new name for the ball club. Perhaps the players were doing so poorly because they figured any team called Phillies was supposed to lose.

One suggestion came from Dee Moore, a former Phillie catcher

who had gone into the Marines. He wrote to offer the name "Philadelphia World's Champs," reasoning "they may get ideas."

The winning entry from among 635 proposed names came from a
Mrs. Elizabeth Crooks, who got a $100 war bond and a season's pass
for coming up with "Blue Jays."

"The Blue Jay will reflect a new team spirit. This bird's aggressive
spirit never admits defeat," she explained.

The *Philadelphia Record* hailed the name as a boon to headline
writers, noting that with the Athletics also tail-enders, the day's results
could be captured with a simple "A's, J's Bow."

Considerably less enthusiastic was Johns Hopkins University in
Baltimore, whose teams had long been called the Blue Jays. The
student body passed a resolution denouncing the Philadelphia club
for "a reprehensible act which brought disgrace and dishonor to the

*Herb Pennock, general manager of the Phillies and/or Blue Jays, presents war
bond to contest winner Mrs. Elizabeth Crooks.*

good name of the Johns Hopkins University." G. Wilson Shaffer, the school's athletic director, suggested that to avoid plagiarism, the Phils call themselves the Philadelphia Cyanocittea Cristatae instead—employing the bird's zoological name. The university worried itself needlessly. Blue Jays was used interchangeably with Phillies in the newspapers, but never really caught on.

One of the most popular wartime reincarnations involved a man whose name was synonymous with another inept, but considerably more lovable collection—the Brooklyn teams of the 1920s, fondly known as the Daffiness Boys. Immortalized for his starring role in the "three men on a base" fiasco with Wilbert "Uncle Robbie" Robinson's 1926 club and always a good source of copy for sportswriters, Babe Herman would be a natural for bringing the fans out to Ebbets Field in the waning days of the war.

Herman had last worn a Dodger uniform in 1931, moving on to the Reds after that season and later appearing with the Cubs, Pirates, and Tigers. He had seemingly concluded his major league career in 1937, then went on to play for the Hollywood club of the Pacific Coast League while tending to his Glendale, California, ranch. At the end of the 1944 season, hobbled by a bad knee and forty-one years old, Herman told the Hollywood club he was through.

But one day, as the 1945 season moved into July, there came a phone call. Babe Herman, still living in Glendale and a familiar face at Dodger Old-Timers' Day games, recalls how he came out of retirement for few final swings at Ebbets Field:

"Branch Rickey called Tom Downey, his Pacific Coast scout, and told him if he'd give him a left-handed and a right-handed pinch hitter, the ball club could be up in the pennant race a little while. And Tom said, 'Babe Herman's the best hitter out here that I know of.' So Tom called me and asked if I'd consider going back.

"I had quit playing ball, retired the end of '44. I was up at the ranch; I had an orange grove up there and a house. On the back part I had five thousand turkeys, which I had a hired man running. But I thought maybe I would just like to try it one year and see how it went. I said I've gotta find out if Rick, my hired man, would take charge of the ranch. So I called him and he said, 'Sure, go on tomorrow if you want,' and he took charge until we marketed the birds."

Wartime travel conditions made getting from the West Coast to Brooklyn easier said than done.

"You were knocked off planes then," Herman continues. "They assured me of a seat until Fort Worth. From there I'd have to go to a ticket agent and find out when I could continue the flight. I got a plane ride to Fort Worth. There I met Roxy Middleton. He was an old Coast League ballplayer when I was a kid and I knew Roxy pretty well. I told him I'm trying to get to New York. Around Fort Worth there were some camps. He said, 'Well, wait a minute' and he went and got his kid, who was a colonel in the Air Force, and he went and talked to somebody and the guy said, 'Well, take a walk for a while, come back in a half-hour.' I did and they put me on a plane and I got to Washington, then I took the train to New York.

"So anyway, I finally got there. They were gonna give me two weeks to get in shape; I hadn't seen a ball since the past September. But Durocher wanted to know if I could hit and I said, 'Sure, I'll go up.'"

After only three days of batting practice, tape wound around blistered hands, Babe stepped into the batter's box to pinch hit for Eddie Stanky in the first game of a July 8 Sunday doubleheader against the Cardinals. Wild cheers from the crowd of 36,053 drowned out the announcement of his name. It was the seventh inning, the pitcher was Red Barrett and Luis Olmo was on third base.

"It was nice. I went up and got a big hand," Herman remembers. "The first ball I swung at, I cracked the bat. I went back and got the other bat, and the next ball I got a hit to right."

Babe climaxed his reappearance by providing the fans with a reminder of the base-running foul-ups of Uncle Robbie's days. He fell down rounding the first base bag.

Herman wryly recalls another pinch hit he got at Ebbets Field:

"I went up and hit with three men on. I hit it about six inches from the top of the screen. The ball came right back to the right fielder's hands so I only got a single out it, but I drove in two runs. I was hitting for Tom Brown; they'd just brought him in from St. Paul.

"Durocher gave me a runner and I went back to the bench. When I got there, Tom said to me, 'Babe, when did you start playing for Brooklyn?' and I said, '1926, Tom' and he said, 'Gee, that's about two years before I was born.' So I said, 'Well, then, I think I'd better quit.' But I went on and finished the season."

The year actually ended a bit early for Herman, who fell victim to an overeager catcher hurling batting practice.

"I had torn cartilage in my knee. I'd been playing with it taped and a steel brace on it the last two years in Hollywood," Herman says. "In Chicago, about a week before the season ended, one of our catchers, I think his name was Peacock [Johnny Peacock], was trying to put a little extra on the ball and he wound up hitting me right in the bad knee. I got one leg out of the way, but I couldn't get the other one out.

"They taped it up real tight, but the trainer said I wouldn't be able to move on that knee very much so Branch Rickey said, 'You want to go home, Babe, go ahead, and if you want to stay here, stay here.' I stayed till the end of the season, but I didn't get into uniform that last week.

"It was kind of different from Robbie's day, but I enjoyed it. Just to get back and see a lot of old friends in Brooklyn, it was great. I took the kids and the wife and we all had kind of a reunion."

Babe did all right for a forty-two-year-old with a gimpy knee who hadn't played in almost a year, hitting a home run and batting .265 on nine hits in thirty-four trips to the plate. After the 1945 season, it was back to the ranch and a scouting job with the Pirates.

Was he surprised at his performance?

Babe Herman with Uncle Robbie in 1931.

Young admirer welcomes Babe Herman back to the Dodgers.

"Even in these old-timers' games, I'm able to hit the ball pretty good," Herman says. "I've always been able to hit."

The 1944 Dodgers provided a reunion, however brief, for baseball's greatest brother act.

As the game entered its last peacetime season, Paul "Big Poison" Waner and his brother, Lloyd "Little Poison," found themselves gone from the Pirates after fourteen years of banging out base hit after base hit. Paul was sent to the Dodgers before the 1941 season began and Lloyd was traded that May to the Braves, their careers apparently close to an end. But with the coming of the war, the brothers would creak their way through a few more seasons with a succession of clubs.

After playing with Brooklyn briefly, Paul finished out 1941 with the Braves and was in Boston again the following campaign. Recalling many years later how getting through a game in his last few seasons could be agony, Paul told of one afternoon in 1942 when he had been pressed into service in center field because of a rash of injuries. A triple was smashed to right center and he chased it down. The next batter hit a three-bagger to left center and he chugged after that one.

Then came a blooper he dove for but couldn't reach. The ball plopped to a stop, but "I just lay there. I couldn't get up to reach that ball to save my life."

Still, there were some hits left in him and as one of the game's great students of batting, Paul also served as an unofficial coach.

Tommy Holmes, remembering his days as a young ballplayer with the Braves, says, "I would not have been as successful as I was if it had not been for Paul Waner. Casey Stengel saw to it that Paul Waner taught me what to do with the ball. He made me a smarter hitter. You see, I was always swinging at the first pitch if it would be a strike. He told me that the first ball had to be where I wanted it or don't swing. He taught me how to look for a pitch, how to set up a pitcher. You know, he said the ball looked like a grapefruit to him. He was the master of the bat."

After the Braves, it was back to the Dodgers for the elder Waner. Playing in about half their 1943 games, he hit for a .311 average at age forty. Paul spent most of 1944 as a part-timer with the Dodgers before going over the Yankees. There was a single trip to the plate as a pinch hitter early in the 1945 season—he walked—and then his release from the Yanks and the end of a twenty-year career that had produced 3,152 hits.

When his playing days were over, "Big Poison" served as a batting instructor, first with the Cardinals and later for the Phils, for whom he was working when he died in 1965.

Lloyd Waner, Paul's junior by three years and 693 base hits, lives in Oklahoma City, not far from the brothers' birthplace of Harrah, Oklahoma, and keeps active during his retirement years by playing golf. The day he took time to reflect on the war era, the seventy-three-year-old Waner was looking forward to a seniors' golf tournament.

"If I shoot around ninety-five I'm happy. The fact is, though, I'm happy just to play. Your muscles don't react like they used to," he chuckled.

After getting into three games for the 1941 Pirates, Lloyd, like his brother before him, was let go, traded to the Braves for pitcher Nick Strincevich.

"I pretty near quit baseball right there," he says, "but then I decided I'd go on to Boston because Casey Stengel was the manager and I thought a lot of him."

His stay with the Braves was a short one. Lloyd moved on to the Reds before the year was over and then it was off to the Phillies for the 1942 season. He batted .261 with Philadelphia, fifty-five points below what would be his lifetime average, then was traded in March '43 to the Dodgers along with Al Glossop for Babe Dahlgren.

Lloyd did not, however, report to Brooklyn, obtaining a war-related job instead. The alternative would have been a call to military service at age thirty-seven.

"They told me, the draft board, that I'd have to work in a government defense business, I couldn't play baseball," he explains. "Here in Oklahoma City they had Douglas aircraft. I started with Douglas and worked there, I guess, about six months or more and then I transferred to Will Rogers Army Air Base."

Working as a fireman at the Oklahoma City Air Corps installation provided some moments almost as exciting as those on the baseball diamond.

"I had quite some experiences there, I got a medal here someplace for bravery," Waner says. "We put out a bomber that crashed. He'd come in about a mile short of the field. It was on instruments on a bad night. He shouldn't have been flying. He hit a ditch, just kind of nosed into it. There were three of them in it, they jumped out and ran. When we got down there, the thing had started on fire. They had flares in there and it started throwing those out everyplace. We had quite a job; we were there from three o'clock in the morning till nine o'clock, putting the thing out. A couple of the boys got burned a little, be we saved part of the plane."

The baseball days were not, as it developed, at an end. By 1944, Waner no longer interested the Selective Service authorities. He was not, however, so ancient as to be overlooked by the manpower-starved Dodgers, who still held title to him from the previous year's trade.

"Branch Rickey called me just before the '44 season opened and he said he's gonna lose two or three of his outfielders to the Army. I think he mentioned Olmo and Galan. He wanted me for insurance and he wanted to know if I could get in shape," Waner recalls. "I says yeah, I thought I could, I had a little softball and a little handball and volleyball over at the fire department. So he offered me a pretty good contract and I went to Brooklyn. And Paul was there."

"We weren't reunited very long," he continues, laughing, "because Branch, before cutting down time in June, called me into his office and told me he wasn't gonna lose any of his outfielders after all so he's gonna have to release me. But he had talked to [Pirate owner William] Benswanger in Pittsburgh and he says, 'You call him and he'll take over your contract.' So I called Benswanger and he says 'come on over' so that's what I did."

Though he hadn't realized it at the time, Waner had given Rickey a farewell present. He remembers, "The last game I played, I won the game for him. Olmo was on third base, one out. They put me in to pinch hit. It was the last of the ninth and tied. We put on a squeeze play and I just bunted the ball out about halfway between the pitcher and home plate. Olmo was running when the pitch was made and he pretty near slid over me. I no more than bunted the ball and he was sliding in home. The next day Rickey called me in and told me how he was gonna have to release me."

Lloyd saw only limited action for the Pirates as he closed out his career, but the club made sure the Forbes Field fans saw his face.

Lloyd (left) and Paul Waner during their brief reunion on the 1944 Dodgers.

"The young boys were all in the Army. Everyone had a bunch of old fellas then, you know, and they had to put them in and out, shuffle them around in other words. I played with Pittsburgh through 1945 and I also coached at first base a few games, kind of changed off with Pie Traynor," he recalls.

"I enjoyed it over there, it was like being back home. I was about thirty-nine or forty; the only thing's wrong, you can't run too good. I could hit the ball as good as ever."

When the war was over, Lloyd joined Paul in retirement, scouting for the Pirates in the Midwest for a couple of years and then going to work as a clerk in the Oklahoma City street maintenance department.

"I worked for the city for pretty near eighteen years and never did miss a day," he says.

Over their long careers, the Waner brothers amassed a total of 5,611 hits. They were not, however, dubbed "Big Poison" and "Little Poison" (both were about 5-feet 9-inches and 150 pounds) because of their toxicity to pitchers. The nicknames derived, rather, from a perversion of English by a New York fan. Lloyd Waner tells the story:

"It was in the Polo Grounds back in 1927. We were hittin' pretty good, Paul led the league and I had .350 or something like that (Paul Waner batted .380 that year, Lloyd a mere .355) and we hit extra good in the Polo Grounds. We were playing a doubleheader and it happened to be that a fella, a big, heavy-set Italian in the bleachers, was always hollerin', you could hear him all over the park. And he'd begin to holler at Paul and I and he called us 'big and little poison.' He meant persons, you know, but it was his slang. The way he hollered it, it sounded like he was saying big and little poison. It just happened that Paul and I, we beat the Giants a couple of games, I think we got fifteen hits in the doubleheader. It came out in the papers that Big and Little Poison beat the Giants twice.

"I never will forget the old boy. Paul and I got him a baseball, got it all signed up for him, and he was as happy as he could be. He says, 'I'm for the Giants, but as long as you boys come to town, I'm goin' to pull for you all, too.' Every time we went to the Polo Grounds, he'd start hollerin' for us, 'There go big and little poison.' We'd wave at him. He was a character, Paul and I had fun with him."

The manpower crisis, while driving managers to distraction, might also drive them right off the bench and back to the playing field. A couple of over-the-hill shortstops named Leo Durocher and Joe Cronin decided they couldn't do much worse than some of the so-called ballplayers in their lineups.

Durocher had played in only eighteen games for the 1941 pennant-winning Dodgers, happy to give way to young Pee Wee Reese. The manager stayed on the bench for all of the 1942 season, his playing career apparently at an end. But the following year, Reese was in the Navy and so Durocher tried a comeback, moving into the lineup in June while approaching age thirty-eight. He lasted a total of six games before retreating to the dugout. Arky Vaughan, alternating between third base and shortstop, with a supporting case, in alphabetical order, of Red Barkley, Boyd Bartley, Bobby Bragan, Al Glossop, Bill Hart, and—for one game—Mickey Owen, would have to do.

When Billy Herman followed Reese into the Navy before the 1944 season, Durocher gave some thought to playing second base, but dispensed with the notion when his thumb was broken by Gene Mauch's exhibition game toss. By now, Arky Vaughan was also gone, having retired to his California ranch. Eddie Stanky was obtained from the Cubs about halfway through the season to play second. Otherwise, an endless stream of infielders were in and out of the lineup with less than scintillating results.

As the Dodgers opened their 1945 spring training camp, Branch Rickey, never known as an easy man with a buck, promised Durocher an extra $1,000 if he would play the first fifteen games of the season, declaring, "Leo, if he knuckles down and gets in shape, would still be our best shortstop."

Durocher had been a slick fielder with the Reds and Cardinals in the 1930s, but by the final wartime season he was turning forty. Nonetheless, he gave it another try, opening at second base as a fill-in for Stanky, who was recovering from pneumonia. The comeback didn't last very long. The manager took himself out of the season's inaugural after a few innings, complaining of leg cramps. He was back again the next day, but again could not go a full nine innings. And that was it for Leo Durocher the ballplayer. (Later, Leo said he would not have taken the $1,000 even if he got through the stipulated fifteen games.) Stanky moved in as the regular second baseman while Eddie Basinski, a professional violinist in the off-season, fiddled around at shortstop.

Still a regular in his sixteenth season, Joe Cronin had batted .311 for the 1941 Red Sox, but by Pearl Harbor Day he was thirty-five years old. The first wartime season saw the shortstop job taken over by rookie Johnny Pesky, who went on to hit .331. Getting into only forty-five games that year, Cronin seemingly had come to the end of his playing days. But Pesky, like Reese, was in Navy blue when the 1943 season arrived and so Cronin, like Durocher, tried to fill in a bit.

The Red Sox manager had a few moments of glory, hitting five pinch homers in '43, three of them in one series with the Athletics. The following year he played some first base. Overweight and slow, his reflexes gone, Cronin was ready to give it another try in 1945, hoping to take up the slack left by third baseman Jim Tabor's departure for military service. But in his third game, Cronin broke his right leg sliding into second base at Yankee Stadium. His twenty-year playing career was over.

By the '45 season, all the ball clubs were counting on old men—by baseball reckoning—along with 4Fs.

The Detroit Tigers won the AL pennant and World Series with a double-play combination comprised of two 35-year-olds, Eddie Mayo on second and Skeeter Webb (manager Steve O'Neill's son-in-law) at shortstop. The thirty-six-year-old Paul Richards did much of the catching while Roger "Doc" Cramer played regularly in the outfield at what the record book said was age forty (he claimed to be forty-three). Hank Greenberg, who returned from the Army in July and proceeded to hit .311, was a mere thirty-four.

The Tiger–Cub World Series had some moments of high comedy in which the baseball graybeards figured prominently.

Cramer provided the following explanation as to why he and Roy Cullenbine had allowed a routine fly ball hit by Phil Cavarretta to drop between them in the ninth inning of the fifth game:

"I could have caught the ball, but Cullenbine kept shouting 'all right, all right.' When I heard this I stopped and then to my surprise, the ball plopped to the ground. I asked Cullenbine why he didn't make the catch and he told me, 'When I called all right, all right, I meant all right, you catch it.'"

The Tigers won the game anyway, 8–4, but lost a chance to wrap up the Series the next day thanks to a baserunning gaffe by another oldster.

Cramer cracked a single to left field in the seventh inning of game six with pinch-runner Chuck Hostetler on second base. As Hostetler rounded third, manager O'Neill, on the coaching lines, threw up his hands in a signal to stop. Hostetler finally did—about twenty feet down the line toward home plate, where he stumbled and fell on his face. He found himself in a rundown and was finally tagged by Cub catcher Mickey Livingston, who had taken the peg in from left fielder Peanuts Lowrey.

Virgil Trucks, who started the game and was knocked out in the fifth inning, says, "He fell down and then scrambled. He didn't know which way to go and they got him. It was a very sad occasion for him."

The Cubs won the ballgame, 8–7, on a twelfth-inning two-base drive by Stan Hack that skipped past Hank Greenberg in left field. The official scorer initially gave Hack a single and charged Greenberg with an error but later changed his mind and awarded the Cub batter a double.

The 1945 season was Hostetler's second (and last) in the big leagues, but he could have hardly pleaded inexperience as an excuse for his basepath blunder—he was forty-two years old. Hostetler had knocked around in the minors for many years, managing to join the Braves for a 1928 road trip although he didn't get into a game, and finally retired. He was working in a Boeing plant in Wichita, Kansas, when, while playing semipro ball, he was spotted by former Tiger pitcher Red Phillips. Phillips recommended him to the Detroit club, and in view of the manpower squeeze, the old-timer was invited to the 1944 spring camp at Evansville. He caught on as a spare outfielder.

The war era provided a shot at the big time for many a ballplayer who, like Hostetler, had spent long years in the vast minor leagues.

Buck Fausett rose from the dead to become a major league rookie at age thirty-six. In 1942, Fausett's name was placed on the list of deceased members of the Association of Professional Ball Players of America, an organization of retired athletes. He happened to be alive, however, and playing third base for the Little Rock club of the Southern Association, plugging away at a minor league career dating back to 1929. Still among the living in 1944, Fausett finally got into a big league lineup, called up by the Cincinnati Reds as a third baseman and pitcher after a .362 season at Little Rock. His career in the majors was to amount to thirteen games, after which, slugging away at an .097 clip and sporting a 5.91 earned run average, Fausett was sold to the Hollywood Stars.

When Joe McCarthy gazed out at shortstop, he saw Mike "Mollie" Milosevich instead of Phil Rizzuto. Milosevich had been a coal miner and steel mill worker as a young man, then turned to baseball, figuring it would be an easier and more lucrative way of life. Things had not quite worked out, however. In nine years with Yankee farm teams at Washington, Pennsylvania; Joplin, Missouri; Binghamton, New York, and Kansas City, Milosevich never hit .300 and not once had he been invited to a Yankee spring camp. But in 1944, the call finally came. Milosevich was to get into 124 games for the Yanks during the last two wartime seasons. When Rizzuto returned from the Navy in 1946 "Mollie," thank you, was shipped back to Kansas City.

Bill Steinecke had also paid his dues. When he opened the 1944 season as the catcher and manager for the Portsmouth, Virginia, club of the Piedmont League, it was the twenty-first minor league team for the balding thirty-seven-year-old whose career dated back to 1928. His major league experience consisted of four games with the 1931 Pirates. Then the unbelievable happened. With Rollie Hemsley (a successor to Bill Dickey, then in the Navy) entering military service himself in mid-August, the Yankees needed someone to back up Mike Garbak, their other wartime fill-in behind the plate. They reached out for none other than Bill Steinecke. Jimmie Foxx took over the Portsmouth club and Steinecke, saying he'd been "released from Sing Sing," headed for New York to don pinstripes.

"I could tell you stories of bus rides through the night, of buses stuck in the mud, of sleepless nights and doubleheaders, of night games and day games and pay days that passed without pay. But the big thing is this: Here I am with the Yankees and the good hotels and the kids want my autograph," he exclaimed.

The dream, unfortunately, was not quite fulfilled—Steinecke never got into a ball game for the Yanks.

Ray Prim, who had pitched in the mid-1930s for the Senators and Phillies with but a 3–7 record to show for his exertions, was recalled to the majors by the wartime Cubs. Dubbed "Pop" because of his silver hair, the thirty-eight-year-old won thirteen games for the 1945 NL pennant winners.

Then there was the Hawaiian-born Hank "Prince" Oana, who may or may not have been of royal blood. Oana broke into pro ball with the San Francisco Seals in 1929, then knocked around the minors as an outfielder for the next thirteen seasons, his only taste of big league competition a six-game stint with the 1934 Phillies. His fortunes began to change in 1942 when he was converted into a pitcher and compiled a 16–5 record for Fort Worth of the Texas League. In June '43, Oana joined the Tiger staff and managed a 3–2 mark. After going back to the minors, he was recalled by Detroit to do some pitching for the 1945 world champs.

What set Oana apart from the average wartime retread was his supposed royal heritage. When he arrived in Detroit, Oana denied all, saying, "When I first joined the Seals, stories were published that I was a Hawaiian prince. The more I denied them, the more people believed them. They're still untrue. I'm just plain Henry Oana; just call me Hank."

Virgil Trucks heard a different story in private.

"I really and truly believed Hank was a prince," he says. "I talked with Hank, I got to know him real well, and he said he definitely was a prince. But, you know, not like being next to a queen or a king or something like that. He wasn't that type of a prince."

Trucks adds, chuckling, "He was just, you'd say, probably a minor league prince."

Another pitcher with a Hawaiian connection was Sig Jakucki, given a second life in the majors by the Browns, with whom he'd had a brief fling in the mid-1930s.

Jakucki had managed to join the Army when only sixteen years old. He was stationed in Hawaii, and after his discharge, toured Japan with a baseball team from the Hawaiian islands. He subsequently pitched in the minors and was brought up by the Browns in 1936, but a 0–3 record sent him back to the minor leagues and two years later, Jakucki left organized baseball. In 1944, he was rediscovered pitching semipro ball in Texas. With wartime hitting being what it was, Jakucki finally found success, contributing a 13–9 record to St. Louis' pennant-winning miracle.

Jakucki was known as a man who didn't mind taking a drink, but in view of the war era's shortage of help, the Browns put up with him. To a point, that is. He was rolling along with a 12–10 record in 1945

Sig Jakucki (third from right) and fellow Brownie pitchers (left to right) Nelson Potter, Denny Galehouse, George Caster, Bob Muncrief, and Jack Kramer await 1944 World Series opener with Cardinals.

when the end came on a September road trip. Having shown up at St. Louis' Union Station in what management deemed less than a properly sober state, Jakucki was put off the team's Chicago-bound train in the St. Louis suburb of Delmar. The next day, however, the ball club had an unwelcome guest at Chicago's Del Prado Hotel—Jakucki had hopped a freight into town. He was denied a room and this time it was aloha for good.

Suddenly reappearing as well were men who had pitched their first major league games as far back as the 1920s.

Clay Touchstone had a modest career to look back on: a total of six games pitched for the Braves in 1928 and 1929 with no won-lost record. The sidearmer had retired in 1943 after spending seven years in the Southern Association and six seasons in the Texas League trying to get back to the majors. When the last wartime season began, he was forty-one years old and a diabetic, dependent on daily insulin injections. But one day he packed up and left his Beaumont, Texas, tavern, explaining, "I suddenly got the hankering to try it again and figured what with manpower conditions being what they are, now would be the best time for a whirl in the majors." Getting a chance with the White Sox, he made a half-dozen relief appearances.

The Cincinnati Reds, having proved in the case of Joe Nuxhall that one was never too young to join a wartime pitching staff, were also breathing some life into baseball fossils. The 1945 club had three hurlers whose major league careers dated back to the 1920s: Hod Lisenbee, age forty-six; Guy Bush, age forty-three; and Boom-Boom Beck, who was forty years old.

The Senators' Tom Zachary gained trivia immortality by yielding Babe Ruth's sixtieth home run in 1927. The pitcher responsible for serving up number 58 was Hod Lisenbee, a colleague on the Washington pitching staff. Lisenbee pitched on and off in the majors until 1936, spent a few years in the minor leagues, and then retired to his Clarksville, Tennessee, farm. In 1944, he decided to return to the game and compiled a 15–15 record with the Syracuse Chiefs of the International League. A year later he was in a Reds' uniform, getting into thirty-one games, mostly as a reliever.

Bush had been a quality pitcher, achieving a record of 176 wins and 136 losses between 1923 and 1938, most of his career having been spent with the Cubs. Like Lisenbee, Bush had retired and then worked his way back with a minor league club. After a 5–3 season in 1944, with the Chatanooga Lookouts of the Southern Association, he was obtained by the Reds for the last wartime campaign and pitched in four games.

Beck, who started out with the 1924 Browns, was not a reincarnation case, having stayed around in the majors through the war years. Boom-Boom pitched in eleven games for the 1945 Reds.

Paul Schreiber was a month shy of his forty-third birthday when summoned by the Yankees to relieve against the Tigers, resuming a major league career that had seemingly ended more than two decades before. Schreiber had hurled in ten games for the Dodgers back in 1922 and 1923, and since the mid-1930s had been the Yanks' batting practice pitcher. By the last month of the 1945 season, the New York pitching staff was so depleted that he was asked to try pitching for real again.

Presumably acting on the theory that not much more damage could be done, Joe McCarthy called on Schreiber to relieve Al Gettel one afternoon in the sixth inning of a game in which the Yankees were trailing the Tigers, 10–0. Perhaps Schreiber should have been the starting pitcher. In three and one-third innings, he gave nary a hit.

"I felt a little nervous. I had to try keeping the batters from hitting instead of giving them the kind they could hit into the grandstand," he commented afterwards.

Schreiber reverted to his batting practice form later on, yielding two runs to the Tigers in a second relief stint.

The years seemed to sit well with pitchers, their ranks even producing a grandfather—reliever Joe Heving, who stuck around with the wartime Indians and Braves. By the time Heving called it quits at age forty-four, midway through the 1945 season, his grandson was three years old.

There was no telling where a ballplayer of yesteryear might be found. Eddie Boland, who played the outfield briefly for the 1934–35 Phils, was plucked by the Senators from the ranks of the New York City Sanitation Department baseball team. Boland joined the Washington club in mid-July 1944, stayed around until his summer vacation ran out, then returned to his clerk's job in time for the sanitmen's big game with the police department. The thirty-six-year-old didn't do badly in his second life as a major leaguer, batting .271 in nineteen games.

John Miklos, a Chicago policeman, took a leave from his traffic directing duties at Monroe and Wabash streets to try out at the Cubs' 1944 spring camp. While Miklos had pitched in the minors from 1936 to 1940, his more recent baseball activity had been confined to hurling the North Side cops to victories over their South Side colleagues. He was described as having "a blazing fastball and exceptional control" but the big leagues, even in wartime, were a bit tougher than the police department circuit. The thirty-three-year-old lefty got into two games for the Cubs, amassed a 7.71 earned run average, then returned to his street corner.

Eddie Basinski, the Dodgers' sometime shortstop in 1945, was another man with a career outside of baseball. In the off-season he was a violinst with the Buffalo Philharmonic. The bespectacled Basinski, signed out of the University of Buffalo after a tryout though he hadn't played for either his high school or college teams, not only had to prove he could play major league baseball, but also encountered a tough time convincing teammates he was really a musician. Durocher wagered a suit of clothes and outfielder Morris Aderholt, a man of more modest means, put up ten dollars, challenging Basinski to show what he could do with a fiddle. He promptly sent for his violin, and prior to a July '45 game against the Cardinals, gave a dressing room concert of classical music.

The search for warm bodies to fill baseball uniforms extended at times to the nation's defense plants. A few ballplayers who had taken full-time war jobs exempting them from military service were coaxed into playing ball at night or on weekends.

Traditionalist Ed Barrow didn't think much of the idea, asserting, "A man is either a major league player or a bricklayer. Using part-timers would demean big league ball. It would give us a semipro tone."

The Browns, who in years gone by might have passed for a semi-pro outfit, had no such qualms using pitcher Denny Galehouse and outfielder Chet Laabs in part-time roles.

Galehouse, working at a Goodyear aircraft plant in Akron, Ohio, when the 1944 season opened, was a Sunday pitcher. He would take an overnight train to wherever the Browns were playing on a weekend, hurl the first game of the customary Sunday doubleheader, then return to his job. Although the right-hander pitched well, he could not get into top shape and felt he was handicapped by being unable to study the hitters on a daily basis. So when he was told he probably wouldn't be inducted immediately if he left his war job, Galehouse joined the Browns as a full-time hurler in late summer. He wound up with a 9–10 record for the '44 pennant winners. The following year, Galehouse did his pitching for the Great Lakes Naval Training Station.

Laabs was employed at a Dodge factory in Detroit at the start of the 1944 season, but later transferred to a job inspecting pipe lengths at a St. Louis war plant owned by the father-in-law of Browns' general manager Bill DeWitt. He eventually learned that the pipes had been shipped to a Tennessee facility helping to build the atomic bomb. Laabs was available for most home games and weekend trips to Cleveland, Chicago, and Detroit, but like Galehouse, eventually quit his job to concentrate on the Browns' bid for an unprecedented pennant. Although he batted only .234, it was Laabs' two home runs that powered the Browns to a 5–2 victory against the Yankees on the final day of the season, giving St. Louis the pennant by one game over Detroit.

Another part-timer was Buddy Rosar, who caught for the Indians when he wasn't working at the Whitehead aircraft plant in Cleveland.

The Senators' hunt for wartime personnel went beyond the nation's borders and into Latin America, particularly Cuba. Latin ballplayers presumably would be draft exempt because of their alien status and they might play for salaries that wouldn't make much of a dent in a ball club's pocketbook.

The man who found the Latins for Clark Griffith was a chunky, Italian-born ex–minor league owner and laundryman named Joe Cambria.

"I used to catch for Cambria's semipro team in Baltimore on Saturdays and Sundays. I got gasoline money for going over there," Calvin Griffith recalls. "Clark Griffith became acquainted with Cambria when he used to go over to see the semipro games. Cambria then became a real good friend for many years. At one time, he and Joe Engel were practically the only scouting system that the Senators had."

Preston Gomez, who was one of Cambria's prospects, tells how he operated:

"Joe was one of the first American scouts to go into Cuba, he went there in the thirties. He signed Bobby Estalella [a journeyman outfielder with the Senators, Athletics, and Browns] way before the war and then during the war days, that's when he signed a lot of Cuban players because most of the good American players were in the Army.

"He used to sign ten, fifteen, sometimes even twenty a year. The ones he thought had a chance to play in higher baseball, even to play on the major league level, he used to send to the Washington club. The other ones he'd send to various minor league clubs, his friends were always looking for ballplayers."

Gomez continues, "What Joe used to do, he normally scouted the teams that were playing in Havana. But his secret was, he had former players he knew in every town, what you'd call 'bird-dogs.' They'd contact him when they saw a young boy that looked pretty good and Joe used to go to that town. The majority of American scouts, they'd

Among Latin imports at Senators' 1945 spring camp are (left to right) infielders Armando Gallart, Angel Fleitas, and Manuel Hidalgo, pitcher Luis Arago, outfielders Augustine Delaville and Jose Redondo, and pitcher Santiago Ullrich.

only stay in Havana, but Joe traveled all over the island. He always had one fella with him, he was the guy who would kind of translate. I do feel Joe understood the Spanish language, but I don't think he spoke Spanish."

Gomez himself was signed in Havana, recalling, "He saw me playing in '43 and signed me in the spring of '44. I was playing amateur baseball. In those days I think they had twenty-two leagues and we played during the summer every Sunday."

By the late stages of the war, some fifty Cubans were playing organized baseball in the United States; about two-thirds of them belonged to the Senators' organization.

While none of the Latin players achieved star status, a number made it to the major leagues. Ten Latins got into the Senators' 1944 lineup at varying times, though the only regular was Gil Torres, a light-hitting infielder whose father, Ricardo Torres, briefly caught and played first base for Washington in the 1920s. Roberto Ortiz saw some outfield action and poked an occasional homer while Mike Guerra backed up Rick Ferrell behind the plate. Alejandro Carrasquel, a sidearming curveballer from Venezuela, won fifty games for the Senators over a seven-year stretch. Gomez was kept as infield insurance for the entire 1944 season, but appeared in only eight games.

The Senators let some of the other clubs have a Cuban player or two as well. Besides Estalella, there was Tommy de la Cruz, the Reds' spring training rhumba leader, who had a 9–9 record in 1944; Nap Reyes, an infielder for the Giants; and Rene Monteagudo of the Phillies, a sore-armed pitcher turned outfielder.

The road to the big leagues was not an easy one for newly arriving Cuban ballplayers, who were unaccustomed to the chilly weather at the northern training camps, bewildered by a strange culture, and generally unable to speak much English.

For starters, there was the trip from Havana to the Senators' College Park, Maryland, camp. Gomez recalls:

"We couldn't speak English. We all had a letter Joe Cambria wrote to us, explaining who we were and where we were supposed to go in case we got lost. They even had somebody waiting for us in Miami when we got off the plane to take us to the train station, and when we got out in Washington someone was there to bring us to College Park."

The Cuban players, particularly the youngsters, would stick together while slowly learning English and the ways of a new land.

"Most organizations today have a Spanish-speaking coach or instructor, but in those days there was nobody," Gomez says. "We went together everyplace. Fellows like Gil Torres or Mike Guerra, who had been there awhile, really helped us with English as much as they could. If we went to eat, we'd wait for them to order our food. They were more like our fathers in those days. There was a barber in Washington from Cuba. He kind of led us everyplace. And we used to go out with girls who wanted to learn Spanish and were interested in trying to help us in the English language. Going to movie houses helped. Joe Cambria always told me that the best thing you could do to learn English is to try and watch a movie.

"But it was a different culture," Gomez goes on. "We used to go to a bowling alley. We'd never seen what a bowling alley was before. We had a pitcher, Bob Ortiz's brother [Olivrio "Baby" Ortiz], he was trying to learn the game. One day he threw the bowling ball too hard, it went all across the other lanes. Those are the kind of things that happened to a bunch of boys being in a different country."

Clark Griffith figured there was one problem his Cuban players would not have to deal with—the draft. In May '44, the selective service system granted the Cubans the status of nonresident aliens, allowing them to remain in the country on six-month visas, immune from serving in the armed forces. But on July 13 the picture changed. The Latins were suddenly declared to be resident aliens subject to the draft and were told to register for military service or leave the country.

Gomez, then twenty-one years old and single, decided to stay with the Senators and take his chances with the draft, but three older Cuban teammates, Torres, Guerra, and Ortiz, all of whom were married, packed up and returned to Havana.

Torres, who had a young son, said he was going back to Cuba because of family pressures, telling reporters, "It's no easy decision for me to make. I've worked eight years to get up to the majors and I certainly don't want to get out of the game now. I realize that if I quit and go home rather than register for the draft, I'll never be able to come back here to play ball. The public would want nothing of me under such circumstances."

The Cuban public, it turned out, wasn't overjoyed either at the trio's departure and gave the ballplayers a hostile reception upon their return home. Within three weeks the Cubans had a change of heart, went back to the United States, rejoined the Senators, and registered for the draft. As it developed, none of the three was ever called for military service.

"They were concerned about their families," Gomez says. "The first thing in their mind was 'oh my God, they're gonna send us overseas.' Some of the people connected with the Cuban consulate tried to explain to them that nothing's going to happen in case they will go into the service. They'd be going to several camps and by time they were ready to go overseas, the war was going to be over. But they panicked. When they got to Havana they were criticized by the people and the news media and they just came back."

Gomez continues: "I was single and I said to myself, if I'm here in this country and they give me the opportunity to work and they are in the war [though formally a belligerent against the Axis, Cuba did not send troops overseas], I am going to register. I could have done exactly as the others did, but to me it wasn't right. This is the way I felt personally. I had letters from fans that sympathized with me and congratulated me for my action. I thought I was going to go into the Navy. I passed my examination, but they didn't call me."

Had Gomez entered the armed forces, the blow to his finances would have been considerably lighter than that hitting most big league ballplayers.

"I was signed to a Chatanooga contract for four hundred dollars a month," he recalls. "But during spring training, the Senators decided to keep me and gave me a major league contract. They gave me two hundred dollars more. For six months, I'd get thirty-six hundred. They didn't pay that much in those days."

While Pepper Martin no longer had any use for foolishness, the war years were a perfect time for the eccentric. Desperate for manpower, management could not snub a likely looking candidate just because he wanted to have a little fun.

And so the Giants would put up with the antics of a Danny Gardella. A New York boy with some experience in the low minors, Gardella was playing the outfield for a Bronx shipyard club when he came to the attention of the Giants in 1944. The competition being what it was, he made the team.

To begin with, Gardella's outfield play left him anything but anonymous. Teammate Johnny Rucker was kind enough to show him how to tap the visor of his cap so the sunglasses would fall into place. But early in the '44 season, disaster struck. When Cub pitcher Hank Wyse lifted a simple fly ball, Gardella tapped for the sunglasses as instructed. Instead of the glasses, his baseball cap wound up squarely over his eyes.

Danny's off-the-field activities were even more delightful for the sportswriters.

His entanglement in a locker room with a piece of equipment belonging to Rucker nearly led to consequences more deadly than being conked on the head with a fly ball. Phil Weintraub recalls:

"Rucker, who had a bad back, used a contraption in the clubhouse where he'd stretch himself every day, hang by his neck and stretch the muscles. It was like a loop—you put your neck in there—and of course it had a pad to keep the rope from burning. It was designed for Johnny, who was quite tall. Danny Gardella came along one day and being a lot shorter [Gardella was 5-foot 7-inches compared to Rucker's 6-foot 2-inches] he jumped up to try it. The first thing you know, he started to hang and before we turned around he was getting blue. I remember Danny's expression, the guy actually started to turn blue. If we hadn't been around, he might have hanged himself."

On his first road trip, Gardella crashed a high school prom at a Pittsburgh hotel, made friends with the orchestra, and persuaded it to accompany him for a solo rendition of "Indian Love Call." He was

Danny Gardella (right) with his brother Al, a reserve first baseman.

said to have terrified a hotel maid on V-E Day by donning a false mustache, combing a lock over one eye, and bellowing that Hitler was not dead after all.

Danny's greatest moment came at the expense of his roommate, infielder Nap Reyes. The setting was twenty floors above the streets of downtown St. Louis. Weintraub tells what happened:

"Danny was hell on wheels. He used to pull a lot of things and Nap Reyes was his foil. Danny kept saying 'things aren't going so well, I don't know, I may commit suicide,' he kept building it up. Well, Danny was an early riser and Nap slept a little later. Finally, one morning at the Chase Hotel, Nap's in bed and Danny opened the window and yelled at Nap 'here I go' and 'goodbye' and all this and that. Nap jumped up and couldn't find him. Then Nap went to the window and looked out and there was Danny looking up at him. He'd gone out of the window, but was hanging by his fingertips.

"Danny was very popular with the players, but he came into disfavor with Mel Ott. They never did get along too well," says Weintraub. "I knew Mel as a player before he was a manager. He was a great guy, but it seems from the time he got to be a manager, he changed completely. He did not have the same sense of humor, he couldn't see a lot of these shenanigans."

Gardella played fairly regularly in the 1945 Giant outfield, hitting eighteen homers and batting .272. But when the old cast returned from the war in the spring of '46, Ott got rid of him.

Few wartime ballplayers had more written about them than irrepressible Lou "The Mad Russian" Novikoff.

Novikoff seemed destined for stardom, having won batting titles in four minor leagues—the Pacific Coast League, American Association, Texas League, and Three-I League—his lowest average .363. But in four trials with the Cubs in the early 1940s, although hitting for a respectable average, he could never approach his prowess of minor league days.

There was, of course, an explanation. Novikoff once complained,

"The Mad Russian"—Lou Novikoff.

"I can't play in Wrigley Field because the left-field foul line isn't straight like in other parks, it's crooked."

For every run batted in, he might let another score with his butchery of balls hit to left field. Novikoff had a fear of approaching the ivy-covered walls in Wrigley Field, leading Charlie Grimm to suspect he viewed them as a source of hay fever or perhaps poison ivy. One day Grimm ripped out some vines, rubbed them on his face and hands in the outfielder's presence, and even chewed a few to show they were harmless. But it didn't seem to make an impression.

Novikoff didn't have much use for curfews, loved to sing and play the harmonica whenever there was an audience, and earned a reputation for being able to bolt down huge quantities of food and beer.

Len Merullo remembers his popular teammate:

"He had a nice family, a wife and a couple of daughters, and he was not a hard drinker, but he loved to have as much beer as he could get in him and really enjoyed being around a crowd. He had that big moon face and a big smile, just a very likeable type of guy. He'd tell you stories, he'd lie like hell. You knew he was lying, but he was entertaining.

"People just loved to be around Louie Novikoff and he loved to be around them. He had a good voice and loved to sing and imitate people, loved to entertain. They had radio stations going all the time, broadcasting from taverns, nightclubs, the little local places. I remember turning on the radio at night and there would be Louie. He'd be introduced as somebody else, but we knew who he was. As soon as he saw that mike, he'd be up there."

Novikoff's quest for a good time couldn't quite reconcile itself with playing day baseball at Wrigley Field. Merullo continues:

"He was a natural hitter, a great hitter. Small hands, small feet and he'd have that big, heavy bat in his hands and boy, he could tomahawk the ball. But he wasn't getting his sleep. In the minor leagues, you're playing all night baseball. He could sleep all day and get out to the ballpark. In Wrigley Field, unfortunately we never had lights. Most of the time you'd be away from the ballpark before four-thirty. Louie would get a head start and he'd be up all night. Louie was as good a hitter as there was around in those days, but never in the condition they hoped he would stay in."

The war era's manpower shortage provided a legacy for the statistically minded. With no one worth mentioning to come to his rescue, Frank Hayes caught 312 consecutive games for the Browns, Athletics, and Indians, starting his streak on the final day of the 1943 season and carrying it into April 1946. Reds' catcher Ray Mueller had a consecutive game streak of 217 upon entering the Army in 1945. When the backstop returned in '46, Ford Frick ruled the streak was intact since he had been serving a worthy cause. But it was to last only sixteen more games before Ray Lamanno, also a service returnee, got into the lineup again.

On the negative side, Yankee third baseman Oscar Grimes and Athletics' shortstop Edgar Busch—both highly qualified for the appellation "wartime ballplayer"—each committed three errors in one inning during 1944 games.

They were outdone by Len Merullo, who was charged with four

Connie Mack wasn't really putting himself back into the lineup, but manpower shortages were severe enough so Frank Hayes (shown crouching) could be pressed into catching 312 consecutive games.

Len Merullo and "Boots," four years later.

errors in the second inning of a doubleheader finale at Braves Field on September 13, 1942. Merullo, at least, had an excuse. Early that morning, seven-pound twelve-ounce Leonard Merullo, Jr., had arrived. Observing "they remember me for something," the elder Merullo doesn't mind talking about his exploits that day.

"I'd been with the Cubs down in New York, playing at the Polo Grounds, and we were expecting our first," he recalls. "My wife, who was in Boston, our hometown, had a false alarm. They let me go home on an earlier train rather than waiting for the club train. Just as I got home she started getting the pains again. The baby was born in the morning and I went back to the club. Naturally, you're not as sharp as you should be, but still you should be all excited and have a pretty good day. I did just the opposite.

"Afterward a headline came out: 'BOOTS' IS BORN, MERULLO BOOTS FOUR."

"They pinned that nickname on him, which was very appropriate. My son is now thirty-six years old and they still call him Boots."

7

The 4Fs: Warriors on the Diamond

Testing himself against Mister Robot, the new pitching machine, the batter was annoyed.

"I simply have to have a pitcher's arm to follow and that thing hasn't any," the slender, twenty-eight-year-old hopeful complained after taking his cuts in the cage at the St. Louis Browns' Cape Girardeau spring camp.

An odd statement, considering the right sleeve of the hitter's uniform was empty. The man was Pete Gray, one-armed outfielder, variously described as amazing, courageous, and an inspiration, and so obviously the symbol of wartime baseball.

Ballplayers supporting a family might receive deferments in the early years of the war, but by the end of 1944 only eighty thousand men remained excused from the draft because they were fathers. Kids and oldsters, part-timers and aliens could fill some of the gaps in the major league rosters. The major burden of keeping baseball alive, however, fell upon those sound enough to hit, run, and throw but physically unfit for military service. Gray and his less publicized counterparts around the 1945 spring training camps were getting ready for a season that would see the big leagues dependent on armed forces rejects.

The trend had become noticeable in 1944 when there was an average of ten 4Fs—"physically, mentally, or morally unfit for service"—per ball club. The Browns team that won the only pennant in the club's history opened with a roster of eighteen 4Fs plus catcher Frank Mancuso (bad back) and pitcher Jack Kramer (asthma), equipped with medical discharges from the paratroopers and seabees, respectively.

The numbers of lame players kept climbing. A survey by Ford Frick in January of 1945 showed the National League clubs with 135

197

Pete Gray during pregame practice at Yankee Stadium. Note thin glove, held by fingertips, providing added flexibility for one-handed maneuvers.

4Fs on their winter rosters and the American League teams with 125 —an average of 16 per squad. The Giants' 1944–45 reserve list numbered twenty-two men unfit for the draft and seven others released from military service for physical disabilities. Washington Senator pitchers Mickey Haefner, Dutch Leonard, and Roger Wolff had two things in common—besides being knuckleballers they were all 4Fs.

While the public wanted baseball to continue, there was, of course, an obvious paradox surrounding individual 4F ballplayers. Government officials charged with finding the manpower to win the war and many a mother whose nonathletic son was in a foxhole somewhere wondered how somebody could be fit to engage in professional athletics when deemed too frail for military service.

As a Mrs. F.L.G. put it in a letter to sports columnist Grantland Rice: "I have one son in Italy and another in the South Pacific and am surprised that you, with all your experience, advocate such games as baseball and football. Most of these men are far better athletes than my sons are. Why should they be fighting for their country when these so-called athletes still are playing games demanding speed and stamina for big money against fighting for fifty dollars a month?"

Joe DiMaggio well recognized the dilemma facing ballplayers stamped unqualified by the military. Stationed in Atlantic City during the spring of 1945 while recuperating from an ulcer attack, DiMaggio was asked by reporters covering the Yankees' spring camp in town whether he would return immediately to the club if released from the air corps because of the ailment.

"You say the fans would not hoot a man with a medical discharge. Well, I would not take the chance," he responded. (DiMaggio was released from the service on September 14, 1945, but waited until the following spring before getting back into pinstripes.)

The rationale supporting the 4F athlete was twofold: First, it was noted that many ballplayers unfit for the service were performing only through the aid of special devices and individual treatment programs. Second, the determination as to who qualified was being made by the military itself.

The arguments were aptly summarized by Arthur Daley of the *New York Times,* who wrote in a December '44 column:

"These lads appear physically fit mainly because their dressing rooms are equipped with whirlpool baths, baking machines, massage tables, and adhesive tape. Some of them have to wear special braces and the majority of them are the most artificially 'physically fit' athletes imaginable. They require persistent attention in order to continue for the brief spurts in which they operate. In the Army or Navy they would get none of that and it was the Army and Navy doctors, it should be remembered, who assigned each of them his 4F status in the first place."

Daley's defense was offered in response to mounting pressures on supposedly infirm athletes.

Reacting to criticism against the medical discharge of athletes who would then return to their teams, the War Department had announced in late November 1944 that the power to approve the release of "prominent" personalities serving in the Army would be taken out of the hands of unit commanders. The Washington directive stated:

"The discharge of able-bodied prominent figures to permit them to participate in activities not considered to be essential to the national health, safety, or interest cannot be justified to the general public. While it is not intended to discriminate against any group in the matter of opportunity for discharge, cases involving discharge of nationally prominent athletes, stage, screen, radio stars, and so forth which might occasion criticism of the War Department discharge policies will be referred to the War Department for final determination."

Two months later, a similar policy was formulated by the Navy Department to cover Navy, Marine Corps, and Coast Guard personnel. In announcing his own crackdown, Navy Secretary James Forrestal cited the "discharge of a well-known professional football player for physical disability followed immediately by successful participation by that individual in professional games."

Forrestal didn't identify the man, but he was referring apparently to Frank Sinkwich, who starred at tailback for the Detroit Lions during the 1944 season after being let out of the Marines for flat feet. (Sinkwich was subsequently inducted into the Army and missed the 1945 season.)

While these directives could cut into the future supply of service returnees, baseball was more concerned with the threat to lift 4F deferments from the men then playing the game.

James F. Byrnes, head of the Office of War Mobilization and Reconversion, was most unhappy over the rejection of many professional athletes by the armed forces for what he called "alleged physical unfitness." On December 9, 1944, he sent a note to Selective Service director General Lewis B. Hershey, suggesting that athletes with medical discharges be recalled to military service and that 4F ballplayers be reexamined.

"They prove to thousands by their great physical feats upon the football or baseball field that they are physically fit and as able to perform military service as are the 11 million men in uniform," wrote Byrnes.

Six days after receiving the letter, Hershey took action, directing local draft boards to review the cases of professional athletes released from the service or deferred for physical disability.

Baseball put on a brave face upon getting the news, with Ford Frick declaring, "We're all out to do anything we can to help win the war—and in a hurry."

But as New Year's Day 1945 approached, the prospects of a fourth wartime baseball season were growing dimmer.

Hopes that an early winter offensive across the Rhine might bring a German surrender by Christmas were dashed when Hitler, in a desperate effort to turn the tide, threw twenty-five divisions against Allied lines in the Ardennes region of Belgium and Luxembourg. Eisenhower's armies would suffer seventy-seven thousand casualties and use up munitions at a fantastic rate in the bitter fighting known as the Battle of the Bulge. In the wake of the setback, Washington looked around and decided the country had become too complacent. Where rationing had been eased, it was toughened. Draft quotas were raised. And James Byrnes turned his wrath on the racetracks, viewed as a factor in war plant absenteeism, ordering them to shut down by the first week of January.

While contending he hadn't given any thought to banning other sports, Byrnes again expressed displeasure over 4F athletes in a meeting with reporters on New Year's Day. A man may have a trick knee, he conceded, "but if it doesn't get tricky on a football field, the chances are it won't get tricky at Verdun or in Belgium."

In his State of the Union message on January 6, 1945, Roosevelt renewed a call he had made the previous year for a national service act utilizing the nation's five million 4Fs "in whatever capacity is best for the war effort." In short, the White House wanted a "work or fight" measure like that hitting baseball during World War I, channeling physical rejects into limited military service or war industries.

One baseball official who wished to remain anonymous observed, "Up to now baseball has been operating under that Green Light the president flashed nearly three years ago. It looks to have changed to an amber color and may go red at any moment."

And the game could take little comfort from the views of Representative Andrew J. May of Kentucky, chairman of the House Military Affairs Committee, which was charged with considering "work or fight" legislation.

"Any man who is able to play baseball is able to fight or work in a war plant," said the congressman. "If baseball has a morale value, it can be just as great played in the Army. Let those fellows play their baseball with the Japs and the Germans."

Baseball's gloom thickened when the War Department, supplementing the earlier directive that 4F athletes be reexamined on the local level, announced on January 20 that it would review the case of any professional ballplayer rejected by his draft board. The Pentagon cited "the inconsistency of rejecting an athlete for an ailment which is not sufficiently serious to prevent him from participating in professional games and exhibitions."

Two days later, Ford Frick and Clark Griffith met with Hershey and War Manpower Commissioner McNutt to find out whether the game had much chance of continuing. Sounding like he was ready for baseball's temporary demise, Frick told reporters that the owners would confer in early February and "they will have to decide then whether under these conditions they will be able to open the season."

In their session at the Hotel New Yorker, the club owners decided to go ahead with plans for opening day in the absence of any government order to the contrary. And there would be no grousing, at least in public, about the manpower crackdown. The review by Washington of 4F deferments for ballplayers "will assure the public that the teams on the field are not needed more elsewhere," the baseball management declared in a statement, emphasizing "whatever the government does is right."

Meanwhile, within the government, baseball still had some friends.

FBI Director J. Edgar Hoover made it clear there were no slackers among the stay-at-home ballplayers, stating, "All the publicity about the situation has left the impression that some of the athletes themselves may be at fault. From our part in the war prosecution, we know this is not true. If any ballplayers or other athletes were attempting to dodge service it would be our job to look into such cases, but our records show there were few if any such cases among the thousands of ballplayers and they are entitled to a clean bill of health."

Happy Chandler, a member of the Senate Military Affairs Committee and soon to be elected the new baseball commissioner, took issue with his Kentucky colleague Andrew May, contending that "baseball should have the right to use rejects if that would mean keeping the game going. Playing baseball is the most essential thing most of those fellows can do. That's about all they have ever done. They have no particular mechanical aptitude, not nearly as much as a woman, for war work."

And, added the game's constant friend, "It's foolish to discount the value of baseball as a morale factor. For that reason alone, those fellows would be more valuable playing ball than fiddling around at something else."

On March 12, Clark Griffith made his annual White House pilgrimage to present season's passes for the Senators' games—FDR's in a leather folder and Mrs. Roosevelt's inside a gold-initialed red pocketbook. Griffith told reporters afterward that he hadn't burdened the president with a plea for baseball's continuation, but was able to state that despite a coal shortage curtailing outdoor lighting, Roosevelt came through in their chat with a "high, hard one down the middle" for more night ball.

Griffith wasn't embellishing. At a press conference the next day, Roosevelt was asked, "Would you care to commit yourself on the subject of night baseball?"

Coming after a couple of weighty questions concerning the Yalta Conference, the query drew laughter. But Roosevelt was ready with an answer that baseball viewed as a glimmer of hope.

"Well, I am one of the fathers of night baseball, as you know, and I am all in favor of baseball so long as you don't use perfectly healthy people that could be doing more useful work in the war," the president responded. "I consider baseball a very good thing for the population during the war."

Roosevelt was then asked whether it would be possible for baseball to operate in 1945 within the manpower restrictions he had outlined. "Why not?" he replied. "It may not be quite as good a team, but I would go out to see a baseball game played by a sandlot team—and so would most people."

FDR's claim of paternity for night baseball, probably occasioned by recollections of his boost for it in the Green Light letter, may have astonished Larry MacPhail, who always figured he deserved the honor. And the reference to "sandlot" baseball seemed like a backhand compliment. But the important point was that the president didn't feel baseball should go the way of racing.

A month later FDR would be dead, but his remarks foreshadowed brighter days following the gloomy winter. The nation was surmounting the final crisis of the war. The German breakthrough in the Ardennes had prolonged the fighting at great cost. But as spring arrived, Allied forces were beginning to converge on Berlin from East and West and on April 3, with American troops across the Rhine in full force, the Senate killed an already modified "work or fight" bill.

With the death of the proposed national service act, the 4F ballplayer would not be frozen to a war plant job after all. Baseball would be cutting its travel still more under pressure from the Office of Defense Transportation, but it could look forward to playing a full 1945 schedule with a flock of draft rejects.

A few of the infirm had found, however, that they were suddenly fit for military duty. Early in 1945, a number of ballplayers previously turned down by the armed forces had been drafted simply because they were professional athletes.

The first victim of what appeared to be outright discrimination was Phillie outfielder Ron Northey. A beaning incurred while playing baseball for Duke University had left Northey hard of hearing in one ear, resulting in his flunking induction physicals twice. On December 20, 1944, the draft authorities tried again, summoning Northey to the Valley Forge Army Hospital near Philadelphia for a third examination. Once more he was stamped unacceptable for military service. Then on January 15, 1945, without notice he had been reclassified from 4F, Northey was told to report for induction into the Army. He tried to join the Navy at the last moment, but couldn't pass its physical. On January 29, the New Cumberland, Pennsylvania, Army reception station welcomed Private Ronald James Northey. What did he do in the Army? He became a valued member of the Fort Lewis, Washington, baseball team.

Ten days after Northey was drafted, Ray Mueller arrived at New Cumberland. While the Reds' catcher may have been an iron-man on the field, as witnessed by his streak of 217 consecutive games, his digestive system was made of less sterner stuff. A stomach ulcer had kept him out of the service. But Mueller was called for re-examination in early 1945, and this time he was pronounced fit.

Hugh Poland remembers vividly how he went from a Boston Braves uniform to one reading "Fort Knox." The events at the draft board in Louisville did not seem very amusing that winter day in 1945, but with the passage of years, Poland's southern tones are punctuated with laughter as he relives the absurdity of what happened.

"I tore up my right ankle in school pretty badly playing basketball, tore ligaments loose and I chipped bones. It gave me a lot of trouble when I had to stand on it for any length of time," he recalls. "I'd tried to join the Navy in Cincinnati and they turned me down. I came home then and I was brought up for the draft in Todd County, Kentucky.

"There were quite a few of us on the bus going from Elkton, which is the county seat, up to Louisville to be examined. We first go into a big room where everybody meets and they call your name and so forth. We sit there for a while and the fella that was in charge asked if there were any professional athletes in the crowd. So like a damn fool I stick my hand up. And he said, 'Your name's Poland?' I said 'that's correct' and he said 'who do you play with?' I said, 'I play with the Boston Braves, I'm a professional baseball player.'

"So now, when they hand out all the papers, I've got a big red 'P' and a big red 'A' written right up in the left-hand corner of my application, which stands for 'Professional Athlete.' I started going

"Professional Athlete" Hugh Poland.

down through the line and the doctors examined me and I go down to the final three: Army, Navy, and Marine doctors. And they look over my doctors' recommendations and what they've found about the ankle and the x-ray pictures they've taken and darned if all three of them don't reject me and give me a rejection slip—'rejected for the armed forces.' I still got it here somewhere. I wasn't glad nor wasn't disappointed, but I find I am rejected for the armed services."

The rejection was not, however, in effect for very long, as Poland explains:

"I go back into the room to put my clothes on, then I hear my name being paged over the loudspeaker in the gymnasium. So I figure, well, it's somebody that knows me and wants to see me. So I got my clothes on. They told me to come to a certain room and the fella that was in the room, he said, 'Say , they can't reject you. You've got to have a special examination, you're a professional baseball player.'

"So darned if they don't run me through that line again. They didn't let me go through the Army, Navy, and Marine doctors this time. But I get down to another one, a little pint-sized guy, and he said, 'Mr. Poland, I'm going to tell you something. If you can play baseball on that leg of yours, you can go into the armed services.' I showed him my rejection slip. I said, 'I've already been rejected by the Army, Navy, and Marine doctors, the last three that were in the final line over there.'

"He said, 'That doesn't make a difference, you're a professional baseball player.' So I was in. And I was married and I had two kids."

Asked if he harbors any bitterness, looking back, Poland replies:

"I know a couple of fellas that passed their physicals and passed everything right on through and they gave them a deferment, but they took me right in. They were very unfair to the pro athletes, there's no question about it. They were looking for 'em and they got 'em.

"But I'm glad I went in and served some time. I was treated very good while I was in the service, I'll say that. They didn't hold anything against me, I was treated very, very nicely."

Poland was, in fact, treated to a catcher's mitt and spent his Army career in his home state, playing baseball for Fort Knox.

Danny Litwhiler, who had been classified 4F for a knee injury suffered in the minors, was another ballplayer suddenly finding himself fit for military service. His story is remarkably similar to Poland's.

"I had had six physicals and they rejected me every time because I had no cartilage in my left knee," he recalls. "In fact, I had tried to enlist because of the harassment we had, not so much from the fans, but writers would kind of take off in general about ballplayers not going. I felt I might as well try to get in. I had tried to enlist in the Navy and they rejected me. And I finally made up my mind, well, I guess I'm not gonna go in."

Litwhiler continues, "It was in January when I was called up and the doctor had had me I guess five or six times in a row, and he said 'not you again?' He said, 'I'm just as stubborn as they [the Selective Service authorities] are. You're rejected again. It's the same knee, it's never gonna be any different.' So he rejected me.

"And as I'm going down the hall I heard this 'Mr. Litwhiler?' I said 'Yeah.' The fellow said captain so-and-so wants to see you. So I went in and the captain said, 'Oh, I want to congratulate you. We've decided you should go in the service. You're in limited service.' So I went in the service in '45.

"I felt relieved, because you keep going, it gets kind of monotonous. About every three, four months you go get examined again. But I hated to leave my family. I had two children. Nobody likes to leave their children."

Litwhiler, like Ron Northey, spent his Army days playing baseball at Fort Lewis.

While it would be too late for the Northeys, Polands, and Litwhilers, baseball eventually found a new friend in Congress who pressed the War Department to rescind the discriminatory policy. He was freshman Congressman Melvin Price of Illinois, elected to office while serving as an Army corporal and appointed to the Military Affairs Committee.

Price, who had more than a casual acquaintance with baseball, having once covered the Browns and Cardinals for the *East St. Louis Journal,* an Illinois newspaper, got involved in the 4F controversy as a result of the impending induction of George McQuinn, the Browns' first baseman. McQuinn, who had been rejected by the Army in 1943 for a bad back and could play only with the aid of a brace, was summoned for a new physical at the Camp Lee, Virginia, army hospital in mid-February 1945. As might be expected he was then reclassified by his Arlington draft board from 4F to 1A.

Asked to look into the matter by the Browns' management, which felt its ballplayer was suffering an injustice, Price took up the McQuinn case with Bryce Harlow, an aide to Secretary of War Stimson. Early in May, the congressman went public, openly accusing the War Department of discriminating against 4F athletes.

"No man should be inducted if he is legitimately 4F, but in some instances athletes have been inducted even without their classification being changed from 4F. The history of many of these cases is that they are automatically inducted regardless of their physical condition," Price asserted.

According to the congressman, Danny Litwhiler had a notation on his draft board records that attested to his being unfit for military duty. Price said the notation read: "This registrant cannot be considered a soldier against your quota, whether he is called by the Army or Navy, because he does not meet the minimum requirements for military training.

"If the Army were not showing rank discrimination against ballplayers, it certainly would not accept a man for military service like Litwhiler and numerous others who cannot meet the minimum physical requirements," Price concluded.

The 4F cause was also taken up by Happy Chandler, whose cheerleading for baseball had been rewarded on April 24 with his selection as the late Landis's successor. Chandler discussed the situation with another man in a new job. Harry Truman promised a review.

In response to the complaints, Major General Virgil I. Peterson, the Army's Inspector General, began an investigation and on May 8— perhaps not so coincidentally V-E Day—the War Department suspended its review of local board rejections of professional athletes. Three days later, it was announced that in the future, only ballplayers able to meet combat requirements would be drafted. McQuinn stayed with the Browns, and a number of other players whose cases had been under review by the War Department also retained their 4Fs. The Washington Senators alone were able to keep three men—George Case, Mickey Haefner, and Dutch Leonard—who might have been drafted if not for the policy reversal.

There were some whose presence on a baseball field was not about to be a matter of controversy. These were the 4Fs and the veterans returning with medical discharges who overcame disabilities that would have kept lesser men on the sidelines of life itself, let alone off a major league diamond, wartime variety or not.

Peter Wyshner hitched a ride one day on a farmer's wagon passing through his hometown of Nanticoke, a mining community in eastern Pennsylvania. As the wagon moved along, Peter fell off somehow. His right arm became mangled in the spokes of a wheel. An amputation above the elbow was required. He was six years old.

As time went by, the boy decided he was going to be a baseball player despite the handicap. Possessing native athletic ability and quickness, he slowly taught himself to be competitive. A natural righty, he converted himself into the left-handed batter he had to be and figured out a way to handle himself in the field, removing almost all the padding from his glove to provide a greater "feel" for one-handed catches. After a catch, he would stick the glove under the stump of his right shoulder, draw the ball clear, and get it away.

First came a chance to play the outfield in semipro baseball. Peter started out with a team in Three Rivers, Quebec, then went on to the Bushwicks, the Brooklyn club that would later send Eddie Yost to the majors. In 1942, he landed a pro job, signing with Three Rivers upon its admittance to the Canadian-American minor league. He was twenty-five years old by now and had changed his name. It would be Pete Gray.

Quickly he became a star, batting .381 with Three Rivers, then moving up to the Memphis club for two seasons, winning the Southern Association's Most Valuable Player award in 1944 with a .333 average and sixty-eight stolen bases, ten of them thefts of home.

As the nation moved into the last stages of the war and baseball scrambled for players, the St. Louis Browns, eyeing a potential box office attraction and, who could say, perhaps a useful outfielder, purchased the contract of Pete Gray for $20,000.

Gray would not be the first big league player with such a severe handicap. Hugh "One Arm" Daily had pitched from 1882 to 1887 in the National League and the Union and American Associations (the latter two also considered to have been major leagues), compiling a 68–80 record and once striking out nineteen batters in a single game.

Pioneer or not, Gray was, of course, a curiosity item. As he worked out with the Browns during their 1945 spring camp at Cape Girardeau, youngsters would imitate him, playing ball with one hand. Manager Luke Sewell picked up Gray's glove on one occasion and tried to catch and throw using one hand himself. Sewell, meanwhile, would wait and see. "He's just another ballplayer in my book, he'll stand or fall on what he shows," the manager told reporters at the training camp.

Gray made the team and there were some good moments: five stolen bases, six doubles, and a pair of triples; cheers from a crowd of thirty-six thousand when he trotted out to left field for the first time at Yankee Stadium; a presumably inspirational display of his batting technique before amputees at Walter Reed Army Hospital; the opportunity to give some confidence to four-year-old Nelson Gary, Jr., who had lost his right arm in an electrical accident and hoped some day to be another Pete Gray.

But the major leagues, even in the last wartime season, were too difficult for a one-armed ballplayer. At the plate, while he was tough to strike out, Gray had little power and the infield played in to take away the bunt. He would manage only 51 hits in 234 trips to the plate, a .218 average. And however deft, Gray couldn't avoid giving the runners an edge in that brief extra moment it took to transfer the ball for a throw back to the infield.

Gray knew he was in the majors primarily as a gate attraction and, inclined to be an introvert, he found it was hard to avoid a feeling of exploitation. There was friction, too, with teammates who felt he

Pete Gray shows Nelson Gary, Jr., how it's done.

might have cost them some games in a tight '45 pennant race that would wind up with the Browns in third place, six games behind the Tigers.

After the season, Gray went barnstorming in California, playing against a team featuring a one-armed black outfielder named Jess Alexander. The next stop would be the Toledo Mud Hens of the American Association. When the war ended, so did the brief major league career of Pete Gray. Gray played a few more years in the minors, then went back home to Nanticoke.

Pete Gray wasn't the only ballplayer to talk with wounded veterans at Walter Reed during the 1945 season. Also visiting the Army hospital was a member of the Washington Senators who himself had been a patient there—Bert Shepard, an ex–fighter pilot trying to pitch again despite the loss of a leg.

Shepard had been in the White Sox farm chain when the draft beckoned in the spring of 1942. Soon after joining the Army, he obtained a commission in the Air Corps and was assigned to fly fighter planes out of England. All went well until May 21, 1944, when on his thirty-fourth mission, strafing a truck convoy north of Berlin, Shepard's P-38 Lightning fighter was shot down by antiaircraft fire. He awoke in a German prisoner-of-war hospital to find that doctors had amputated his right leg between the knee and ankle.

Shepard's spirit, however, was not broken. Within a month he was running with the aid of an artificial leg fashioned by a Canadian prisoner using materials supplied by the British Red Cross. In February '45 he returned home on the prisoner exchange ship *Gripsholm* determined to resume his baseball career.

The twenty-four-year-old was convalescing at Walter Reed when his ambitions came to the attention of Undersecretary of War Robert Patterson. The official got in touch with Larry MacPhail, who had served as his aide prior to being released from the military early in 1945. Together they arranged for a tryout at the Senators' College Park spring training base, not far from the hospital.

On March 13, a few days after being fitted with a more efficient though still temporary limb, Lieutenant Bert Shepard arrived at the Senators' camp.

"This is the one thing I dreamed about over there for months," he told reporters after going through a three-hour drill, displaying a slight limp noticeable only to those who might have been watching for it. "Sure I'm serious about playing ball. I can still take a good cut, throw well, and when I get a special leg instead of this temporary one, I'll do okay."

While it was questionable whether Shepard could make the Senator pitching staff, an incident that occurred a few days later made it clear the ball club prized the southpaw, if only for the goodwill he could bring.

Soon after his initial appearance in the Washington camp, Shepard told Patterson he wanted to work out with the Yankees. An Army plane was provided to fly him to the team's Atlantic City training base and along for the ride was MacPhail, who had just bought the Yanks in a partnership with Dan Topping and Del Webb. When Clark Griffith heard that Shepard was gone, he became extremely upset, suspecting kidnap. The Senators were not about to part with their

Bert Shepard is awarded the Distinguished Flying Cross and Air Medal by Undersecretary of War Robert Patterson before September 1945 game at Griffith Stadium. Looking on are Gen. Jacob L. Devers (left) and Gen. Omar N. Bradley.

man. But by nightfall Griffith learned his pitcher had not been stolen, merely borrowed. Shepard spent two hours showing some one hundred wounded vets from England General Hospital in Atlantic City how he could throw and scamper about, then returned to the Senators.

Shepard got into his first game when the Senators visited the Norfolk Naval Training Station. Taking the mound amid cheers from eight thousand sailors, he pitched one scoreless inning and fielded a bunt flawlessly. The next day, he relieved against an Army team from Fort Story, Virginia, giving up one run in a two-inning stint.

While signing with the Senators for the regular season in the official capacity of a coach, Shepard's perseverance was rewarded on July 10 when he got to pitch against major league competition, albeit in an exhibition. Facing the Dodgers before more than twenty-three thousand fans in a benefit game at Griffith Stadium raising funds for a servicemen's welfare agency, he went four innings, yielding but two runs.

Then came the real thing. Manager Ossie Bluege called on Shepard in the fourth inning of a lost game against the Red Sox in early August. Shepard did not embarrass himself. Striking out George

"Catfish" Metkovich to end a twelve-run rally not of his making, he went on to pitch five and one-third innings, giving up only one run and three hits. It was, however, to be his sole appearance in a game that counted in the standings.

"Bert was pretty damn good, it was amazing," says former teammate George Case. "He realized he was exploited to a certain degree, but he was grateful. He had a wonderful disposition and he loved baseball."

"Walter Reed was just up the road from Griffith Stadium," Case notes. "Bert was constantly going up there to show what he'd done. And we'd have a couple of amputees at every game; they'd see Bert throw batting practice."

Another wartime ballplayer with a major handicap was Dick Sipek, who won a part-time job in the Cincinnati outfield despite his almost complete deafness resulting from a head injury at age five.

Sipek had developed his athletic ability at a state school for the deaf in Jacksonville, Illinois, under the tutelage of his house-father, Luther "Dummy" Taylor, an old-time Giants pitcher. Upon Taylor's recommendation, the Reds gave the youngster a chance with their Birmingham Barons farm club of the Southern Association. Appearing in the same league with Pete Gray, he batted .336 in 1943 and .316 the following season.

The final wartime year, Sipek found himself at age twenty-two the third deaf ballplayer in big league history after Taylor and William "Dummy" Hoy, an outfielder who enjoyed a long career around the turn of the century.

Sipek played some right field for the Reds and also pinch hit, batting .244 in eighty-two games. While Gray was withdrawn, Sipek was outgoing and popular. Although able to speak a little, he taught his teammates sign language. Once, when called out on a close play, he gave the umpire the sign for a vulgar word. The ump didn't understand what was happening, but the Reds' bench roared with laughter.

"He was as nice, as jolly a kid as you could be associated with," says Frank McCormick.

The ex-Reds' first baseman recalls there wasn't much of a problem on pop flies that might he handled by either Sipek, the second baseman, or himself. McCormick explains, "I could understand it when he tried to form a word, but mostly he'd wave his arms if he had it."

After the 1945 season, Sipek was sent back to the minors, where h played a few more years before leaving the game.

George "Bingo" Binks, a regular in the Senators' outfield during the 1945 season, was another 4-F ballplayer with a hearing problem. Mastoid trouble in his childhood had led to deafness in one ear.

George Case, who played alongside Binks, says, "On more than one occasion the ball was hit and I hollered him off, but he couldn't hear me. He must have run into me four or five times."

The disability once resulted in Binks being picked off first base on a trick play. After he singled against the White Sox's Eddie Lopat in the ninth inning of a tie game, manager Ossie Bluege ordered Gil Torres to sacrifice. The White Sox had a maneuver of their own in mind. As the first baseman and third baseman charged in, Lopat pitched out and second baseman Roy Schalk sneaked behind Binks. Bluege shouted a warning, but Binks did not hear him and was erased by catcher Mike Tresh's throw.

A number of men were able to stay in big league uniforms because they had punctured eardrums. Leo Durocher had expected to go into the Army, but was rejected over a damaged right eardrum resulting from a 1933 beaning. "LEO HAS HOLE IN HEAD" announced the New York *Daily News.*

A wartime pitcher might get by without an overwhelming fastball or scintillating curve. For that matter, he would be given a chance even if he arrived on the scene with something less than sparkling eyesight.

As the 1944 season got under way, the Dodgers sent pitcher Tom Sunkel to their Montreal farm club and called up hurler Jack Franklin. Both were born in Paris, Illinois, but there was something else more significant that they had in common. Each man was blind in one eye. Sunkel's left eye had been damaged by a popgun missle fired by his brother when they were small boys. He developed a cataract, and in 1941, while pitching for Syracuse, lost all sight in the eye. The left-hander nevertheless went on to do some pitching for the Cardinals, Giants, and Dodgers. Franklin was blind in his right eye, though it hadn't stopped him from serving as an Army MP for eleven months before obtaining a discharge. His big league pitching career would be confined to one game for the '44 Dodgers.

Charley Schanz, a strapping 4F righty who compiled a 13–16 record for the 1944 Phillies in his rookie season, was said to have had such poor eyesight that he wore glasses while shaving.

A story on southpaw Barney Mussill's arrival at the Phils' 1944 spring camp inspired the Chicago *Daily News* headline: "ROOKIE HURLER IS A ONE-MAN GAS-HOUSER." Mussill had received a medical discharge from the Army the previous October, after an encounter with a defective mustard gas container at Fort Warren, Wyoming, which resulted in temporary blindness and a three-month hospital stay. When he reported for his first shot at a big-league job, the twenty-four-year-old was still unable to read for more than an hour at a time. He donned eyeglasses on the mound and wore thick tinted lenses off the field. Though ineffective, Mussill stuck around long enough to pitch in sixteen games.

Head injuries were grounds for separation from the Army or Navy, but not necessarily a deterrent to appearing in a baseball lineup.

Mickey Livingston had suffered a severe concussion while catching in the minors in 1939 when he rammed his head against a concrete dugout going after a popup. The injury didn't stop him from making the majors, nor did it prevent the Army from drafting the backstop after the 1943 season. But once in khaki, it developed that Livingston had an unforeseen problem. Whenever he wore a helmet for any length of time, he got a headache. The ballplayer's military career, therefore, was not especially lengthy. Attired in a soft cap belonging to the Chicago Cubs, Livingston was behind the plate again and on a pennant-winning team in 1945.

The Phillies had an errant medicine ball to thank for obtaining one of their wartime ballplayers. Ted Cieslak had suffered a fractured skull in 1939 when Dizzy Trout felled him with a pitch in a Texas League game. He made an apparent recovery, however, and was able to resume his minor league career. When the war came, the outfielder–third baseman was inducted into the Army and sent to Fort Dix. While tossing a basketball around in the post gymnasium, Cieslak was struck in the back of the head with a medicine ball that had gone astray. The blow to an already vulnerable spot touched off severe headaches, and so, in December '43, after undergoing almost a month of observation in the base hospital, he was discharged from the service. The following year Cieslak finally got a crack at the majors. He was picked up by the Phils, appeared in eighty-five games and batted .245, then was sent back to the minors.

Tommy Warren, a slender right-hander with some minor league experience, was given a tryout by the Dodgers after spending ten months at the St. Albans Naval Hospital in New York, recovering from head injuries suffered in the North African invasion.

"I'll be pitching for the boys overseas. They want baseball to continue and I'll certainly try to do my share," Warren remarked upon arriving at the 1944 Bear Moutain training camp.

He did make the mound staff but was around only briefly, compiling a 1–4 mark.

Elmer "Red" Durrett, who played for the Dodgers during the last two wartime seasons, had a particular problem with the location of the club's training camp during his first spring back from the war. Durrett had been released from the Marines after suffering shell shock on Guadalcanal. Not quite recovered from the effects of combat, the outfielder would hit the ground on the Bear Mountain practice field when artillery went off at nearby West Point.

"I did it twice, not once but twice, and that's no joke," he confided to newsmen.

While woeful underpinnings didn't keep Hugh Poland or Danny Litwhiler out of the Army, there were others whose feet, ankles, or knees were just too tender for even the most zealous induction examiner.

Heinz Becker, a sometime first baseman and pinch hitter for the Cubs, was the only German-born player in the majors during the war era. But the Berlin brewmaster's son had another distinction more relevant to his availability for wartime play—perhaps the worst feet in baseball.

"He had the flattest feet with the bones all out of place, his right ankle bone was on the ground, and the goddamn biggest protruding bunions," recalls ex-teammate Len Merullo. "The Cubs spent a fortune just operating on those feet of his."

Though Becker was of limited value in the field, he did deliver some timely hits for manager Charlie Grimm late in the Cubs' 1945 pennant drive, filling in when Phil Cavarretta was sidelined with an ailing shoulder.

"He had a good stroke, he could hit line drives all over the place, just a born hitter," says Merullo. "He was a big man; strong, and a typical German-looking type, and Charlie Grimm [also of German background] loved him. He called him Heinzapoodle. He was just a natural for Grimm.

"Heinz very rarely played regularly, as good a hitter as he was, since we had Cavarretta around, and he was not a good fielder, he couldn't move," Merullo continues. "I can remember my coming across the bag during infield practice one day and he stretched out for the throw to make the play look as smooth as possible. He never got his hand up in time and that ball hit him right flush in the forehead and he went down. We thought he was dead."

The sorest knee in baseball belonged to Bill Salkeld, who made his major league debut at age twenty-eight with the 1945 Pirates.

Salkeld had banged up his knee in a rundown play nine years before while catching for the San Francisco Seals. As he dove to tag Portland's Moose Clabaugh, Salkeld's shin guards slipped and his right knee got caught in the runner's spikes. A few days later, an infection set in and he was hospitalized for three months, at one point threatened with an amputation. The doctors said he would never play baseball again and the knee would be stiff for life. But Salkeld didn't give up. He got a job as a furniture salesman, then tried sandlot play in California, and following a two-and-a-half-year layoff, returned to professional ball. After spending five years with the San Diego Padres, he was called up by Pittsburgh to help thirty-six-year-old Al Lopez with the catching chores. Salkeld's .311 average over ninety-five games, compared with his .241 mark the previous year in the Pacific Coast League, said something about the caliber of major league pitching. But it was his catching style that drew particular attention.

Lloyd Waner remembers, "He was a good catcher, but he couldn't squat clear down on account of his leg. He kind of went down just on one leg, sideways like. But he was pretty active back there. I don't know how he did it, but he sure did."

There were other assorted medical specimens. Len Rice, a catcher for the Cubs and Reds, and Clancy Smyres, an infielder appearing briefly with the Dodgers, each had one kidney. Pitcher Al Javery of the Braves and infielder Glen Stewart of the Phils could empathize when facing each other—both were deferred for varicose veins. Catchers Mike Garbak of the Yankees and Ken O'Dea of the Cardinals labored with hernias.

Hal Peck played the outfield for the Athletics in 1945 despite the loss of two toes blown off three years earlier when his shotgun accidentally discharged as he hunted down rats outside his Genesee Depot, Wisconsin, home.

A few perfectly healthy ballplayers found themselves in 4F because they exceeded the military's 6-foot 6-inch height limit.

Howie Schultz—one half-inch too tall for the Army—was brought up by the Dodgers in August '43 as a replacement for Dolph Camilli. The popular first baseman had been traded, with pitcher Johnny Allen, to the Giants for infielder Joe Orengo and pitchers Bill Lohrman and Bill Sayles in a deal bringing Branch Rickey howls of outrage. (Camilli never reported to the Giants, going home to California instead, a small consolation perhaps for Brooklyn fans.)

Variously nicknamed "Steeple" and "Stretch," Schultz was awkward around first base but could hit an occasional long ball, and while

Mike Naymick provides a frame for Bob Feller.

the war was on, he would do. During the winter he put his height to use as a center for the Hamline College basketball team, the St. Paul, Minnesota, school belonging to a conference that allowed a collegian to retain amateur status in one sport while playing professionally in another. Schultz dropped back into town in December of 1944, tallying eleven points to help Hamline score a 47–42 victory over City College in Madison Square Garden.

The first baseman was hardly the tallest ballplayer around. The 6-foot 8-inch Mike Naymick and Johnny Gee, at 6 feet 9 inches the tallest man ever in the big leagues, pitched intermittently through a couple of seasons, with minimal success.

Naymick, turned down when he tried to enlist in the Marines and then rejected by the Army, wore a size seventeen shoe.

"My draft board told me if I were fighting on foreign soil and wore out my shoes, I'd be out of luck. I told them I could fight a Jap or a Nazi as well as anyone else, but they won't take me," he reported sadly.

Lou Boudreau, for whose 1943 Indians Naymick posted his best record—a 4–4 mark—says his motion "was like a canoe, he'd kick his left leg up and his foot would be practically in the hitter's face."

"They kept teasing him about the size of his feet," Boudreau recalls. "It was a huge shoe and he was quite sensitive."

Asked whether the teasing affected Naymick's performance, his old manager replied, "He could throw the ball hard, he could've been a good pitcher. It didn't help, I'll tell you that."

Johnny Gee had once seemed headed for great things. Joining the Syracuse club upon graduation from the University of Michigan, he

Johnny Gee seems to be having a good time, but he can't keep up with five-foot-six-inch Dom Dallessandro of the Cubs in seventy-five-yard dash before September 1943 game at Wrigley Field.

compiled records of 17–11 and 20–9, then was purchased by the Pirates late in the 1939 season for $75,000 plus four players. The fastballing right-hander appeared to be worth every cent of what was then an unusually large outlay, striking out eleven Braves in his second big league start. But he developed a sore arm the following spring and never regained his form.

Gee made sporadic comeback tries with the Pirates and later the Giants. Stripped to the waist, he would sit in the outfield during batting practice, hoping the arm would come around from the sun's baking. But it never did. In 1946 he called it quits with a career record of seven wins and twelve losses.

Phil Weintraub, Gee's teammate on the Giants when the end of the line was near, says, "I remember Johnny in the minors. He was so big and could throw the ball by you, he was tremendous. But when we got ahold of him, his arm was pretty much spent, he was a lot of motion and not too much of anything else. Of course, in those days they didn't know a lot about surgery to save the arms. Johnny was trying to use the sun as therapy, but it didn't help him. He made every effort, but he just didn't have it anymore."

A few other skyscraper-sized pitchers appeared at wartime training camps but never made it into a major league game. The Tigers took a look at 6-foot 11½-inch Ralph Siewart while the Phils gave a trial to James Spencer, who stood 6 feet 9 inches tall. The hopefuls had a common legacy from 6-foot 4½-inch Schoolboy Rowe, who had pitched for both Detroit and Philadelphia before entering the Navy— they wore his old trousers.

While the physical disability that made him available may have been the chief asset of many a wartime ballplayer, there were also some top-flight major leaguers among the draft rejects. It was they who provided the war era game with whatever semblance of respectability it retained.

The Tigers were carried to their 1945 AL title and World Series victory on the pitching arms of temperamental southpaw Hal Newhouser and colorful right-hander Dizzy Trout. Newhouser had planned to be sworn into the Army Air Corps on the Briggs Stadium pitching mound but was turned down for a heart problem. Trout was deferred for poor eyesight. Neither could be called a "wartime" pitcher. Newhouser, who won a total of 29 games in 1944 and another 25 in the Tigers' championship year, had 207 career victories over a 17-year span. Trout, contributing 65 victories over the last three war-era seasons, won 170 games in a career lasting 15 seasons. Rudy York, available to play first base for the Tigers throughout the war years because of a knee injury suffered in a basketball game, belted 277 homers over 13 years.

Three shortstops who would be outstanding in any era were draft rejects. Lou Boudreau, a .295 lifetime batter and member of the Hall of Fame, played on a twice-fractured ankle that had become arthritic. Vern Stephens of the wartime Browns, deferred for a knee injury, hit 247 homers during his career. The Cards' slick-fielding Marty Marion played for thirteen seasons hoping a trick knee, souvenir of a childhood accident, would not slip out of place.

Whitey Kurowski, a genuine major leaguer covering the left side of the Cardinal infield alongside Marion, played with a misshapen right forearm, a piece of bone having been removed in childhood when an infection set in following a fall from a fence.

The National League's 1945 stolen base leader (only twenty-six steals, but no one could do any better) was a twenty-two-year-old Cardinal rookie installed in left field after problems stemming from an old eye injury brought an Army discharge. Converted the following year to a second baseman, Red Schoendienst would play for 19 seasons and amass 2,449 hits.

The bats of Phil Cavarretta and Andy Pafko helped the Cubs to the 1945 NL pennant. Cavarretta, deferred for an ear problem, was to hit for a .293 average over twenty-two years while Pafko, unacceptable for military service because of high blood pressure, spent seventeen years in the majors.

George Kell, blossoming as a hitter after being traded from the Athletics to the Tigers following the war —his lifetime average .306 over fifteen seasons—was another of the gimpy-kneed ballplayers.

Head injuries enabled the wartime Pirates to keep third baseman–outfielder Bob Elliott, a future member of the two-thousand hit club, and crafty left-hander Preacher Roe, whose best years were to come with the great Dodger teams of the early 1950s.

Over at Ebbets Field, most of the familiar faces were gone by the latter war years, but Dixie Walker was still around. When picked up by Larry MacPhail in 1939 from the Tigers, Walker's medical history featured a broken leg, broken collarbone, torn ligaments of the right shoulder, and a left knee that had trouble staying in its socket. Dixie's triumph over adversity and perhaps more to the point, a knack for hitting Giant pitchers—he batted .436 against them in 1940—quickly made him the idol of all Flatbush. He rewarded Dodger fans for their adulation by leading the National League in batting during 1944 with a .357 average, but wasn't dependent on wartime pitching for base hits. Over an eighteen-year career, Walker had a .306 average.

Tommy Holmes' 1945 batting streak wasn't a fluke. The Braves' outfielder, kept out of the Army by a sinus condition, would bat .302 over eleven seasons. Reds' first baseman Frank McCormick, deferred because of a disk problem, hit .299 in a career spanning thirteen years.

Perhaps the final word on the question of physical rejects came from Senator William Langer of North Dakota. Langer was unhappy over seeing men supposedly unfit for service cavorting on a baseball diamond. So in the spring of 1945, he called for legislation that would require all big league teams to fill at least 10 percent of their rosters with veterans who had lost an arm, a hand, or a leg.

With the end of the war, the proposal, like many a lesser 4F ball-player, was forgotten.

V

On Foreign Fields

(Opposite) A quick change of uniform and these soldiers and sailors will be ready to do battle with American League all stars in July 1942 benefit game at Cleveland. The servicemen and their last civilian employers are: Front Row —*Frank Pytlak (Red Sox), Sam Chapman and Benny McCoy (Athletics), Morrie Arnovich (Giants), Bob Feller (Indians), Ernie Andres (minor leaguer), Sam Harshaney (Browns).* Middle Row—*Chief O. Mulkey, Chet Hajduk, and Johnny Rigney (White Sox), manager Mickey Cochrane, Lt. George Earnshaw (ex-A's pitcher), Lt. Comdr. J. Russell Cook, Mickey Harris (Red Sox).* Back Row—*Fred Hutchinson (Tigers), Cecil Travis (Senators), Ken Silvestri (Yankees), John Grodzicki (Cardinals), Don Padgett (Dodgers), Joe Grace and John Lucadello (Browns), Vince Smith (Pirates), Johnny Sturm (Yankees), Emmett Mueller (Phils), Pat Mullin (Tigers).*

8

At Bat for Uncle Sam

The Navy was indignant. Rumor had it that Al Brancato, a Philadelphia Athletics infielder who also ran a sporting goods store, had been given a special deal in return for enlisting shortly after Pearl Harbor. The way the story went, Brancato would be assigned to a Navy supply shop in Philadelphia—utilizing his experience as a merchant—and would be free in off-duty hours to continue laboring at Shibe Park.

Untrue, said the naval recruiting office in Philly, insisting "contrary to popular reports, Brancato is going into the Navy to fight."

In a formal statement, the Navy let it be known that while Brancato would be kept busy initially handing out paraphernalia as a storekeeper second class, "he will be assigned to active duty aboard a naval ship. He will not be kept in Philadelphia and he will not play baseball. This is not a powder puff war. To his everlasting credit, Brancato

asked for active service and he will get it. There are no soft jobs in the Navy in wartime."

Brancato would not, in fact, remain in Philly. The Navy eventually shipped him to the Pacific. As for there being no "soft jobs" around, Brancato did not have an easy time of it. For example, he was put in a pressure-packed situation one day in October '44 on the Hawaiian island of Maui. A soldier named Joe Gordon scored the winning run in a 6–5 victory by the Army over the Navy in the servicemen's "Little World Series" only because of an errant throw by sailor Al Brancato.

A touchy business from the outset, this question of how to deal with the ballplayer turned serviceman.

True, it was not a "powder puff war," but soldiers and sailors did have a need for some entertainment, so why not let it be provided by those comrades in arms who had a special skill? And who better could run the military's conditioning programs than professional athletes,

Mickey Cochrane and more formally attired fellow officers, Adm. Ernest J. King, chief of naval operations (left), and Lt. Comdr. Leonard Stack, gather with Mayor Harry Van Wagnen of Lorain, Ohio, before September 1942 game between Great Lakes Navy team and a local ball club. King was in Lorain, his hometown, to dedicate a monument to its men and women in the armed forces.

assigned naturally as recreation specialists? There would, as well, be a third, unstated element making it likely that a big league ballplayer taken by the military would find himself hitting a curve ball instead of a beach—a yearning by commanders at individual installations to carve out their own little athletic empires.

Getting assigned to an athletic program in the service didn't pose much of problem for a major leaguer. Virgil Trucks, who went from the pitching staff of the Detroit Tigers to that of the Great Lakes Naval Training Station Bluejackets, tells how it was done in his case:

"I was supposed to go into the service and I'd already taken my preinduction exam. I'd never met Mickey Cochrane, but I liked what I knew and what I had read about him. He was the manager at Great Lakes, a lieutenant commander. I wanted to go into the Navy and play ball for him. So I sent him a wire—I was living in Birmingham— and told him I was going in the service and I had chosen the Navy, but that didn't necessarily mean I would be in there. He told me to contact a Lieutenant Commander [J. Russell] Cook.

"Cook sent me a wire back saying to transfer my papers to Chicago Draft Board Number One and they would take over from there. That's exactly what I did. I came to the draft board here in Birmingham and told them I was going to Chicago, I had a job there, and I'd like my papers transferred. And they did that. I went on immediately afterwards and I'd spent two days at a hotel in Chicago when I got a notice that I was drafted to Great Lakes. It was handled by the higher-ups of naval personnel."

If Mickey Cochrane didn't grab a ballplayer then Lieutenant Commander Gene Tunney would. The ex–heavyweight champion was designated a physical training adviser to the chief of naval personnel and told to recruit athletes, coaches, and physical education specialists to supervise conditioning drills at Navy bases. Since the headquarters for Tunney's program was Norfolk, Virginia, the local Naval Training Station and·Naval Air Station baseball teams would not be lacking for talent.

While the Army developed few stateside teams that could compete with the Great Lakes or Norfolk powerhouses, it got its share of ballplayers, at least one of whom seemed to have been snatched from the Navy.

Tex Hughson's pitching had helped keep the Red Sox in the 1944 AL pennant race, but by August the time had come for military service.

"I was a little late going in, I was a pre–Pearl Harbor father and over twenty-five with a high draft number and all that," Hughson says. "Finally I went through the physical examination and I was assigned to the Navy. That was changed later. I don't know exactly how it came about."

But he has an idea of the motive for the transfer.

"I left Boston and I came home to Texas," Hughson continues. "Well, there was a San Marcos Army Air Force base near where I live and it was in a service league that included bases in San Antonio— Fort Sam Houston and the San Antonio Aviation Cadet Center—and each of those bases had major league ballplayers; Enos Slaughter, people like that. And there was Randolph Field, maybe it didn't have as many big league ballplayers, but they had four all-American tailbacks. San Marcos, though, had no major league ballplayers, it was sort of an orphan.

"I was transferred from the Navy and into the Army Air Force and assigned here, in my hometown, to play and kind of even up the situation."

Hughson notes, meanwhile, that for all the trouble the Army brass may have gone through to land him, he never pitched a ball at the Texas post. "I went through basic training, but early in March '45, just about the time we were going to start our service league, all of us got shipped out," he explains.

Hughson would do his Army hurling among the palm trees on Pacific islands.

If Great Lakes could vie with Norfolk for the best Navy players, so, too, might commanders at Army posts compete with each other for the talent that happened to be in khaki.

Harry "The Hat" Walker, now coach of the University of Alabama at Birmingham ball club after four and a half decades on baseball payrolls as player, manager, and batting instructor, tells about his entry into the Army after appearing with the Cardinals in the 1943 World Series.

"The next morning after the Series, Al Brazle and I were inducted in the Army at Jefferson Barracks," Walker recalls. "Originally we thought we were going down to Memphis to an air base, but it seems that Pete Reiser's troop commander at Fort Riley, Kansas, had a big pull at Jefferson Barracks. So we went to Fort Riley. We woke up and that's where we were. We didn't have much to say about it."

Walker goes on, "We took our basic training there in the mechanized cavalry. I came up with spinal meningitis about two months before the baseball season started and I almost died with it, but that

*Army-bound Harry Walker, flanked by outfield mates Stan Musial and
Danny Litwhiler, at 1943 World Series.*

spring we got together and started playing and we had a good ball
club there. We had Reiser and Lonny Frey and Joe Garagiola, Murry
Dickson, Ken Heintzelman, Rex Barney. We won everything."

Once snaring a big leaguer, the brass would make sure he played.

Charlie Gehringer entered the Navy at age thirty-nine following
the 1942 season, and after two years' duty in California, was transferred to the naval air station at Jacksonville, Florida. With nineteen
years at second base for the Detroit Tigers behind him, the future
Hall of Famer was, by then, tired of baseball. So when his commanding officer told him of exciting plans for the air station's baseball team,

Gehringer said he would be satisfied merely to coach. The response, as recalled by Gehringer years later, was: "If you don't play, I'll send you so far they won't know where to find you." He played.

Dodger hurler Kirby Higbe completed his initial Army processing at Fort Jackson, South Carolina, in three hours instead of the normal three days. The post ball club had a game the afternoon of his arrival. He pitched.

Pete Reiser almost got a medical discharge from Fort Riley, but was too important to the installation's baseball team to be spared.

An Army doctor studying Reiser's medical records when he came down with pneumonia shortly after arriving at the Kansas post decided he should never have been taken into the service in the first place and recommended a discharge. Reiser had experienced headaches and dizziness since suffering a concussion when he crashed into the center field wall at Sportsman's Park chasing down an Enos Slaughter drive in a July '42 game. Though accepted by the Army, he had been turned down for naval service.

Reiser later would tell how his separation from the Army was about to be finalized when he encountered a colonel who advised how he was "looking forward to having a hell of a ball club here at Fort Riley." The colonel ripped up the discharge papers.

As a consolation, the Dodger star was provided with a private room in his barracks and given a pass allowing him to go anywhere he pleased between 6:00 A.M. and 6:00 P.M.

While in a larger sense Reiser had been discriminated against, he was, however, enjoying privileges not accorded fellow GIs. That situation was not unique.

At Fort Dix, the Army decided to make things easy for another soldier who presumably needed to conserve his energy so that he could bring glory to the post baseball team. Pfc. Phil Masi had been excused from KP for twenty-two straight days during the early spring of 1944. Then one day a sergeant handed Masi a catcher's mitt to break in, noting he soon would be behind the plate for the Fort Dix nine. The soldier's good fortune was now at an end. He informed the sergeant that while he was indeed Phil Masi, he was not the man of the same name who made his living catching for the Boston Braves. Pfc. Masi was on KP the next day and before long found himself at Fort Logan, Colorado.

What was seen as the Army's favoritism toward ex-Cardinal Terry Moore brought an outcry from his fellow soldiers. When Moore, who had entered the Army in the fall of 1942, attended the World Series the following year on a furlough from his duties in the Panama Canal Zone, thirty-three GIs signed a letter to the servicemen's magazine *Yank* complaining "there are many men who have been at this station for three years and never received a three-day pass."

Although they often paid visits to their ex-teammates, ballplayers serving in the military were prohibited by baseball regulations from getting back into their old uniforms while on furlough. The men were placed on a National Defense Service List, remaining the property of their teams but not counted against the roster. Reinstatement would have to await receipt of an honorable discharge.

Dodger pitcher Larry French felt the opportunity to get two hundred career victories merited an exception to the rule. When French entered the Navy after the 1942 season at age thirty-five, he had 197 lifetime wins. Figuring he would be too old by time the war ended to resume his labors, and stationed conveniently at the Brooklyn Navy Yard, he sought permission to pitch in off-duty hours, offering to donate his salary to the Navy Relief Society. Even if baseball would have waived its rules prohibiting such a return, French was out of luck. The matter was referred by local naval authorities to Washington, where Rear Admiral W.B. Young, pleading fear of "a flood of such requests," turned French down.

An exception was made, however, for Cardinal pitcher Murry Dickson so that he could appear in the 1943 World Series. Dickson had gone into the Army during the last week of the '43 season but was able to get an immediate ten-day pass from Fort Riley. He hurled two-thirds of an inning in the fifth and final Series game.

Perhaps the most powerful service clubs were assembled at the Great Lakes naval installation north of Chicago, where the roster, changing each year as men were transferred in and out, might at any one time boast upwards of a dozen former major league players.

Mickey Cochrane, volunteering for the Navy shortly after Pearl Harbor, managed the Great Lakes baseball teams to 166 wins and only 26 losses over the first three wartime seasons, occasionally getting into the lineup himself. When Cochrane was assigned to the Pacific following the 1944 season, having reached the rank of lieutenant commander by then, he was succeeded by Bob Feller, returning from duty aboard a battleship. Feller helped continue the club's winning ways in 1945 by taking to the pitching mound as well, compiling a 13–2 record and striking out 130 batters in 95 innings. Former Tiger third baseman Pinky Higgins guided the squad in its last few war era games after Feller returned to the Indians in August.

Besides Feller and Virgil Trucks, who went 10–0 for the '44 Great Lakes team, the pitching staff at varying times included ex–big leaguers Tom Ferrick, Denny Galehouse, Johnny Gorsica, Bob Harris, Si Johnson, Johnny Rigney, and Schoolboy Rowe. Taking care of the hitting were the likes of Walker Cooper, Billy Herman, Higgins, Ken Keltner, Johnny Mize, Dick Wakefield, and Gene Woodling.

The force behind the sports program was base commander Captain Robert Emmet, the man responsible for training one third of the naval personnel assigned to sea duty. For those who felt athletics might be overemphasized at the installation, Emmet explained, "These men in training are just out of civilian life. They're facing the job of adjusting themselves to military life in addition to undergoing intensive routine. The game of baseball is a genuine incentive for wholesome thinking. They'll discuss the plays and players of an exciting game for days after the last out. When a man's mind is alive with interest and enthusiasm, there is no room in it for homsickness or depressive thoughts."

Virgil Trucks observes, "Captain Emmet was very fond of all sports and he went out and got good athletes. He was enthusiastic about the whole sports program. They had a great foootball squad there; Lou Groza was on the team. Tony Hinkle, who was a great coach at Indiana, was the head of the basketball program.

"Emmet was a regular old Navy man but he wasn't that strict, he pretty much let the athletes have a free reign."

Trucks contends that the 1944 Great Lakes team, which compiled a 48–2 record, "could have won the American League pennant or the National League for that matter."

The squad beat eleven of twelve major league opponents. Trucks himself hurled two-hitters against the Red Sox and White Sox and three-hitters against the Browns and Giants.

An otherwise perfect season was spoiled by a loss to the Dodgers, which could be taken in stride, and a defeat at the hands of a semipro team which, while recalled now by Trucks with great amusement, had sent Mickey Cochrane into a rage.

The Great Lakes club, at the time sporting a 23–0 record, was invited to Dearborn, Michigan, to play a team of Ford Motor Company employees. Somehow the sailors were held to a 1–1 tie going into the bottom of the ninth. With one out, Schoolboy Rowe decided to serve up a blooper pitch, a delivery utilized with considerable success during the war years by the Pirates' Rip Sewell. Rowe's blooper, however, proved to be a disastrous experiment. A young man named

Gene Malish promptly walloped it for a homer and an astonishing 2–1 Ford victory.

"Mickey Cochrane was so mad at Schoolboy Rowe he could have killed him," says Trucks. "Cochrane probably didn't catch ten innings all year, but this was sort of a reminiscing deal. Being that he had been with Detroit, the people in Dearborn wanted him to catch, and he did. He signed for a fast ball but Rowe throws up this blooper pitch and the kid hit it about four hundred feet in an open field, an inside the park home run."

Trucks continues:

"When we got back on the bus, I thought Cochrane was gonna give Rowe a dishonorable discharge, he was so mad at him. He said, 'If I ever catch another ball game and I call for a fast ball, or whatever pitch I call for, you better throw it. You'd better not throw the opposite pitch or I'll have you shipped out so far you'll never get back.'

"Cochrane told him, 'I'll guarantee you, the next time we play 'em I got somebody that'll beat 'em,' meaning me. They came to Great Lakes later. He put me in and I threw about six, seven innings, struck out about fifteen, just threw the ball right by 'em, and we won, I think, eleven to one or something like that; it was an ungodly score. And he felt he had revenge."

Did Rowe ever throw another blooper pitch?

"Never, no way. That broke him of that," Trucks laughs.

While they seldom played major league opponents, the Navy teams in Norfolk were also impressive.

The Norfolk Naval Training Station swept to a 92–8 record in 1942 on the arms of Fred Hutchinson and Bob Feller. Hutchinson, who would become a fine pitcher for the Tigers after the war, won twenty-three games; Feller had nineteen victories, his last one a 7–0 shutout against an unlikely opponent—the Washington office of the FBI. Vince Smith, a former Pirate, did the catching.

While the club had to make do the following year without Feller, who had gone to sea, the pitching staff was still formidable, featuring Hutchinson again, along with newcomers Charley Wagner of the Red Sox, Walt Masterson of the Senators, and Tom Early of the Braves. Smith was behind the plate while Phil Rizzuto and former Athletic Benny McCoy formed the double-play combination. The lineup also included Dom DiMaggio of the Red Sox, Don Padgett of the Dodgers, and Eddie Robinson of the Indians. Paced by Wagner's 17–5 mark and Rizzuto's .317 batting average, the 1943 edition rolled up a 75–25 record.

Norfolk's Bob Feller is reunited with ex-Indian catcher Frank Pytlak on 1942 servicemen's all-star team playing in Cleveland.

Most of the big leaguers were transferred out after the second wartime season. But Tommy Byrne, a promising Yankee southpaw, and Johnny Rigney of the White Sox, the latter moving over from Great Lakes, were fresh pitching arms helping the 1944 club post an 83–22 mark.

There was more than enough talent for both naval outfits in Norfolk.

When Pee Wee Reese was unable to beat out Rizzuto for the shortstop job on the '43 naval training station team, he was transferred to the naval air station club. Already there were Reese's exteammate, pitcher Hugh Casey; infielder Murray Franklin of the Tigers, and catcher Al Evans of the Senators.

Captains Harry A. McClure and C.C. Champion, Jr., the respective commanders at the naval training station and naval air station, were anxious to field strong clubs. Before throwing out the first ball at his squad's 1943 season opener, McClure gave a little pep talk suggesting baseball games were "point-blank proof to our enemies that they cannot succeed in overhauling our way of life."

While he liked to fraternize with his players, McClure did not forget the prerogatives of rank. George Case recalls: "He used to sit on the bench. One time the Senators were playing a game at Norfolk, the Navy had sent us down on a plane. Dom DiMaggio went after a ball and crashed into the fence. The commander went out to see if Dom was all right—in his jeep.

"They said if you didn't produce, you were on your way," adds Case, grinning. "One game I beat Masterson with a wrong field homer and two days later he was shipped out to the Pacific. He always claimed if I didn't get the hit, he'd have stayed there."

The baseball team attached to the Navy's preflight training program at the University of North Carolina had some pretty good ballplayers of its own—Ted Williams and the Reds' Harry Craft in the outfield, Johnny Pesky at shortstop, and Johnny Sain on the pitching mound. Also in the lineup were two ex–big leaguers named Buddy, both of whom happened to be first basemen. Buddy Gremp of the Braves moved over to third base while Buddy Hassett of the Yankees kept his customary position.

The 1944 team at the Sampson Naval Training Station in upstate New York, featuring the Reds' Johnny Vander Meer—famed for his consecutive no-hitters in 1938—was strong enough to wallop the Red Sox, 20–7, and the Indians, 15–2.

The Bainbridge, Maryland, Naval Training Station had four ex–big league shortstops on its 1944 club: Dick Bartell of the Giants, Buddy Blattner of the Cards, Fred Chapman of the Athletics, and Ray Hamrick of the Phillies. None of them was the team's leading hitter; that honor went to first baseman Elbie Fletcher, of late with the Pirates, who batted .344. While Bainbridge took five of eight games from major league opposition that year, it was only able to manage a 5–5 split against the Norfolk Naval Training Station. A young Cardinal outfielder named Stan Musial—the 1943 National League batting champ—was among the crop arriving at Bainbridge for the '45 season. Musial credits his days there with helping him develop as a long ball hitter, saying he altered his stance to pull the ball better so that he could belt some home runs for the sailors in the stands.

Not far away was the Curtis Bay, Maryland, Coast Guard ball club, starring Sid Gordon and Mickey Witek of the Giants, Lou Klein of the Cardinals, and Hank Sauer of the Reds.

The Army talent was hardly confined to the Fort Riley team. When an outfielder for the Santa Ana, California, Army Air Corps base singled in three trips to the plate against the Los Angeles Police Department in a June '43 contest, it was noted he had run up a thirteen-game hitting streak. There was a long way to go before Joe DiMaggio would match his old record.

The following month, when his club faced the Army Air Transport Command team from Long Beach, California, DiMaggio struck out and popped up twice. In times past he had been on the same side as the opposing pitcher that day—Red Ruffing.

Although thirty-eight years old at the time and minus four toes on his left foot, the result of an old coal mine accident, Ruffing had been inducted into the Army following the 1942 World Series. In the fall of '43, he would pitch his Long Beach squad to a 4–1 victory over Camp Pendleton for the Southern California service championship, besting Ted Lyons, another pretty good veteran hurler, who had left the White Sox at age forty-one to enlist in the Marines.

Luke Appling, who like Lyons had seen many seasons at Comiskey Park, let it be known upon reporting for induction in December '43 that "ducking bullets can't be much worse than ducking some of those bad hops in the infield." He did the latter, the Army putting him to work as manager-shortstop of the Camp Lee, Virginia, quartermaster post team.

Hugh Mulcahy and Johnny Beazley would continue their pitching careers with an Army Air Transport Command club in Tennessee. Hank Greenberg, having been loaned by Camp Custer to a prison team early in his service career, later did a little swatting for the Army itself in Florida.

It cannot be said, however, that the military kept ex–big leaguers back in the States for their entire service careers. Most would be sent abroad eventually—for some more baseball.

Army Chief of Staff Marshall ordered the dispersal overseas of servicemen-athletes under his jurisdiction following a survey in the

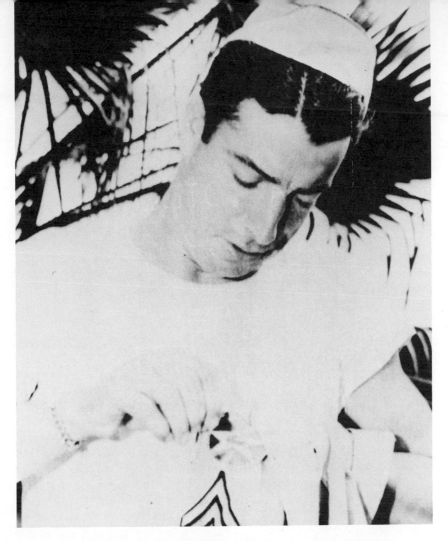

Army's baseball fortunes in the Pacific soar with Joe DiMaggio's Hawaii arrival in June 1944. Wearing sergeant's stripes instead of pinstripes these days, DiMaggio sews on shoulder patch of Seventh Army Air Force.

spring of 1944 showing 280 former professional baseball players—some never having finished basic training—still assigned to domestic bases.

The first stop for many would be Hawaii. By the summer of '44, the Army's Seventh Air Force, headquartered in Honolulu, had in its ranks a host of former major leaguers, including DiMaggio, Gordon, Ruffing, and Beazley.

The Navy did not issue a formal directive aimed at its domestic ballplayers until the spring of 1945, waiting until the war's waning months to pronounce "deliberate concentration of professional or publicly known athletes within the continental United States for the purpose of exploiting their specialties. . .detrimental to general morale."

But long before the directive was issued, the Navy had shipped its best ballplayers to Hawaii to counter the Army presence there.

Virgil Trucks tells how the Navy reinforcements were assembled in Hawaii during the late summer of 1944:

"I had just come home for boot leave. I had it coming after the Great Lakes season was over because I didn't take any after I got out of boot camp. We went right into our spring training program. I'd ridden a train all night to get home to Birmingham. I walked in the front door and immediately there's a telegram saying, 'Report back to Great Lakes immediately. Remainder of leave canceled.' I didn't know what had happened. So I get right back on the train and go back to Great Lakes and get in around noon the next day.

"I reported to the ship's company office and they asked, 'Can you get a plane out of Midway [the Chicago airport] at four o'clock this afternoon?' I said 'I guess so,' there wasn't any use saying anything else because they'd tell you to do it.

"So I flew first to Olathe, Kansas. I met up there with Schoolboy Rowe, who'd been at Great Lakes with me, and then Vander Meer comes in. We're just to report to San Francisco, we don't even know what our orders read. We were flying on a high priority. It took a commanding officer, and I mean a high commanding officer, to get our flying priority. We were bumping people like lieutenants and captains in the Army, left and right. We were knocking them off the plane for flying space.

"We get to San Francisco and they have a jeep meet us and take us someplace. The next morning we fall in line and they come find us guys and say, 'You're getting a plane out of here tonight from Alameda at ten o'clock.' We got on that plane and flew to Hawaii and a jeep met us there and took us straight to a sub base.

"And here are all these ballplayers assembled and I find out what we're there for—to play in the Army–Navy World Series."

The order came from the top, Trucks believes, continuing, "The Army out in Hawaii had DiMaggio and all those ballplayers and the Navy didn't have as much. The Navy was looked down on and Admiral Nimitz didn't go for that. He brought out all of those major league ballplayers who were in the Navy back in the States and challenged the Army to that World Series."

By September '44, the 14th Naval District in Hawaii had imported Trucks, Rowe, Vander Meer, Pee Wee Reese, Johnny Mize, Hugh Casey, Walt Masterson, and Al "No Soft Jobs" Brancato from domestic bases. Phil Rizzuto, who had been organizing recreational activities for wounded sailors at a fleet hospital in Brisbane, was deemed more essential battling the Army. So Rizzuto and Dom DiMaggio, also stationed in Australia, were flown to Honolulu.

The Army accepted Nimitz's challenge, but had to do without Dom's more illustrious brother, who was sidelined with ulcers.

Throwing out the Series' first ball at Furlong Stadium on the

Admiral Nimitz gets Army-Navy World Series under way.

grounds of the Schofield Army barracks in Honolulu, Nimitz sounded a call for unity, declaring, "We are all in a bigger league. We plan to keep the Japs in the cellar until they learn to play ball with civilized nations." Niceties out of the way, he then unleashed the Navy.

Trucks got things started, outpitching Johnny Beazley as the Navy defeated the Army, 5–0, in the opener. Nimitz's men won the second game, 8–2, behind the pitching of Vander Meer and Casey and a bases-loaded homer off the bat of Joe Grace, a former Browns outfielder. The series was originally scheduled for seven games, but was stretched to eleven contests to give as many soldiers and sailors as possible a chance to see the ballplayers. When it was all over, the Navy had won eight games, the Army had taken two, and one ended in a tie.

"We sure went to work, we sure demoralized the Army," Trucks chuckles.

Having presumably justified his mission to Hawaii by rapping out twelve hits and playing errorless ball, Rizzuto was flown back to Australia when the series was over. His Navy teammates were scattered among various installations in Hawaii, but a few months later they, too, would be heading elsewhere.

Early in 1945, the Navy divided its Hawaii ballplayers into two teams, one representing the Third Fleet and the other the Fifth Fleet. Under the supervision of Mace Brown, an ex–big league pitcher and Marine lieutenant, the men were flown to play on a string of Pacific islands taken in the preceding months from the Japanese.

"Some of those spots where we played, like in the Palau group, weren't big enough to make landing strips on, so you'd land on one island and take landing-craft boats over to the next island and play," Trucks recalls. "They'd go in with bulldozers and scrape off a big level field and line it up and that's where we'd play. Mize hit several right over the palm trees into the ocean.

"We were playing before Army, Navy, and Marine people and one thing's for sure, we always had a great crowd. We played hard. Some of those games we'd knock batters down just like we were playing big league baseball."

The plan had been to have the two teams go back to Hawaii after the tour with the ballplayers being returned to their respective bases there. Things did not, however, work out that way because, according to Trucks, one member of the group had a little too much to say.

Tennis star Bobby Riggs had been tapped to play matches on the tour with Buddy Blattner, who besides being a big league infielder was also a Ping Pong champion and an outstanding tennis player.

It's not quite the Forbes Field water cooler, but lister bag will have to do for ex-Pirate catcher Vince Smith, cooling off before March 1945 Navy baseball game on Guam.

"Bobby Riggs is the one that got us in trouble," says Trucks. "He said we're gonna take a tour in the South Pacific and come back to Hawaii. Somehow or other this got on the news broadcasts and was played back in the States and here, we're still in a war yet, the war isn't over by any means. So Nimitz says yeah, they're going on tour, and when they finish they're gonna stay out there. That's exactly what happened. They dumped us on several islands when it was over. I guess the most guys at any one base were Connie Ryan, myself, Del Ennis, and Johnny Vander Meer. We were all stationed in one group on Guam."

The Army ballplayers also would make their way to Pacific outposts, but not without a snafu or two.

Tex Hughson picks up the story from the Army side as of March '45 when he was pulled out of the San Marcos, Texas, air corps base just as its baseball season was about to begin.

"Orders came out of Washington to get the remaining Army athletes out of the States; there were naturally some complaints about us having good hideouts and all," he says.

"We met at Kearns Field in Salt Lake City; this was kind of a jumping off point before going overseas. We had football players there, too. The football players, who didn't have to play for several months, were processed through in about three days and flown to

Hawaii. The baseball players spent several weeks at least in Salt Lake City and went through basic training all over again and then went to Seattle and then by Liberty ship to the Hawaiian islands.

"The other ballplayers over there who'd been waiting on us wanted to know where the hell we'd been. It was an Army screw-up on the orders."

By the time the Army athletes arrived in Hawaii, the Navy ballplayers had long since departed for their Pacific tour. So the fresh crop of Army men busied themselves facing each other.

"We were divided into three teams while we were on the Hawaiian islands," Hughson remembers. "One was at Hickam Field, one at Camp Wheeler, and the team I was with, we were stationed at a little fighter base about twenty miles out of Honolulu. Buster Mills [a former big league outfielder] was the head of my ball club, he was a first lieutenant. We had no involvement with the Navy whatsoever, except we played a naval air station a game or two."

The delay in dispatching the Army ballplayers to Hawaii was not the only foul-up, Hughson continuing, "I remember one instance where there was supposed to have been an outstanding softball team on one of the Pacific islands—Eniwetok or someplace—so they came up with this idea of sending the Camp Wheeler team from Hawaii down there to play a seven-game series. They flew the team two thousand miles in an old flying boxcar, a B-24. But they only played seven innings before the club lost all the balls, knocked them in the ocean. They weren't used to these major league hitters that could hit the ball four hundred feet. This was just another one of the goof-ups."

After spending about six weeks in Hawaii, the three Army squads were shipped out to entertain the troops that had taken the Mariana island group.

In midsummer, Hughson's ball club, whose headquarters were now on Saipan, paid a visit to play some games against the other two Army teams, which were based on another of the coral islands making up the Mariana chain fifteen hundred miles southeast of Japan. The athletes would learn later of a secrecy-shrouded hangar on that island not far from their ballfield. The shed belonged to the Twentieth Air Force's 509th Composite Group. The island was Tinian where on August 6, 1945, at 2:45 A.M. the "Enola Gay" lifted off on a mission to end the war.

"There was a lot of scuttlebut that something big was going to happen," Hughson says. "But you know how rumors can get around in the Army. We had no inkling of the magnitude of what it was, of course. We weren't too far from where they took off with the atomic bomb and we did see all the films and reconnaissance reports the next day. They were blown up in the orderly room."

The Army ballplayers tried to appear before as many troops as possible, but conditions sometimes stymied them.

"The ballparks were all what you'd call skin infields; there was no grass," Hughson recalls. "They were well prepared by the Seabees but it rained quite often. About every other day we were rained out because when a shower would come, the red clay would be wet and we'd get our cleats all clogged up."

While most of the Army games were played on the Mariana islands of Saipan, Tinian, and Guam—the GI crowd seated on wooden bomb crates—Hughson also recounts a visit to what is today perhaps the best remembered Pacific outpost of the war:

"We went up to Iwo Jima after it was secured and instead of having three teams, we were divided back into two—American and National League all-stars—and we played a series.

"We played in a natural amphitheater-type place and the GIs sat all the way around on the bank of this gradual slope. They estimated up to twenty thousand were at some of the ball games."

"I kid everyone," Hughson says. "I tell them I fought World War II with a baseball bat and glove."

After MacArthur returned, as promised, to the Philippines, a lot of baseball was played in Manila's bullet-scarred Rizal Stadium, which could hold up to thirty thousand GIs. Some eight hundred booby traps, along with the body of a Japanese soldier found between third base and home plate, had to be taken out, however, before the ballplayers could move in.

The stadium was home for an Army team managed by Kirby Higbe and dubbed, appropriately enough, the Manila Dodgers. The pitching staff, which included future National Leaguers Jim Hearn and Vern Bickford besides Higbe, was so strong that Senator hurler Early Wynn played some shortstop. Much of the catching was done by Joe Garagiola, who became linked with a man of somewhat greater renown who had appeared in the park years before.

"The Manila ballpark had been shot up quite a bit, but it had its traditions," Garagiola explained upon joining the Cardinals after the war. "They painted your name on the wall if you hit a homer. They had Babe Ruth's name up there. I got mine in alongside his, I hit two."

The stadium was used by other service teams as well, one of whom employed a ringer to win a bet.

Eddie Waitkus, who played in Rizal for the 544th Regiment, later recounted how $60,000 was wagered by soldiers from his unit and the 594th Regiment on a game between the two outfits. Just before the contest, Waitkus, who would go on to play first base for many years in the majors, encountered Fred Martin, a pitcher in the Cardinal chain whom he knew from his Texas League days. Martin was with a field artillery unit that had no connection with either of the contending regiments. No matter.

"I had no trouble getting him to agree to pitch," Waitkus recalled. "Martin didn't belong to our regiment, but we made it legal by having him attached to the 544th for rations and quarters. He pitched a great game for us, winning 1–0."

Far be it from the Army, meanwhile, to slight the GIs stationed in Europe. In the months after V-E Day, the soldiers who weren't being shifted to the Pacific had a lot of time on their hands. They could be kept busy rooting for former big leaguers representing their outfits.

The Army appropriated soccer stadiums for use as ballfields, putting on baseball tournaments in Austrian cities such as Salzburg, Traun, and Linz. In Germany, Nuremberg Stadium, where the Nazis had goose-stepped before enormous throngs, would now be known as Soldiers Field. A section of the grounds became a baseball diamond.

Harry Walker tells how he came to be the playing manager of the 65th Division ball club:

"At Fort Riley we won seven straight games at a tournament in Wichita. Then they sent six of us down to Camp Shelby, Mississippi. George Archie and George Scharein, Kenny Heintzelman, Rex Barney, Al Brazle, and myself went to join the Sixty-fifth Division. And we went overseas together and landed in Le Havre. We stayed pretty much together all through, went about five hundred miles in combat. Our whole group was in a reconnaissance outfit.

"When we moved into Austria, the general talked to me—General [Stanley] Reinhart, he was a real nice guy—and said he'd like to have a ballclub to entertain the soldiers. So we put together a club. First we played in a town called Traun, about fifteen miles out of Linz; then we moved into Linz, built a ballpark on what used to be a soccer field. Tom McKenna, who's now the trainer with the Mets, was our trainer, and the fella that did the announcing was Lindsey Nelson."

Though it had half a dozen former big leaguers, Walker's 65th Division squad wasn't good enough to win even the Third Army championship. That honor went to the 71st Division, whose pitching star was a 6-foot-6 sidearmer named Ewell Blackwell, later a standout with the Cincinnati Reds. When the 71st went on to play for the European championship against a team from Reims, France—Allied headquarters on the continent and site of the German surrender—it was, however, taking no chances. The best players from the other clubs in the Third Army were borrowed, among them Harry Walker. Two games of the series were played in Reims, the other three at Nuremberg.

Walker recalls, "We'd have close to sixty thousand GIs watching at Nuremberg. It gave them a chance to feel like they were back home, to be out there drinking beer and cokes and eating peanuts. The field was beautiful; the infield was red-looking, real fine crushed brick, and with the green grass it was very pretty. We had just one corner of the place, it was so big. L-5 planes (Stinson Sentinels—light observation and transport craft) landed out in center field where Hitler used to parade his big guns and everything. They had a small fence, about five-foot high, I guess, around the area, and all the guys that could fly in would land right inside."

The Reims team won the European servicemen's title, three games to two, then, adding Walker and a few others from the Third Army, defeated the Mediterranean theater champs.

"We went over to Italy and played on a soccer field near the Leaning Tower," Walker remembers, "then we came back and played for about a week in Nice, on the Riviera. The other team was an all-colored unit."

Walker, meanwhile, had his own plan involving the use of former major league ballplayers who, like himself, had seen battlefield action:

"They were talking about promotional events. I said why not take a team that had been in combat and go back to play in New York, Brooklyn, maybe five major cities. We'd take all the money from that and give it to the veterans who had lost arms or legs or eyes. I thought maybe we could raise half a million dollars.

"It was about July '45 when I started this thing. They thought it was a little too late, they liked for me to start on it the next year. I said the only thing was, most of your ballplayers that would mean something would be out of the Army by then. I certainly knew wasn't any of 'em gonna stay in the Army just to play it. And by next spring we had gotten out."

While the Army and Navy put together teams of professional caliber, they also used ex–big leaguers to set up recreational programs for the ordinary serviceman. The most prolific organizer was Zeke Bonura, dubbed the "Judge Landis of North Africa." A less than graceful first baseman, but a long ball hitter with the White Sox, Senators, Giants, and Cubs, Bonura was one of the first major league players taken into the Army. By the summer of 1943, operating out of Oran, Algeria, he had set up ten GI baseball leagues with eighty teams and was also running boxing, basketball, and touch football programs. The efforts were not without reward. Citing him for "a substantial contribution to the morale and efficiency of troops in the field," Eisenhower personally decorated Corporal Bonura with the Legion of Merit.

Now living in retirement in his native New Orleans, Zeke Bonura recounts how he became the Army's unofficial commissioner of sports:

"Greenberg and I got drafted about the same time. I left for the Army in '41. I'd been with the Cubs, but at the end of the '40 season, when my draft number came up and it looked like I was about to go in, they got rid of me, sold me to Minneapolis. It was under condition. Mike Kelly, the Minneapolis owner, told Jimmy Gallagher, the Cubs' general manager, if I came back alive, he'd give him ten thousand. The Cubs figured, well, hell, they weren't gonna lose anything. It was like I was a dead fish. I'd be too old to come back to them anyway. And I was. Hell, I was close to thirty-eight when I got out.

"So I played about a month with Minneapolis before going into the service. I was inducted at Camp Shelby and I made a ball diamond up there with the help of the other GIs. They said gee whiz, this fella can do more overseas than he can do here, he's a helluva promoter. So I went over in special service.

"I didn't play much, just a little bit with a headquarters team. I wasn't over there to play ball, but to have the GIs play, keep the fellas busy till they got up to the front lines."

In addition to the baseball leagues, there were softball lessons to be given. Bonura recalls, "My commanding officer, General Arthur A. Wilson, said, 'Now, Zeke, you gotta get the nurses to do something because they're always there in the operating room, they need to have some play.' So I organized softball games for the nurses. We put on a big leg show, I had 'em put on tights for the GIs. I had a helluva time, they didn't want to put the shorts on, they said they'd rather play with slacks. I said all we're doing is putting on a show for the GIs."

"Eisenhower pinned the Legion of Merit on me one day out there," Bonura remembers with pride. "There were about six of us

Army nurses in North Africa—this group shunning shorts—get batting tips from Cpl. Zeke Bonura.

got it. He shook my hand and all for this promotion I did. He was a baseball fan, he'd be sitting there watching the games."

The citation accompanying the commendation stated that Bonura had "established twenty baseball fields in the area through the use of voluntary assistance."

He tells about the "vounteers":

"The Italian prisoners of war we had did the work. They didn't know a baseball diamond from Adam and Eve but I could speak a little Italian. I showed 'em what we had to do and I stayed out there with 'em till we got it organized, dragging the infield and marking it off. I'd get a detail of forty-five or fifty men, they had a helluva time, they all wanted to come out. I treated 'em good, saw they'd eat the GI rations."

When POWs weren't busy as groundskeepers, they set up boxing rings, Bonura recalling:

"I got a bunch of boxers, all amateurs, GIs who liked to box. They wouldn't have tights. All they'd do is take their shirt off and wear their big, big gloves. Nobody would get hurt. I was the referee, the timer, and every damn thing. The Italian prisoners would build the rings and we'd have a little gooseneck light for when they'd fight at night. You couldn't have a big light because the German planes would see it, they'd come and bomb the shit out of us."

"We had German prisoners of war, too, but they weren't kept together with the Italians, they didn't like each other," Bonura notes. "I once put them both together to play a soccer game and boy, you talk about blood and guts. So they stopped me and said, 'Don't do that anymore.'"

Bonura would meet directly with the brass to go over plans for organizing servicemen's activities throughout North Africa. He explains he was not an easy man to pry loose from the assignment:

"One time this priest came over to me. He said, I'm Father so-and-so, I'd like to get you to join our outfit. He was with a tank batallion waiting to be assigned to fight the Germans at the Kasserine Pass. He said, 'If we get you, we'll make you a captain in the athletic department.' Not a lieutenant, he wanted to make me a captain right off the bat.

"I said, 'I appreciate that Father, but you'd have to go see my boss, General Arthur A. Wilson.' He said, 'Don't you have some colonel ahead of you?' and I told him, 'No, the big boss over here, he's the man to see. I'm assigned to General Wilson.'

"So he went to see the general and he came back and said, 'Boy oh boy, you stay in strong with that man, there wasn't a Chinaman's chance for me to get you. The general said no, he couldn't let you go with one outfit, he'd have to keep you here for all the boys.'

"So I stayed there, I was kind of a freelancer."

But it wasn't all fun and games for the athlete turned soldier or sailor. More than a few ballplayers went into combat in the air, on the ground, or at sea.

No one on a big league roster at the time of Pearl Harbor was to die in action. Two men who had made brief appearances in the majors in 1939, however, did lose their lives. Elmer Gedeon, who played five games in the Senators' outfield, died on April 15, 1944, when the plane he was piloting was shot down by a Luftwaffe fighter over St. Pol, France. It was his twenty-seventh birthday. Two years before, Gedeon had been decorated for pulling a fellow crewman from the wreckage of an Army bomber that had crashed in North Carolina, returning to the plane despite broken ribs and shock. He suffered burns in the rescue and was hospitalized for three months. Harry O'Neill, who caught one game for the Athletics, was killed on Iwo Jima in March of 1945.

There was a far heavier toll among minor league ballplayers who, being younger than their big league counterparts and without celebrity status, were more likely to get into the fighting. By December of 1944, a total of forty-one men from the minors had died in combat.

Bomber pilot Billy Southworth, Jr., was the most highly publicized minor leaguer on the war front. An outfielder on the roster of the International League Toronto Maple Leafs when he joined the Army Air Corps in December 1940—the first man from organized baseball to enlist in the service—the son of the Cardinal manager was much the dashing aviator. Credited with popularizing baseball headgear among pilots, Southworth made twenty-five bombing runs over Europe wearing a St. Louis cap given him by his father. It seemed to be a good luck charm—his B-17 Flying Fortresses were never hit. By the time he returned to the United States for reassignment early in 1944, Southworth had reached the rank of major and wore the Distinguished Flying Cross and Air Medal. A chance meeting with Hollywood producer Hunt Stromberg resulted in a ten-year movie contract to take effect after the war.

But then his luck ran out. The morning of February 15, 1945, Southworth took off from Mitchel Field on Long Island for a routine flight to Florida. Suddenly, one of the four engines on his B-29 Superfortress gave out a heavy stream of smoke. He tried for an emergency landing at LaGuardia Field, but the bomber overshot the runway and plunged into twenty-feet of water in Flushing Bay. Five crewmen were picked up by the Coast Guard. Southworth and four others couldn't be found. Almost six months after the crash, a New York City police launch discovered the body of Billy Southworth, Jr., off a beach in the Bronx. He was twenty-seven years old.

The best-known airman from major league ranks was Buddy Lewis of the Senators, a third baseman and outfielder who had been among the American League's top hitters in prewar days.

Lewis went off to war with a flourish. The Senators and Athletics were in the fourth inning of a doubleheader nightcap at Griffith Stadium one Sunday in June '43 when a plane appeared behind center field. The twenty-two thousand spectators were startled to see the craft swoop low over the diamond. The Washington ballplayers had, however, expected it.

George Case tells the story:

"Buddy had gone into the Air Corps and we hadn't heard much

from him. All of a sudden before batting practice that day, in comes Buddy in his uniform. He'd flown to Washington from Georgia, taken some VIPs up. We smothered him, asked him 'how're you doing' and all that. He said, 'I can't stay, but when I leave I'll buzz the field.'

"I'm in the on-deck circle in the second game, ready to hit, and here comes this DC-3 straight out of center field, breaking all air regulations. The fans didn't know who it was, but we did. He cut the field in half, almost hit the flagpole. He wiggled his wings and I threw my bat in the air. That was the most thrilling thing that ever happened to me. He told me later he got reprimanded for it."

Lewis was to make better use of his aviator's skills as a transport pilot in the China–Burma–India theater, flying numerous missions over the "Hump" in a C-47 he named "The Old Fox" after Clark Griffith. He received the Distinguished Flying Cross and Air Medal.

Another airman from the American League was Phil Marchildon, a native of a tiny Ontario farming community who joined the Royal Canadian Air Force after managing a 17–14 record pitching for the 1942 Athletics.

The hurler received a commission and was assigned as a gunner aboard Halifax bombers. On the night of August 16–17, 1944, while flying his twenty-sixth mission, Marchildon's plane was shot down laying mines in Kiel Bay off Nazi-occupied Denmark. Parachuting eighteen thousand feet into the water, he swam for four hours before being picked up by a Danish fisherman, only to be turned over to the Germans. Marchildon spent the next nine months in a prison camp, losing almost forty pounds before his repatriation with 256 other Canadian airmen.

The ordeal left him a bad case of nerves. Sleep did not come easily and his appetite was slow in returning. Yet after resting at home, Marchildon was able to rejoin the Athletics in July '45 and made three appearances that season.

"When he came back he was very quiet and very serious about everything he did," George Kell recalls. "Mr. Mack said he'd really changed. He'd been through a lot. But he said very little about it."

By the 1946 season, Marchildon was able to regain his form, posting a 13–16 record with a last-place Athletics club.

Hank Greenberg had a close call while in an administrative post with the Army Air Corps. Serving in 1944 as the commander of a headquarters squadron at a base in China, Greenberg was in the control tower with a priest one day when a B-29 taking off for a raid

Phil Marchildon (left) and Jack Knott (center)—considerably tougher days lying ahead—warm up with Les McCrabb at Athletics' 1942 spring camp in Anaheim, California.

on Japan suffered a mishap on the runway. As Greenberg and the chaplain raced to rescue the crew, the plane's bomb load exploded. The force sent the pair sprawling into a drainage ditch. Greenberg had trouble hearing for a few days, remarking later, "That was one occasion when I didn't wonder whether or not I'd be able to return to baseball, I was quite satisfied just to be alive." As it turned out, his rescue effort had not been needed. The twelve crewmen had scrambled to safety just before the plane blew up.

Red Sox lefty Earl Johnson spent his early days in the Army pitching for the Camp Roberts, California, Rangers, taking the opportunity to develop a fork ball. He saw considerably more action later in a rifle platoon of the 30th Division, 120th Infantry, participating in Bradley's St. Lo breakthrough following the Normandy invasion and in the Battle of the Bulge. Johnson received a battlefield commission and was awarded the Bronze Star for braving German fire to recover a jeep stranded with valuable electronic equipment. He was also to win the Silver Star.

In between playing baseball at Fort Riley and Nuremberg, Harry Walker experienced his share of the real war. He tells how he won the Bronze Star with the Sixty-fifth Division:

"It happened right near the end. You realized the war couldn't last much longer and it scared the hell out of you. You've always read about how many people were killed after the war was over because nobody knew it. I thought, my God, why don't they just go ahead and quit. The last bunch we captured were boys fifteen to eighteen years old.

"I was in a recon outfit. You look at a western movie and see the scouts going forward. That's pretty much what we were doing, except on a mechanized basis. You'd try to find roadblocks or bridges blown up and report back so you wouldn't have your infantry or artillery pieces bottled up where the enemy's artillery or planes could get to them. You'd try to keep out in front, from five to ten miles, and one time we got seventy miles back of the enemy lines.

"One night about 11 o'clock we were trying to get to a bridge going out of Germany into Austria. It was on a river not too far from Passeau. We didn't have but thirty men. We were just about a half-mile from the bridge when we had to stop. It was sleeting and raining, and we ran into three guys, guards that were patrolling the thing. At first they thought we were Germans because we were so far ahead of the lines.

"I tried to get them to surrender. Well, one guy pulled his gun up in my face. I had a .45 revolver that I'd bought in the States. That little thing saved my life. The guy that pulled the gun, I shot him in the chest and then I shot the others. Killed the first two and wounded the third guy. It was so damned quick, it was almost like a machine gun went off. It was just one of those deals that you didn't want to happen, but your reaction was to live and that's about it."

There was more action ahead, the following day. Walker continues: "I was on point with a .50 caliber machine gun when we ran into a bunch that were trying to get across the bridge. I shot a few with that. It would tear up most anything. And we captured a bunch of soldiers and some big guns, 88s."

In addition to the Bronze Star, Walker received the Purple Heart, though he was not seriously wounded.

"First I got hit in the hand with a piece of artillery, shrapnel from an 88.

"Later," he laughs, "I got hit in the rump with a piece of our own. I took a rifle grenade and threw it. It hit this building before we could get out. But it wasn't too bad. I was real lucky."

Walker sums up:

"It was quite an experience. I wouldn't ever want to go through it again, but I certainly feel good that I got to be in this thing, to see what it was all about. It makes you appreciate what you've got here so much more. We've got faults, we bitch and complain, but I think our country is the greatest in the world."

When it came to the battlefield, the Philadelphia Athletics were a lot tougher than the club's past fortunes in the American League would indicate. Besides Phil Marchildon, A's pitchers Jack Knott and Bob Savage and shortstop Jack Wallaesa saw plenty of combat.

Knott, entering the Army at age thirty-five, won a battlefield commission and was wounded in the Battle of the Bulge.

Savage received a shrapnel wound of the right shoulder during the fighting in Italy. Undaunted, he wrote to Connie Mack from a hospital bed, "I hope they will be able to dig it out because more than anything else, I want to pitch." Savage did return to the mound in 1946, and though his record was 3–15, three others on that last-place club lost more games.

Wallaesa, assigned to an Army port batallion as a stevedore, spent forty-three days unloading ammunition at Anzio. "I don't think any pitcher will ever scare me again after that experience," he remarked later. "Dozens of times I got down on my knees and prayed as I saw ships blown up around me and my buddies tossed into the water."

Pitcher Lou Brissie, like Bert Shepard, was a symbol of courage for wounded servicemen. While a teenager, Brissie had been given a tryout by Connie Mack but was advised he was not ready for professional baseball. He enrolled at Presbyterian College in South Carolina and then, when the war came, joined the Army. Fighting with the paratroopers in the Appenine Mountains of northern Italy during December '44, he suffered shrapnel wounds of the feet, legs, hands, and shoulders from a bursting German shell. A total of twenty-three operations would follow. But in the spring of 1946, Lou Brissie was ready to give baseball another try, turning up at the Athletics' training camp. Strapped to his left leg was a whittled-down catcher's shin guard with a rubber sponge underneath, protection for bones and nerves left exposed by his injuries. He was sent to the minors, but made it back to the A's a few years later, winning fourteen games in 1948 and sixteen the following season.

John Grodzicki, a promising young pitcher with the Cardinals before the war, suffered a shrapnel wound of the right thigh five weeks before V-E Day as his paratroop unit fought in the final battles on German soil. A few months after discarding crutches, Grodzicki

Navy antiaircraft gunner Bob Feller.

went to the Cards' 1946 spring camp, wearing a steel brace and taking massage treatments in efforts to strengthen his right leg. He pitched some, but was never effective.

Cecil Travis, a star shortstop for the Senators who entered the Army after batting .359 in the 1941 season, suffered frozen feet in the Battle of the Bulge. He returned to baseball eventually but had lost mobility and could not regain his hitting form.

Kirby Higbe went from the baseball team at Fort Jackson to a combat infantryman's job with the 86th (Blackhawk) Division. His rubber boat was narrowly missed by a German artillery shell in the crossing of the Danube.

On the Pacific front, Bob Feller helped take care of the Japanese. While he could have spent the war in the Navy's physical training program—in short, playing baseball—Feller took gunnery courses at Norfolk and Newport, Rhode Island, and requested sea duty. After finishing up the Norfolk Naval Training Station's 1942 baseball season, he was assigned to the U.S.S. *Alabama.* The battleship was stationed in the North Atlantic for the first half of 1943, then went through the Panama Canal to the Pacific to provide protection for aircraft carriers.

Placed in charge of an antiaircraft gun crew, Feller blazed away at low-flying Japanese attack planes with Bofors .40-millimeter guns in naval campaigns off the Gilbert Islands, the Marshall Islands, and Truk. He served twenty-seven months at sea before returning home to join the Great Lakes baseball team.

George Earnshaw, best known for pitching twenty-two consecutive scoreless innings for the Athletics against the Cardinals in the 1930 World Series, obtained a Navy commission at age forty-one, five years after his retirement from baseball. Assigned initially to coach the Jacksonville Naval Air Station baseball team, Earnshaw, like Feller, requested combat duty and was given command of a gunnery team aboard the aircraft carrier *Yorktown.* He received a commendation from Admiral Nimitz in the fall of 1944 for directing fire against Japanese torpedo planes in the battle for Truk. By the end of the war, Earnshaw had risen to the rank of commander.

Larry French, having been denied a Navy furlough to try for the two-hundredth-victory mark, proceeded to more serious matters, participating in the Normandy invasion and Pacific operations. When mustered out of the service in the fall of 1945, he was a lieutenant commander. He was also thirty-eight years old. It was too late to go back to the mound and pick up those last three elusive wins.

There were some athletes who emerged from military service a little worse for wear without having fired a shot.

Finishing up his Army career with the Camp Lee, Virginia, baseball team, Pete Reiser fell into a ditch while chasing a fly ball and aggravated a shoulder injury incurred in his confrontation with the Sportsman's Park fence.

Cardinal second baseman Frank "Creepy" Crespi broke his left leg playing for Fort Riley in the summer of 1943 and was confined to an Army hospital. Not one to remain inactive for long, he proceeded to get into a wheelchair race. It ended with patient and wheelchair slamming into a corridor wall. Crespi broke the same leg in another place. He never made it back to the majors.

VI

The Road to Peace

9

Hellos, Good-Byes, and a Man Named Robinson

Southpaw Charley Gassaway of the Athletics went into his windup, delivered to the right-handed hitter, and then watched in dismay as the ball soared off the bat toward Briggs Stadium's left field pavilion, clearing the wall 375 feet away.

The 47,729 fans on hand—hardly a turnout one would expect the sad sack A's to draw—roared with delight as the batter circled the bases. He had been hitless in four previous trips to the plate, but now in the eighth inning the spectators had been rewarded.

On this first day of July 1945, after four years and two months in the Army, Hank Greenberg had returned to baseball. It was the beginning of the end for people like Charley Gassaway.

At first the exodus was a trickle. Only 9 percent of the big leaguers in military service were discharged during the '45 season, and some of them decided to wait until the following spring to make their comeback. But a few stars were back in uniform for the latter stages of the final wartime pennant races, and judging from their performance, it seemed they had never been away.

The Tigers, the first team to be hurt by the war, with the early loss of Hank Greenberg, reaped the biggest rewards.

He hadn't played much baseball in the service and returning at age thirty-four, after an extended layoff, was plagued with a charley horse, sore arm, blistered hands, and a sprained ankle. Yet Greenberg had little trouble regaining his batting form against wartime pitching.

Appearing in seventy-eight games, he batted .311, knocked in sixty runs, and hit thirteen homers. The final one, a ninth-inning, bases-loaded drive against the Browns, gave the Tigers the '45 pennant over the Washington Senators on the last day of the season.

The starting pitcher for Detroit in that final game at Sportsman's

259

Park had himself shed a uniform of another kind. Virgil Trucks received a medical discharge from the Navy at Norman, Oklahoma, the last Tuesday of the season, worked out with catcher Paul Richards on Friday, and pronounced himself fit to pitch on Sunday.

"I had a bad knee for a long time and the problem recurred on Guam," Trucks recalls. "The war was about over and I wanted to get out, so I turned in to sick bay in Guam and stayed there about three weeks, a month, and they decided to send me back to Hawaii. I stayed there a few weeks and they shipped me to San Francisco and then to the Norman naval station.

"They had no ball club there, but I found a kid who had caught a little baseball. I threw to him and I just ran around the base hospital and got myself into the best condition I could. I was discharged just before the season ended, caught a train out of Norman to St. Louis, and started that ball game. I didn't try to throw any sliders or curves, I just threw all fastballs."

Trucks had enough stuff to last into the sixth inning when, with the Browns leading, 2–1, he was relieved by Hal Newhouser, who received credit for the 6–3 pennant-clinching win.

The two service returnees led the Tigers to a 4–1 victory in the second game of the World Series against the Cubs, Greenberg blasting a three-run homer off Hank Wyse and Trucks pitching all the way.

Bob Feller was discharged from Great Lakes in mid-August of 1945, went right back to the Indians and in his debut before 46,477 hometown fans, hurled a 4–2 victory over the Tigers, scattering four hits and striking out twelve. He finished out the season with a 5–3 record.

The twenty-six-year-old Feller was in his prime, but the wartime lineups posed no problem either for Red Ruffing, in a Yankee uniform again at age forty-one after a two-and-a-half-year service hitch. Ruffing weighed 245 pounds—30 pounds over his last playing weight—when released from the Army Air Corps in early June. But he managed to shed half the excess poundage in workouts and returned to the mound on July 26, pitching shutout ball for six innings against the Athletics before needing relief help. An old man by baseball standards, Ruffing, like Greenberg, had assorted aches and pains—blisters and arm, leg, and back muscle cramps—but remembered enough about pitching to go 7–3 for the last half of the '45 season.

Athletics' pitcher Dick Fowler, returning after three years in the Canadian Army, promptly threw a no-hitter against the Browns.

Virgil Trucks (left) and Hank Greenberg whoop it up after starring roles in second game of 1945 World Series.

Buddy Lewis, coming back to the Senators just before his twenty-ninth birthday, found his batting eye quickly, hitting .333 in sixty-nine games. Luke Appling, thirty-eight years old when he returned to the White Sox after two years in the Army, hit for a .362 average in eighteen games. Charlie Keller, once again in the Yankee outfield following his release from the U.S. Maritime Service, batted .301 over forty-four games.

There were some fine welcome-home tributes, the biggest splash accorded Bob Feller. A reception arranged by Cleveland Mayor Tom Burke drew one thousand people to the Hotel Carter's Rainbow

Senators welcome pitcher Walt Masterson (left) and shortstop Cecil Travis back from military service with $500 war bonds. Baseball commissioner Happy Chandler seems a lot happier about the whole thing than Washington owner Clark Griffith.

Room. In festivities at Muncipal Stadium, ex-Indian greats Cy Young and Tris Speaker, heading a civic committee, presented Feller with a jeep for his Iowa farm.

Buddy Lewis, Walt Masterson, and Cecil Travis received war bonds from the Senators in pregame ceremonies.

Travis returned to the Washington lineup for a Saturday afternoon game with the Browns on September 8, but the attention of the Griffith Stadium crowd that day was elsewhere. With a Navy band doing the honors, the strains of "Hail to the Chief" were heard in a ballpark for the first time since the opening day of the 1941 season. Harry Truman, accompanied by military aides, cabinet members, a thirteen-member congressional delegation, and wife Bess, was on hand to throw out the first ball.

The president's appearance, like the return of a few stars, seemed to be a sign that things were getting back to normal. But soon after the close of the 1945 season, it became clear that while the familiar faces would be back, the world of baseball would never be quite the same again.

The new era dawned on October 23 with the signing by the Dodgers' Montreal farm club of an ex-Army lieutenant and four-sport UCLA letterman named Jackie Robinson.

The war years had seen some strides toward racial equality in American society. Roosevelt banned discrimination in defense industries and established a Fair Employment Practices Commission to investigate complaints. With the home front economy booming, the black man was bound to receive some slice of the more generous economic pie. On the political front, the Supreme Court struck down the all-white primary. Negroes were organizing themselves in greater numbers to battle the hypocrisy of a nation fighting totalitarianism abroad while maintaining segregation at home. NAACP membership, 50,000 in 1940, had increased tenfold by the end of the war.

As for the baseball scene, the last segregated seating arrangement in the major leagues was eliminated in May 1944 when the Cardinals and Browns announced that Negroes would no longer be confined to the screened-in right field pavilion at Sportsman's Park. Otherwise, so far as America's national sport was concerned, time seemed to be standing still.

Representatives of CIO unions including the auto workers and

Harry Truman, flanked by the First Lady and Adm. William D. Leahy, takes in September 1945 Senators-Browns game, marking the first presidential visit to a ballpark in four and a half years.

longshoremen—all but one of the delegates white—went to the December 1942 baseball meetings in Chicago to take up the question of baseball's color barrier with Commissioner Landis. He refused to see them.

Bill Veeck, in his autobiography *Veeck As In Wreck,* says he tried to buy the financially ailing Phillies early in 1943 with the aim of stocking the club with players from the Negro leagues. Veeck maintains that Phillie President Gerry Nugent was agreeable to selling, but as soon as Landis was informed of what was in the works, the National League took over the team and sold it to Bill Cox's syndicate for half the price Veeck was willing to pay.

Paul Robeson, the distinguished black actor, and a delegation of black publishers met with Landis and other baseball officials in December 1943 to ask that the racial barrier be lifted. Landis's response: "Each club is entirely free to employ Negro players to any and all extent it desires. The matter is solely one for each club's decision without restriction whatsoever."

In the spring of 1945, members of the Negro press and the sports editor of the pro-Communist *Daily Worker* showed up at the Dodgers' Bear Mountain camp with two ballplayers from the Negro leagues, Terris McDuffie, a thirty-four-year-old pitcher, and Dave (Showboat) Thomas, a thirty-nine-year-old first baseman, demanding they be given a tryout. Branch Rickey agreed to let the pair work out before him, apart from the Dodger squad, but was not impressed. Perhaps dropping a hint of things to come, Rickey told the writers, "I'm more

Paul Robeson chats with reporters after visiting December 1943 major league meetings in New York.

for your cause than anybody else you know, but you are making a mistake using force; you are defeating your own aims."

There was pressure, too, in Boston where Isadore Muchnick, a city councilman whose constituency was largely black, led a fight to block permits required for Sunday baseball unless the local clubs took steps to end discrimination. The Red Sox agreed to provide a tryout in April for three black players: Jackie Robinson of the Kansas City Monarchs, Sam Jethroe of the Cleveland Buckeyes (later an outfielder with the Braves), and Marvin Williams of the Philadelphia Stars. Manager Joe Cronin and his coaches put the trio through a one-hour drill at Fenway Park. The ballplayers then went home, heard nothing more, and the Sunday licenses were approved. The Red Sox would not have a black player until the arrival of infielder Pumpsie Green in 1959.

When the Yankees opened their 1945 home season against Boston, pickets marched outside the Stadium demanding an end to the color barrier. "If We Can Stop Bullets, Why Not Balls?" read one sign.

The major league owners then appointed a two-man committee—Branch Rickey and Larry MacPhail—to study the issue. In August, the pair joined a unit set up by Fiorello LaGuardia to probe discrimination in baseball.

Rickey, meanwhile, was quietly taking steps of his own. Upon coming to Brooklyn from St. Louis, he had secretly received permission from the Dodgers' board of directors to sign black ballplayers when he felt the time was ripe.

To find the right man, Rickey knew he had to engage in extensive scouting efforts. Early in 1945, he devised a cover for his talent search, announcing plans to start a team called the Brooklyn Brown Dodgers to play at Ebbets Field in a new Negro circuit called the United States Baseball League. Rickey sent his top scouts to look at the existing Negro clubs with the ostensible aim of stocking the Brown Dodgers. His real objective was finding a candidate to break the racial barrier.

The prime prospect seemed to be a college-educated former Army officer playing shortstop for the Kansas City Monarchs. Dodger scout Clyde Sukeforth was dispatched in August to Comiskey Park in Chicago to watch the ballplayer in a game against the American Giants. The shortstop was out of the lineup owing to a shoulder injury the day of Sukeforth's visit. But the verdict on him was pretty much in by that point, and so he was invited to meet Branch Rickey.

On August 28, 1945, Jackie Robinson went to Brooklyn, expecting to be recruited for the Brown Dodgers. Instead, after graphically describing the racial slurs he would encounter and receiving assurances he would have "guts enough not to fight back," Rickey offered Robinson a contract in organized baseball. He would get $600 a month and a bonus of $3,500 to play for the International League Montreal Royals, Brooklyn's top farm club.

Rickey asked Robinson to keep the agreement secret, hoping to delay an announcement until December when, with the football season over, the news would receive wider attention. But the word was to come earlier than he had desired. LaGuardia was dropping hints that baseball's color barrier would be broken because of efforts by his anti-discrimination committee and in mid-October the mayor asked Rickey for a go-ahead to announce that a black ballplayer soon would be signed.

Jackie Robinson of the Kansas City Monarchs.

Not wanting the public to believe he was bowing to political pressure, Rickey asked LaGuardia to hold off on a statement for a week, then had Robinson fly to Montreal to sign his contract. Reporters summoned to a press conference at the Royals' office on October 23 thought there might be an announcement that Montreal was being admitted to the major leagues. They were startled to meet Jackie Robinson.

In February 1946, the Royals signed another black man, a twenty-seven-year-old pitcher named John Wright, hoping his addition would ease the pressure on Robinson. Wright would not make it in organized ball. But in the spring of '46, the Dodgers' Nashua, New Hampshire, club of the New England League signed two other blacks who would be heard from in years to come—Roy Campanella and Don Newcombe.

Robinson would have an outstanding 1946 season at Montreal before breaking the major league color barrier in the face of almost unbearable abuse.

As baseball went into its first postwar spring, there were many new faces around—or at least faces that had not been seen on a major league diamond in three or four years. The ball clubs returned to Florida or California training camps to find themselves with a glut of players coming back from the service. The year before, bodies had been hard to find, but now there was a surplus.

Some of the younger ex-GIs seeking a minor league job got a head start. Declaring "baseball owes it to the servicemen," Bob Feller set up a three-week school at Tampa in January '46 to develop the skills of returning veterans—both aspiring ballplayers and those with some organized baseball experience. The men paid for their own transportation to the school as well as room and board and equipment, but the instruction—by a staff of big league ballplayers—was free.

The ball clubs were anxious to find out what talents the discharged soldiers and sailors were bringing with them.

The Cubs organized a camp at Lake Worth, Florida, in mid-January for their returning minor league ballplayers and free agents. The Dodgers had a similar facility at Sanford, Florida, generally starting each day with a one-hour lecture by Branch Rickey. When the Giants' main contingent gathered at Miami, farm director Carl Hubbell was in Jacksonville, looking over two hundred youngsters.

In early February, the Yankees took thirty-eight returning servicemen—big leaguers and top minor league prospects—to the Panama Canal Zone for three weeks of preliminary training. The Senators

Hugh Mulcahy gives pitching pointers to young ex-serviceman at Bob Feller's instructional camp.

had ex-GIs Sid Hudson, Jake Early, and Cecil Travis work out at Hot Springs, Arkansas. Buddy Lewis, who along with Travis had seen some action in 1945, was also asked to attend the workouts, but refused to go, pleading the press of business at his North Carolina auto dealership.

With the nation's housing situation still tight and ballplayers on hand in abundance, the clubs had a problem finding space for their men.

Pitcher Hal Klein spent his first night at the Indians' Clearwater, Florida, spring camp sleeping on a sofa in the lobby of the team's hotel, there being no rooms to be had.

Browns' general manager Bill DeWitt told the sixty-five players invited to the club's Anaheim, California, spring camp not to bring their families, pleading lack of accommodations. Pitcher Fred Sanford responded, "I didn't see my wife and kids for two years while I was serving in the Pacific theater and I intend seeing something of them now. They will be at Anaheim." He showed up with his family and made his own living arrangements.

As the prewar ballplayers trooped home from the military, the baseball senior citizens who had added a few years to their careers were told their services would no longer be required.

There would be no more baserunning blunders by Chuck Hostetler—he was let go by the Tigers in January of 1946. Pitcher Vern Kennedy, a veteran of twelve seasons in the majors, was given a present by the Reds on March 20, his thirty-ninth birthday—an unconditional release.

Impressive statistics didn't count for much when considered alongside advanced age and the caliber of wartime play.

Paul Derringer, a fifteen–year man, was released by the Cubs despite his 1945 record of 16–11. A more meaningful figure was the pitcher's age—thirty-nine. None of the other big league clubs wanted him either, so he signed with Indianapolis of the American Association.

Debs Garms was bid farewell by the Cardinals despite batting .336 over seventy-four games during the last wartime season. And Garms was not merely a war era hitter. The outfielder–third baseman had led the National League in batting in 1940 while with the Pirates. He was, however, thirty-seven years old by V-J Day.

The White Sox's Tony Cuccinello, playing third base on ailing legs, batted .308 in 1945, losing the American League title by a single percentage point to the Yanks' George "Snuffy" Stirnweiss. But the following January, the thirty-eight-year-old veteran of fifteen years in the majors was given his walking papers.

"I'm the most surprised guy in baseball," said a bitter Cuccinello upon receiving the news. "When the season ended, Jimmy Dykes definitely assured me I'd be back with the White Sox."

Even angrier were the men who returned from the armed forces to find they were no longer wanted by baseball. The front-liners were welcomed back eagerly, but fringe ballplayers and those at an advanced age might have a tough time getting their old jobs back.

The so-called GI Bill, perhaps best remembered for the educational benefits it accorded returning servicemen, also spelled out re-employment rights. A veteran was entitled to his former job for at least a one-year period, providing he was still qualified for the position and there were no unusual circumstances making it unreasonable for his ex-employer to rehire him. The Justice Department was empowered to bring legal action on behalf of ex-servicemen if efforts at persuasion were unsuccessful.

Baseball had drawn up its own regulations which, it maintained, fell within the provisions of the GI Bill. A returning serviceman was guaranteed a trial of either thirty days in spring training or fifteen days during the regular season to show he could still do the job. He would be given fifteen days' pay at or above his old salary level. At the end of the trial period, management had three alternatives. It could keep the ballplayer, send him to the minor leagues if waivers could be obtained from all the other clubs, or hand him his unconditional release.

An ex-GI dispatched to the minors would be entitled to his old big league salary for one year. His former major league club would have to make up the difference between the pay he would receive from a minor league team and his prewar salary level. Those who were released got fifteen days' pay and a thank you.

Approximately three hundred service returnees were kept on major league rosters during the 1946 season. There were others, however, who were unable to regain their old jobs despite the GI Bill. A few fought back.

Tony Lupien seemed to be your average ballplayer, but he was, in fact, not quite so ordinary. Lupien happened to be a Harvard graduate. The first baseman would not accept meekly what he considered to be a violation of his government-sanctioned rights.

Lupien had put in two full years with the Red Sox and another year with the Phillies before entering the Navy in March of 1945. He was discharged late in the '45 season, returned to the Phils in time to get into fifteen games over a twenty-two day period in September, and hit for a pretty fair .315 average.

The following winter, the Phils made a deal with the Reds to obtain first baseman Frank McCormick and, deciding Lupien was dispensable, put him on waivers. When no team claimed him, the twenty-eight-year-old Navy veteran was traded to the Hollywood Stars of the Pacific Coast League.

Lupien cried foul, writing to Happy Chandler to protest that his rights to his old job had been ignored. When he received no satisfaction from the commissioner, he filed a complaint with the U.S. Attorney's office in Philadelphia.

Tony Lupien (left) with Jimmie Foxx.

"The GI Bill was designed to protect for at least a year the jobs of men who entered the service," Lupien observed.

"Now that bill either applies to ballplayers or it doesn't," he told reporters. "That's what I am trying to find out. And if it means that I am the goat or the ball carrier, I am perfectly willing to assume that role. If the GI Bill does apply then I may help many other veterans in the months to come by following through with my action."

The Phils had fulfilled their obligations under the regulations drawn up by baseball to deal with veterans. Lupien had been given more than the minimum trial upon his discharge. So Phillie general manager Herb Pennock felt no pangs of conscience. Pennock said the Phils had offered Lupien to the Braves free of charge but they refused to take him. He contended that a 1946 spring training trial for the ballplayer was "not necessary" because he "had every opportunity to make good the twenty-two days he was with us last year." (A curious statement, though, in view of the fact Lupien had hit .315 during that period.)

Lupien eventually had second thoughts about carrying through with a legal challenge. Since he had a wife and two young daughters to provide for, he decided to report to Hollywood and drop his protest. He was given a contract at his old $8,000 big league salary—part of the money was to be paid by the Phils. Lupien would return to the majors for one more season, playing first base with the White Sox in 1948.

The next man to squawk was outfielder Bruce Campbell.

Campbell had played thirteen years of major league ball before joining the Army Air Corps following the 1942 season. Upon returning to the Washington club in the spring of 1946, he was thirty-six years old. The Senators kept Campbell for thirty-five days at their Orlando, Florida, training camp (five days beyond the minimum exhibition-season trial guaranteed by baseball) and then bid him goodbye, paying him off with the obligatory fifteen days' salary accorded a returning GI given his outright release.

Campbell managed to land a job with the Buffalo Bisons of the International League, then in early July went to the AMVETS—American Veterans of World War II—to seek help in getting paid his old big league salary for one year. The veterans organization asked the government to look into the matter and issued a statement urging baseball to devote itself "to the principle of a full year's salary for the unwanted professional baseball-playing GI as well as for the star."

Five days after stories on Campbell's protest appeared in the papers, he was released by Buffalo.

Campbell then held a news conference in Washington with a representative of the AMVETS and announced that a formal complaint had been filed with the office of the U.S. Attorney in the District of Columbia seeking payment of his former $9,000 salary. Echoing Lupien's remarks, Campbell said he was willing to be a "guinea pig" in the interest of other ex-GIs who had been released by their old teams.

Clark Griffith responded that he was "as much for the GIs as anyone." But, said the Washington owner, Campbell "just couldn't make the team."

By the end of July the dispute was settled out of court. Griffith got Campbell a job with the Minneapolis club of the American Association and agreed to make up the difference between his old $9,000 salary and the money he would make during 1946 playing with Buffalo and Minneapolis. The Senators' tab as estimated by Campbell was $5,000.

Griffith warned, however, that his action was not to be viewed as a precedent, explaining, "I was prompted in making this settlement by my friendship and good feeling toward Campbell for what he has meant to baseball in the past."

Campbell was never to play in the majors again.

A few of the other ex-servicemen who had been discarded also reached settlements with their old teams after threatening legal challenges.

Pinky May, the Phils' third baseman for five seasons before entering the Navy, went to the U.S. Attorney's office in Philadelphia upon being released by the ball club soon after his return in the spring of 1946. May sought $6,950, the difference between the money he had been paid in his brief '46 trial and the amount he would have made if kept by the Phils for a full year. The team agreed to come up with two-thirds of the remaining money and averted a suit.

Bob Harris, a pitcher released by the Athletics after his return from the Navy, demanded $3,300 from the club—the difference between the money he made pitching in the American Association during 1946 and his old big league salary. An undisclosed settlement was reached following a meeting among Harris, Connie Mack, an A's lawyer, and Gerald A. Gleeson, the U.S. Attorney in Philadelphia.

But some of the disputes found their way into federal courtrooms, where judges would be asked to weigh such matters as the ability of the plaintiff to make a double-play pivot or deliver a fastball.

When Navy veteran Al Niemic took the Pacific Coast League Seattle Rainiers to court upon losing his infielder's job, manager Bill Skiff testified for the defendant. Skiff explained that the thirty-five-year-old Niemic had been dismissed because he "was getting mixed up on double plays."

Federal Judge Lloyd Black was not, however, impressed by the presumably expert witness and ordered the Rainiers to pay Niemic's back salary claims.

Steve Sundra, who had won fifteen games for the Browns in 1943 before entering the Army, went into St. Louis federal court with help from the AMVETS after being dropped by the ball club two months into the 1946 season.

The Browns' front office personnel testified that while Sundra possessed an effective fastball before his service stint, he had slowed down so much that he could no longer pitch in the majors. Also trooping before Judge Roy W. Harper to offer evidence on Sundra's ability, or lack thereof, were Brownie manager Zack Taylor, the successor to Luke Sewell; two of his coaches; J. Roy Stockton, sports editor of the *St. Louis Post-Dispatch*; and J. G. Taylor Spink, whose *Sporting News* was based in St. Louis.

This time management won. Judge Harper, who perhaps didn't need to hear the testimony since he was said to be a fan of the Browns, turned down Sundra's bid for $5,400 in retroactive wages. The judge found that Sundra was indeed no longer qualified for his old job, and provisions of the GI Bill notwithstanding, observed:

Elbie Fletcher makes himself at home in tent he's pitched at Forbes Field to dramatize housing scarcity as 1946 season gets under way. Coach Spud Davis tucks the first baseman in.

"Baseball not only is a business but also a sport and a source of entertainment. The position of each player is constantly subject to personal competition and the public demands the best in skill and ability. The will of the public is supreme."

Then there was the minor league ball club that focused on provisions of the GI Bill allowing veterans engaged in on-the-job training programs to receive subsistence payments. The Jackson, Mississippi, club of the Southeastern League asked the Veterans Administration to pay out such stipends to ex-servicemen on the team. The players, management contended, were essentially involved in training programs for future big league careers. The VA wouldn't go along, finding there was no "reasonable assurance" that a minor league player could be permanently established in his profession after such "training."

As baseball went into the 1946 season, there were other reminders of the war days.

Housing remained in short supply. The Senators had to improvise sleeping quarters in the Griffith Stadium dressing room for ten players who couldn't find accommodations by the start of the schedule. A plea in the newspapers directed at Senator rooters read: "If you possess an extra tent, igloo, or lean-to, kindly get in touch with President Clark Griffith of the Washington baseball club."

The Braves set up an around-the-clock phone number for fans to call if they had a room available; the White Sox offered a season's pass to anyone taking in a ballplayer.

One man found a temporary solution to the housing crisis thanks to Bill Veeck. One of Veeck's first steps toward livening things up after buying the Indians in June '46 was to erect tepees at the club's two ballfields, League Park and Municipal Stadium. The way Veeck told it, a local resident, supposedly evicted from his apartment, came to him one day and asked if he could be put up in the League Park tent. Veeck told the fellow to find himself a cot and move in.

A continuing shortage of consumer items such as nylons provided baseball showmen like Larry MacPhail and Veeck with opportunities for promotional stunts. MacPhail, having bought into part ownership of the Yankees, attracted women to the Stadium for a game in May with the Red Sox by giving out 500 pairs of stockings and staging a fashion show. Veeck outdid MacPhail in August, distributing 503 boxes of nylons before an Indians–Red Sox game.

Baseball was, of course, anxious to put squabbles with angry exservicemen and other wartime legacies behind it.

Ballparks that had been neglected due to a shortage of labor and materials were spruced up for the 1946 season.

At Forbes Field, the wooden outfield fences—a fixture since 1909

Yankee Stadium fashion show, staged along with nylon giveaway to bring out the ladies in first postwar season, has its attractions for visiting Red Sox as well.

Bill Veeck takes personal charge to make sure women receiving free nylons for attending August 1946 Indians game know the source of their good fortune.

—were replaced by brick walls. Restrooms were renovated and a Pirates' Den added to the press facilities to provide appropriate repast and liquid refreshment for the chroniclers of the game.

With traditionalist Ed Barrow no longer in charge, the Yankees finally installed a lighting system. A crowd of 49,917 turned out on a windy, misty night, the temperature only in the forties, to watch New York host Washington on May 28 in the first Yankee Stadium game under the lights. General Electric President Charles E. Wilson, whose technology had made it all possible, was accorded the honor of throwing out the first ball.

Lights were also put in at Braves Field, a development that went off without a hitch. But another bit of enterprise—the laying on of a fresh coat of green paint—brought the Boston management grief. Some three hundred fans among those attending the season's opener with the Dodgers appeared at the Braves' office after the game with a momento on the seat of their pants—a layer of paint that had not quite dried. The ball club took out an apologetic ad in the papers and offered to pick up dry cleaning costs.

The initial postwar season saw the Yanks become the first team to travel regularly by air, flying aboard the "Yankees Mainliner," a chartered four-engine United Air Lines plane capable of cruising at all of 230 miles an hour. There were those, however, who were not quite ready for the future. When the club made its first trip in the forty-four-seater—a hop on May 13 from LaGuardia Field to Lambert Field in St. Louis—five players excused themselves and journeyed via train instead.

The baseball world emerging from wartime found turbulence in areas other than the skies. Although the ball clubs could once again field truly major league squads, things were far from serene.

The first ball club taking to the air on a regular basis, '46 Yanks are about to embark on their maiden journey—a four-and-a-half-hour flight from New York to St. Louis.

Players who lost good money during the war years because of military service were given a chance to make it back by "jumping" south of the border. Businessman Jorge Pasqual and his four brothers threw around big dollars during the spring of 1946 to lure American ballplayers to their Mexican League.

Commissioner Happy Chandler warned the deserters that they would be suspended if they didn't return to their clubs by opening day. The most prominent player to defect, shortstop Vern Stephens of the Browns, came back before the season began and escaped punishment. More than a dozen others succumbed to the Pasqual money —among them pitchers Max Lanier of the Cards and Sal Maglie of the Giants and catcher Mickey Owen of the Dodgers—and were ordered banished for five years. Most of the men soon became disillusioned with alleged broken contract promises and poor conditions and came back to the United States, seeking to rejoin their old clubs. Chandler refused, however, to relent, and it was not until 1949 that the ban was lifted.

The big league owners were also in for a headache or two from a domestic organization—the American Baseball Guild, a fledgling union. Robert Murphy, a Boston attorney and Harvard Law School graduate, set out to organize ballplayers for collective bargaining. His first stop was Pittsburgh, a strong union town. Murphy's efforts almost resulted in a walkout by the Pirate ballplayers. In response to management's fight against a union certification election, the players took a strike vote prior to a scheduled June night game against the Giants. A strike resolution passed by a slim margin, but the players had agreed that a three-fourths majority would be needed for the vote to be binding, so they took the field. By the late stages of the 1946 season, the union drive had petered out. In August, Murphy won the right to hold a union election among the Pirate players, but they voted 15–3 not to join the Guild.

The baseball hierarchy, not unmindful of the threats posed by the Mexican League and unionization, took steps to deal with some of the players' major grievances. An owners' committee set up a series of meetings with representatives designated by the ballplayers, out of which came a $5,000 salary minimum, a pay-cut limit of 25 percent for any one year, and provisions for a pension plan. The reserve clause was not yet an issue.

As for the ballfield, the stars discharged from military service generally had little trouble getting into the groove.

Stan Musial, returning from the Navy, led the National League in hitting with a .365 average, while outfield mate Enos Slaughter, back from the Army, batted .300. Paced by their bats and the pitching of Army veterans Howie Pollet and Murry Dickson, winners of twenty-one and fifteen games, respectively, the Cards won the 1946 NL pennant, though forced into a playoff by the Dodgers.

The Red Sox took the American League race with ease, finishing twelve games ahead of the Tigers and seventeen in front of the Yankees. Navy veterans Ted Williams, Johnny Pesky, and Dom DiMaggio led the way with .300 seasons. Ex-GI Tex Hughson was a twenty-

Joe DiMaggio works out at New York Athletic Club, getting his legs in shape for return to baseball after three years in the Army.

game winner for Boston, while Mickey Harris, returning after four years in the Army, had seventeen victories.

Bob Feller was 26–15 and struck out 348 batters. Joe DiMaggio, hampered by injuries, hit only .290 but he would go on to bat over .300 during the next four seasons. Hank Greenberg led the American League in homers with 44 and RBIs with 127.

The '46 season was capped by the Cardinals' seven-game World Series victory over the Red Sox.

With the likes of Musial, Williams, DiMaggio, Feller, and Greenberg displaying their powers once again, the baseball world would get along quite well minus the men who had kept the game alive through the preceding years of struggle.

Mel Ott made the point clear one day during the 1946 spring training season.

When Danny Gardella arrived in Miami a holdout, then got into a dispute with traveling secretary Eddie Brannick over the Giants' dining room dress code, the eccentric outfielder was given the gate.

"We have put him on the auction block and he will go to the highest bidder. Several minor league clubs have expressed an interest in him and that is that," announced Ott.

(Gardella would leave the country altogether, taking his high spirits to the Mexican League.)

In what amounted to an epitaph for wartime baseball, manager Ott declared:

"The time has passed when we have to worry about players like that. His type are no longer of great importance in the major leagues, now that the war is over.

"It was different in the days when we often didn't know when we would be able to put nine men on the field. But now we have a camp full of fine players.

"I don't think any of the others will be missed."

Sources

Aside from interviews, my most valuable sources were the newspapers of the day. The *Sporting News* and *New York Times* were especially helpful. I also reviewed the sports sections of the *Chicago Daily News, Detroit News, New York Herald Tribune, New York Journal–American, Philadelphia Inquirer, St. Louis Post–Dispatch,* and *Washington Evening Star.*

General interest magazines furnishing additional material on wartime baseball were *Collier's, Newsweek, The Saturday Evening Post,* and *Time.*

The following books provide an overview of life in America during the Second World War:

BAILEY, RONALD H., and the editors of Time-Life Books. *The Home Front: U.S.A.* New York: Time-Life Books, Inc., 1977.

LINGEMAN, RICHARD R. *Don't You Know There's a War On? The American Home Front, 1941–1945.* New York: G.P. Putnam's Sons, 1970.

PERRETT, GEOFFREY. *Days of Sadness, Years of Triumph: The American People 1939–1945.* New York: Coward, McCann and Geoghegan, Inc., 1973.

PHILLIPS, CABELL. *The 1940s: Decade of Triumph and Trouble.* New York: Macmillan Publishing Co., Inc., 1975.

I found these baseball books to be of particular interest:

ALLEN, LEE. *The National League Story.* New York: Hill and Wang, 1961.

ALLEN, LEE. *100 Years of Baseball.* New York: Bartholomew House, 1950.

BARBER, RED, AND CREAMER, ROBERT. *Rhubarb in the Catbird Seat.* Garden City, N.Y.: Doubleday and Co., Inc., 1968.

ENRIGHT, JIM. *Baseball's Greatest Teams: Chicago Cubs.* New York: Macmillan Publishing Co., Inc., 1975.

FRISCH, FRANK, as told to STOCKTON, J. ROY. *Frank Frisch: The Fordham Flash.* Garden City, N.Y.: Doubleday and Co., Inc., 1962.

GRAHAM, FRANK. *The Brooklyn Dodgers: An Informal History.* New York: G.P. Putnam's Sons, 1945.

HIGBY, KIRBY, with QUIGLEY, MARTIN. *The High Hard One.* New York: Viking Press, 1967.

HIRSHBERG, AL. *From Sandlots to League President: The Story of Joe Cronin.* New York: Julian Messner, Inc., 1962.

HONIG, DONALD. *Baseball When the Grass Was Real.* New York: Coward, McCann and Geoghegan, Inc., 1975.

KAUFMAN, LOUIS; FITZGERALD, BARBARA; and SEWELL, TOM. *Moe Berg: Athlete, Scholar . . . Spy.* Boston: Little, Brown and Co., 1974.

LIEB, FREDERICK G., and BAUMGARTNER, STAN. *The Philadelphia Phillies.* New York: G.P. Putnam's Sons, 1953.

MANN, ARTHUR. *Branch Rickey: American in Action.* Boston: Houghton Mifflin Co., 1957.

MEAD, WILLIAM B. *Even the Browns: The Zany, True Story of Baseball in the Early Forties.* Chicago: Contemporary Books Inc., 1978.

OBOJSKI, ROBERT. *The Rise of Japanese Baseball.* Radnor, Pa.: Chilton Book Co., 1975.

PARROTT, HAROLD. *The Lords of Baseball.* New York: Praeger Publishers, Inc., 1976.

PETERSON, ROBERT. *Only the Ball Was White.* Englewood Cliffs, N.J.: Prentice-Hall Inc., 1970.

RITTER, LAWRENCE S. *The Glory of Their Times.* New York: Macmillan Publishing Co., Inc., 1966.

SEYMOUR, HAROLD. *Baseball: The Golden Years.* New York: Oxford University Press, 1971.

SPINK, J.G. TAYLOR. *Judge Landis and Twenty–Five Years of Baseball.* New York: Thomas Y. Crowell Co., 1947.

VEECK, BILL, WITH LINN, ED. *Veeck As In Wreck.* New York: G.P. Putnam's Sons, 1962.

VOIGT, DAVID QUENTIN. *American Baseball: From the Commissioners to Continental Expansion.* Norman: University of Oklahoma Press, 1970.

WHITING, ROBERT. *The Chrysanthemum and the Bat.* New York: Dodd, Mead and Co., 1977.

WILLIAMS, TED, as told to UNDERWOOD, JOHN. *My Turn at Bat: The Story of My Life.* New York: Simon and Schuster, 1969.

Invaluable sources of statistical material were:

Neft, David S.; Johnson, Roland T.; Cohen, Richard M.; and Deutsch, Jordan A. *The Sports Encyclopedia: Baseball.* New York: Grosset & Dunlap, 1974.

The Baseball Encyclopedia. New York: Macmillan Publishing Co., Inc., 1969.

The baseball financial data cited on pp. 151–152 is from Hearings Before the Subcommittee on Study of Monopoly Power of the Committee on the Judiciary, House of Representatives, 82nd Congress, 1st session, Part 6, Organized Baseball, U.S. Government Printing Office, Washington, D.C., 1951.

The text of President Roosevelt's "Green Light" letter (pp. 19–20) and his remarks on baseball at a March 13, 1945, news conference (page 203) are from *The Public Papers and Addresses of Franklin D. Roosevelt,* compiled by Samuel I. Rosenman. New York: Harper and Bros., 1950

Index